BUSINESS

and

GOVERNMENT
RELATIONS

Partners in the 1990s

D. WAYNE TAYLOR

gage EDUCATIONAL PUBLISHING COMPANY
A DIVISION OF CANADA PUBLISHING CORPORATION
TORONTO ONTARIO CANADA

Canadian Cataloguing in Publication Data

Taylor, D. Wayne
    Business and government relations

Includes bibliographical references.
ISBN 0-7715-5695-0

1. Industry and state — Canada. I. Title.

HD3616.C32T3 1990   338.971   C90-093932-X

Acknowledgments
For permission to reprint copyrighted material, grateful acknowledgment is made to the following:

Canadian Alliance for Trade and Job Opportunities—advertisements, "Will free trade diminish our sovereignty?" (Figure 10-1) and "Trade is our bread and butter" (Figure 10-2).
Canadian Cancer Society— "Mail Campaign Postcard regarding Bill C-51"
Canadian Journal of Administrative Sciences, Chief Ed. Jean-Charles Chebat— "An Interpretative Approach to Understanding and Improving Business-Government Relations" by D. Wayne Taylor. From *Canadian Journal of Administrative Sciences*, Vol. 4 No. 4 (Dec. 1987).
Canadian Medical Association—Excerpt from Bill C-51: "The Tobacco Products Control Act."
Canadian Public Administration (CPA), Ed. V.S. Wilson— "An Interpretative Understanding of the Non-Fulfilment of Business-Government Relations" by D.W. Taylor and V.V. Murray. From *CPA* Vol. 30 No. 3.
Canadian Tobacco Manufacturers' Council (CTMC)— "Postalgram" (Exhibit 3); "Letter to Industry" (Exhibit 4) and advertisements, "There's a major problem . . ." (Exhibit 5); "Why the Proposed Government legislation . . ." (Exhibit 6); "Every cultural and professional sports group . . ." (Exhibit 7).
Outdoor Advertising Association of Canada—letter to all Federal Cabinet Ministers and Members of Parliament re implementation of Bill C-51: "The Tobacco Products Control Act."

Cover design: Susan Weiss

ISBN: 0-7715-5695-0
1 2 3 4 5 WC 95 94 93 92 91
Written, Printed, and Bound in Canada

To

Mom, Dad,
and Karen, my best friend.

Plus ça change, plus c'est la même chose.

Alphonse Karr, 1808–1890

The invasion of armies is resisted; the invasion of ideas is not.

Victor Marie Hugo, 1802–1885

CONTENTS

PREFACE

Canada's most famous novel,
Two Solitudes,
talks about cultural isolation
of Anglophones and Francophones . . .
but another two solitudes exist—
business and government.

Pierre Elliott Trudeau, 1981

Since the Great Depression of the 1930s, the governments of most industrialized nations have increased their involvement in the economies of
these countries. As a result, nearly every sector of society has challenged
the classic assumptions about the roles of both business and government in
the economy. Among these are: the traditional role of business as provider
of all goods and services not of a collective nature; the ability of business to
satisfy societal goals and needs; the efficacy of the market system; and the
capacity or willingness of government to develop the economic climate
required for private investment and growth.

Today, not only do governments fulfil their traditional roles; i.e.,
providing national defence, justice, and the protection of life and property,
but they also regulate the actions of industry and, in some cases, provide
actual goods and services.

In essence, the basic philosophy of capitalism has been modified worldwide into various concepts of collectivism. Societies once viewed as capitalist have, in fact, "mixed economies" today. Thus, most Western
nations have public ownership of property, state-regulated markets, price
allocation mechanisms other than consumer sovereignty, oligopolies, and
state direction of enterprise.

The invisible hand of the marketplace has been transformed into the
two *visible* hands of "rational" business management and state intervention. In the absence of a pure laissez-faire economy, private sector financial
performance has been influenced as much by management's response to,
and more important, use of government, as by its response to the
marketplace.

No industry in Canada today is unaffected by the state. In 1986, governments in Canada (federal, provincial, and municipal) accounted for 43% of the country's *Gross Domestic Product*.[1] About half of this was in the form of transfer payments and the redistribution of income.

None of this is new for Canada. In fact, many have argued that Canada has had a mixed economy since the chartering of the Hudson's Bay Company in 1670. Business-government interaction, therefore, has been a reality for over three centuries. Borrowing from political science's lexicon, one could describe the process by which Canada's business-government relations have been managed as "elite accommodation."

This process was particularly evident during the early 1950s when C.D. Howe, as Minister of Trade and Commerce, saw his role as one primarily of enforcing the "public interest." For him, this was ultimately business' interest. Ironically, those business managers who publicly display the strongest affection for the free market system are usually managers of firms with a fair degree of market power, thanks to their industry's particular structure. This situation often results from business' requests for and receipt of government assistance to close entry or control prices.

However, this is all changing. Academics, business people, and government officials have been closely following the reported breakdown of elite accommodation and the overall deterioration of Canadian business-government relations since the 1970s. Much of the research on this theme has assumed a problem exists: that government intervention is emasculating the private sector; that business' interests are no longer synonymous with the "public interest"; *that what was once the workplace of a national socio-economic partnership is now the battleground for two disparate solitudes, each growing increasingly antagonistic, mutually suspicious, and ignorant of the other.*

According to the press, the private sector regards cabinet ministers as political advantage-seekers and sees civil servants as paper-pushing, bumbling, irresponsible time-wasters. Civil servants, on the other hand, regard the private sector as people looking for a handout. Both sides have described present business-government relations in Canada as futile, adversarial, prejudiced, and little more than a carnival sideshow.

It should not be surprising that some degree of conflict exists between business and government. After all, government's task is to build a consensus from among an increasing number of competing interests and needs, and to provide strong leadership when no consensus exists. In a pluralist democracy such as Canada, the public interest can no longer be defined solely by business leaders or any other single interest group.

---

[1] *Gross Domestic Product* (GDP) refers to the total national output of goods and services for a year, excluding foreign income. *Gross National Product* (GNP) adds foreign income to the GDP figure.

But are the halcyon days of C.D Howe and elite accommodation really over? Do two new solitudes exist? What *is* the present state of business-government relations in Canada? Is there more to the subject than popular theories suggest? Until now, these questions have been largely neglected by Canadian social scientists and students of administrative studies.

Business and Government Relations provides an up-to-date, practical guide to studying and understanding Canadian business-government relations. It is an empirically based examination of this integral variable in the strategic management of business and government enterprises today. Until Professor James Gillies started his research ten years ago, almost every business-government study had been mostly conjecture, prescription-without-diagnosis, or anecdotal case study. The tools of social science had not been applied with much rigour.

Business and Government Relations is appropriate for either graduate or advanced undergraduate courses in business policy, political science, public administration, economics, or sociology. It is my personal belief that students, no matter how well versed in management or government, need an understanding of the history and environmental framework of Canadian business-government relations. Only then can they interpret the present status of these relations and the constraints on modifying them. *Business and Government Relations* provides such a background, as well as up-to-date analysis.

To say the least, *Business and Government Relations* should prove to be a controversial book. It has not been written in the normal textbook style because it is not a "normal" textbook. It is a book designed to inform student and practitioner, layman and expert alike about the uniquely Canadian underpinnings and manifestations of business-government relations.

Business and Government Relations is also a book strong in its opinions. If the success or failure of the Meech Lake Accord is to determine the political future of Canada, the success or failure of business-government relations in the 1990s will likewise determine Canada's economic future. Just as Canada can either remain a shining example of confederalism or become a victim of nationalist balkanization, so can it either remain a world industrial leader or retreat into the colonial backwaters of a new global order. The first will be decided by our eleven first ministers; the second by our business and government elites.

If this book is used as a textbook, as I hope it is, then instructors should use it to provide background and a departure point for classroom debate. The cases are appended to help you do this. The opinions, conclusions, and generalizations of this work can spark, rouse, and even incite students not only to learn, but to think critically for themselves—the greatest gift an educator can bestow.

This book will also serve as a valuable addition to the manager's bookshelf. It should be an easy, yet informative read for the business

executive who recognizes the importance of business-government relations to his or her firm. In short, *Business and Government Relations* is a
comprehensive self-learning medium, combining text and figures with
illustrative cases.

This book was written to provide an *interpretive* understanding of
business-government relations in Canada. What does that mean? First, for
business and government to interact more effectively *and* to their mutual
benefit, a better understanding of each other's values, attitudes, beliefs, and
perceptions is absolutely necessary. Second, this understanding can only be
attained through increased interaction at the appropriate levels and at the
appropriate times. Finally, both sides need to become fully aware of the
historical and environmental backgrounds which will inevitably shape
their relationship.

As the five section headings of this book suggest, if the *key players* in the
Canadian economy first, *understand* the historical and environmental
backdrop to business-government relations in this country, and second,
interpret current events correctly within their proper context, they will
then be able to constructively and co-operatively *manage* their interrelationships to meet the serious economic challenges which face them in
the 1990s. Or, to work backwards, business and government need to work
co-operatively as *partners* to forge strategies that will guarantee Canada
continued economic prosperity, at less cost to the natural environment,
and within an increasingly turbulent, complex, and global order. To
become partners, both business and government must strategically manage
their interface. Each side must develop a full understanding of the values,
attitudes, beliefs, and perceptions that the other possesses; must learn how
these variables are dependent upon the role and structure each has assumed
in the Canadian polity; and must see how the latter are grounded in over
three hundred years of neo-corporatist history and pragmatic culture.

Sounds simple, does it not? Then why do business and government
continue to have problems? Perhaps common sense does not always
prevail in business-government interactions, as we know it does not in
most complex, longstanding relationships among people. Sometimes it
takes a third party to re-introduce common sense into a long-time relationship. That is what this book hopes to accomplish.

For the purposes of this book, *business-government relations* shall refer
to the entire gamut of interaction between business and government elites
as it affects business strategy and/or government policy, rather than
matters of a purely administrative, routine nature. However, this book
does fall short of being a definitive encyclopedium, and for good reason.
The research for this book overwhelmingly indicated that the lion's share
of discernible business-government relations was between the federal
government and big business. This book concentrates on that relationship.

There is another reason for concentrating on big business and big
government. Increasing importance is being accorded to national

industrial strategies, liberalized trade, increasing global competitiveness, and the restructuring of the world economy. But only when big business and the federal government can work together in a national partnership can these events be turned to Canada's advantage.

Business and Government Relations focuses upon the policy-making level of government and the strategic management level of business. Without successful business-government relations at these levels, routine chores of interaction, such as tax law interpretation and occupational safety standards administration, become meaningless.

This book is concerned with the long-term survival of the private sector in Canada, the appropriate and most effective role of the state in post-industrial society, and the continuing survival of the Canadian economy in an increasingly challenging global commercial environment.

Irksome to some may be the comparison of Canadian business-government relations to those of the United States. This has been done, not to ignore what is transpiring in the rest of the world, but to redress the injustice done to this field of study by the sometimes incorrect parallels drawn between these two quite different sets of business-government relationships. In this management situation, we have more to learn from ourselves and our past, than from others.

The Identification of Strategic Skill Requirements of Management: A Framework for Integrating Theory and Practice in Public and Business Policy Studies

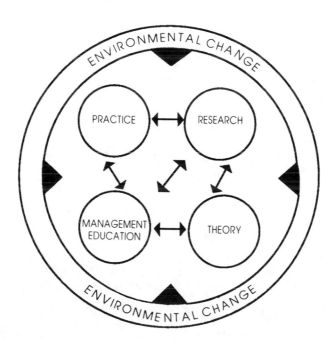

This book integrates practice with theory, using the framework set out on page xiii. It identifies what managers must know and do to improve their personal business-government relations, and to help create a positive working partnership between the private and public sectors. *Business and Government Relations* has deliberately not been structured for the classroom, as are many business administration books. If the study of business-government relations must avoid the trap of structuralist and reductionist thinking, then so should its prophets and their media.

Above all, this book is written to make you think, to challenge you (and to have you challenge it), to encourage you to question conventional wisdom and popular reporting, and to scratch beneath the surface of public posturing and political rhetoric. I hope it does.

ACKNOWLEDGMENTS

As in any endeavour of this nature, I would be remiss not to acknowledge those individuals and institutions who assisted me in my research. First, I would like to thank the Max Bell Business-Government Studies Programme for its financial support of the research which preceded the writing of this book. Second, I wish to thank Bill Bruce of the Institute of Social Research at York University for his assistance in the statistical analysis of the survey data. I must also extend my eternal gratitude to Jim Gillies, Vic Murray, and Tom Wilson, all of York University, for their time, ideas, suggestions, guidance, and encouragement over the last ten years or so during which I have been privileged to be both their student and colleague. Thanks also to all of the business and government managers who took the time and had the interest to complete the questionnaires and/or to be interviewed, as well as to suggest ways in which to improve business-government relations in Canada. Finally, I must thank my wife, Karen, who typed, and typed, and typed—thank you.

D. Wayne Taylor

UNDERSTANDING BUSINESS-GOVERNMENT RELATIONS IN CANADA

To fully appreciate the problems and questions that business and government face, and the difficulties they have in facing them, one must first understand from where Canadian business and government come. The next three chapters respectively identify the strategic problem of management today, the history of business-government relations, and the socio-cultural (environmental) framework within which business and government interact.

CHAPTER 1

INTRODUCTION

CHAPTER 2

A BRIEF HISTORICAL BACKGROUND

CHAPTER 3

ENVIRONMENTAL FRAMEWORK

CHAPTER

1 INTRODUCTION

He that goeth about to persuade a multitude that they are not so well governed as they ought to be, shall never want attentive and favourable hearers.

Richard Hooker, 1554–1600

For the first one hundred years of Confederation, Canada lived off its natural resources. For the past twenty years, Canada has lived off its credit!

In the years immediately following World War II, Canada possessed the world's third most robust economy and was the world's third greatest military power. Wheat exports had doubled, and production of oil, iron ore, uranium ore, aluminum, and hydro-electric power had quadrupled. By 1958, the population had grown from 11 million to 17 million. Sir Wilfrid Laurier's dream of a world-class nation was being built by a flood of immigrants from the four corners of the world.

Canada was blessed with the best aspects of all worlds: the British tradition of government, the influences of French culture, and the dynamism of the American economy. Its only shortcoming was a small domestic market. In fact, it was far smaller than what economists would consider to be of minimum efficient size for industrial self-sufficiency at an affordable price. But this, too, was turned to advantage. Canada became a trading nation—one of the best in the world—with 25% of the economy trade-based.

However, such is no longer the case. What happened?

OURS IS A CHANGING WORLD

The world is a dynamic place. Nothing remains the same. The world's economy has undergone radical changes since World War II, and certainly since the Kennedy Round of the General Agreement on Tariffs and Trade (GATT) during the early 1960s. World trade has grown disproportionately compared with real growth in the world's Gross Domestic Product (GDP). A dramatic rise in exports due to fluctuating currencies, new natural resource discoveries, and Third World development is restructuring the global economy. One day, it will give rise to a whole new economic order.

These challenges are shared by the seven industrialized nations which, including Canada, have become known as the *G-7.* The other six are France, West Germany, Italy, Japan, the United Kingdom, and the United States.

In 1987, for example, the United States—formerly the engine of the economy of the non-communist world—faced a U.S. $144.3 billion deficit in its trade balance in goods and services. In 1984, however, Americans had enjoyed a surplus of U.S. $112.5 billion. Meanwhile, as seen in Figure 1-1, Japan and West Germany (which just thirty years ago were reeling from the devastation of the Second World War) collectively held a 1987 positive trade balance of U.S. $123.7 billion.

Figure 1-1

G-7 Trade Accounts 1984, 1987

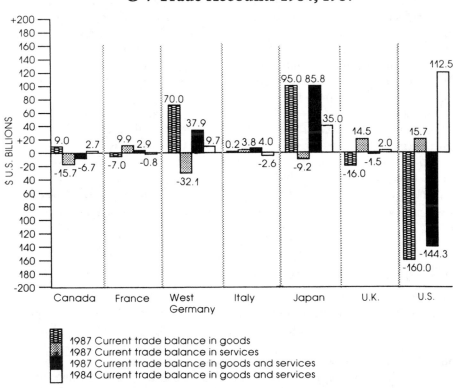

1987 Current trade balance in goods
1987 Current trade balance in services
1987 Current trade balance in goods and services
1984 Current trade balance in goods and services

Source: Organization for Economic Co-operation and Development, 1988.

Who will drive the world's economy tomorrow? The United States, to regain its title, must drastically reduce its level of imports, probably increase taxes while reducing government services, and endure escalating prices. Not an enviable path to hegemony. To compound matters, the American dollar's value has dropped 21% since 1984, compared with the combined currencies of the other G-7 countries. At the same time, Japanese holdings of U.S. paper debt have increased threefold since 1984. However, Japan is not without difficulties. Formerly low manufacturing and production labour costs—once a powerful competitive advantage—have crept up to within 16% of the average American rate.

There are also vast and forbidding differences among the G-7 nations themselves. One significant variation is in nominal rates of industrial output between 1982 and 1988. During that period, Canada led the pack with a 40% increase in industrial output. France, on the other hand, trailed behind the others with only a 7% increase. When inflation is taken into account, this translates into an actual contraction in France's industrial output since 1982. Nor has inflation—or even standard of living—been consistent throughout the group. Italy's standard of living today is almost half that of the United States.

To place all this in the proper perspective, only five countries had a real economic growth rate greater than 5% last year. All were totalitarian states, led by the news-breaking South Korea. On the face of it, pluralist democracies and industrial success no longer seem mutually congruous.

Where, then, does Canada fit into this gloomy picture for liberalist capitalism? According to the 1988 annual competitiveness scorecard produced by the Swiss-based European Management Forum,[2] Canada recently ranked five out of twenty-four OECD countries for overall competitiveness, only lagging behind Japan, Switzerland, the United States, and West Germany (in order of rank).

In 1987, Canada's Gross National Product (GNP) grew at the rate of 8.1%, while the Consumer Price Index (CPI) climbed 4.6%. This yielded a real growth rate of 3.5%, compared with 2.5% for the United States, 3.5% for the United Kingdom, and 2.4% for Japan. Canada's real growth in Gross Domestic Product (GDP) over the past five years has outperformed that of all other G-7 countries (see Figure 1-2). Income rose a nominal 6.9% in 1987—well ahead of inflation—for a real gain of 2.3%. Labour market participation climbed 2.4%—higher than in any other G-7 nation. OECD forecasts for 1988 predicted a real economic growth rate for Canada second only to that of Japan.

---

[2] A non-profit, self-supporting research organization conducting much of the research used by the Organization for Economic Co-operation and Development (OECD) and the World Bank.

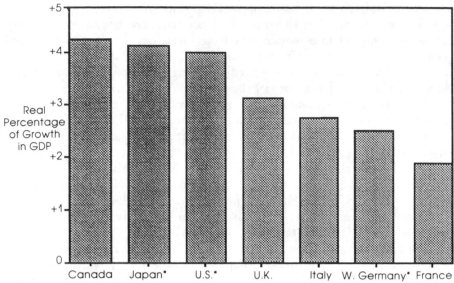

Figure 1-2

**Real Gross Domestic Product
Average Annual Percentage Change: 1983-1988**

* Real change in GNP

Relative to other industrialized countries, Canada's banking system is strong, second only to that of Switzerland. In fact, Canada enjoys the fifth-best credit rating in the world. However, this country's strong banking sector has achieved some of its success by charging the highest short-term interest rates of all 24 OECD countries. This has, at times, made borrowing by small Canadian enterprises almost prohibitive.

Unfortunately, Canada's world-class financial reputation has been achieved at the cost of indigenous industrial entrepreneurism. This situation is perpetuated by the dienneal review of the Bank Act by Canada's non-elected Senate, composed of a disproportionately high number of bank directors.

This country's solid financial ranking is also offset by its industrial relations system. High initial labour costs and a very low annual growth rate in productivity result in high production costs, which in turn reduce the competitiveness of the small number of manufactured goods produced and traded. Canadian labour is also plagued with high absenteeism, high turnover, and many days lost due to work stoppages.

On the positive side, however, Canada ranked first among OECD countries in per capita expenditure on education. Canada ranked second in the percent of population enrolled in higher education. Ironically, however, the ranking was only twelfth for availability of skilled labour. Apparently, the products of this expensive educational system, with its high participation rate, do not match the skills required by industry, further hindering Canada's international competitiveness.

Furthermore, although inflation has declined since the double-digit days of the early 1980s, prices in Canada are still rising faster than those of many major trading partners. Unemployment remains high, at a rate of 7.5%. Worse still, regional economic disparities have also widened. While the jobless rate for Ontario and Quebec has dropped below that of ten years ago, unemployment elsewhere in Canada is still much higher than in the late 1970s.

Once again on the plus side, Canada ranked second in natural resource self-sufficiency, and first with respect to the role of the state not hindering private-sector competition (very surprising indeed). *In other words, according to the European Management Forum, government in Canada hinders private-sector competition the least of all OECD countries!*

In fact, Canada has been remarkably successful on most grounds for the past decade or so. It had the strongest economic growth of all the G-7 industrialized countries, including Japan, despite generally depressed world prices for commodities and natural resources.

However, there is a significant structural weakness in all of this for Canada. Only 19% of the labour force was engaged in manufacturing, as compared to 30% in Japan; 33% was employed in services, of which Canada is still a net importer. In 1987, Canada was a net *exporter* of forest products, minerals, energy, grain, and fish, but a net *importer* of fruits, vegetables, textiles, clothing, machinery, and equipment. The largest contributor to the deficit was the net outflow of investment income to foreign investors. Canadians remain "hewers of wood and drawers of water." Most economic growth has been, and will continue to be, in low value-added natural resources. Canada actually ranked at the bottom of the OECD countries in growth and investment in capital and industrial goods. More services, manufactured goods (78% of all imports), high value-added goods, and technology-based goods were imported than were exported.

As a result, Canada's trade surplus in 1984 of U.S. $2.7 billion was transformed into a deficit of U.S. $6.7 billion by 1987 (see Figure 1-3).

As William Mulholland, then President of the Bank of Montreal, said in a speech to the Canadian Institute of Mining and Metallurgy in 1980:

> For purposes of both mineral development and labour costs, environmental standards and labour organization, Canada must be counted as a developed country. In terms of the existing infrastructure of secondary manufacturing industries, however, Canada must be considered a developing country. Thus, we face the worst of both worlds.

Figure 1-3

Canada's Trade Balance 1978-1988

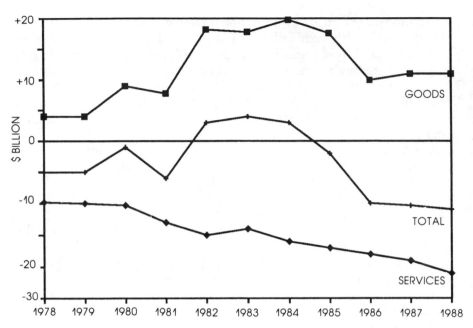

Source: *Financial Post* September 19, 1988.

Of course, Mulholland did not add that his bank's high short-term interest rates and risk aversity in its loans management policy were among the reasons why that infrastructure was not in place. Was Mulholland being overly pessimistic? Are the critics of Canadian banks missing the mark in their criticism? After all, trade *was* the prime reason for the successful postwar rebuilding of the economies of West Germany, France, Italy, and most notably, Japan. Besides, even though merchandise imports had risen by only 14.6% per year since 1965, Canada's exports had grown at a favourably comparative rate of 15.2%.

Many contend that it is *what* Canada is exporting—natural resources—that has become the problem. What had been a competitive advantage since the days of the *coureur-de-bois* in the 1600s and 1700s has become a competitive disadvantage.

By definition, a supply of non-renewable resources means an eventual end to this source of prosperity, and escalating margins as the supply diminishes. Yet world prices for metals and minerals are at an all-time low. Stockpiles grow larger each day, thanks to Japan's strategy of financing natural resource development around the world. By offering unheard-of cheap loans, excess production was assured, along with lowest-cost inputs for Japan's manufacturing industries. Just as Canada's recoverable reserves were starting to show signs of depletion, substitutes were abounding everywhere.

Similar is the situation regarding renewable resources. Japanese-financed development of alternate sources of supply is springing up everywhere, providing lower-cost substitutes for Canadian renewable resources. Yet these are still being harvested in this country at a much greater rate than that of replenishment.

In general, Canada has become a nation of low technology and high wages in an era when the competitive edge lies with high-technology, low-wage countries, such as the emerging industrializing bloc along the Pacific Rim of the Far East. Nor does the dilemma for Canada and its G-7 partners end there.

The industrialized world has also entered an era where public-sector deficit financing has become the norm, rather than the exception. The West is living in an "age of entitlement," wherein the public's demand for more government services parallels its demand for less government taxation and spending. Politicians and public servants oblige and yield to this "catch-22." Most of the member nations of the OECD now carry substantial operating deficits financed by borrowing—not a new phenomenon for many industries but, as some economists argue, an unacceptable one for governments.

Canada is no exception. With total government spending equal to 43% of the GDP in 1987, the federal government alone spends over $100 billion annually. The provincial, territorial, regional, and municipal governments combined spend that much again. In 1987, government deficits in Canada equalled 4.4% of the GDP, hovering around $30 billion for each of the previous three years.

Is Canada worse or better off than other countries? The Canadian federal net debt in 1987 was $11 386 per capita—10% greater than it was in 1986, 500% what it was in 1977, and 14.4% of the total net worth per capita. Of that figure, 76.9% was foreign-held debt; i.e., $8 750 per capita was owed to foreign creditors! In contrast, the foreign debt per capita for the United States was only $2 300 in 1987.

According to successive annual reports of the Auditor General and the Report of the Royal Commission on Financial Management and Accountability (Lambert Commission) in 1979, Parliament has lost all financial accountability and management control of the public purse. (Of course, the same had been said of Congress in the United States, where government spending as a percentage of GDP is much less than in Canada.)

What is the problem with increased government spending and, above all, increased government deficit spending? Is there a correlation between government upsurges in spending and a country's poor economic performance? Does greater government intervention financed through foreign debt result in lower productivity, higher unemployment, higher costs and prices, and a poorer international competitive position?

Or does government intervention actually lessen the blow of general economic fluctuations? The government cushion for the price of oil, for example, accomplished this throughout the 1970s after the Organization of Petroleum-Exporting Countries (OPEC) struck the West's economy in full force.

Overall, the evidence is at best mixed. Sometimes government intervention works, and stimulates or protects the economy. Sometimes it actually makes matters worse, both over the short and long term, by masking the real problems which then go unaddressed.

Comparing Canada to Japan and West Germany does not help much either: Japan has a lower level of government spending and much less government intervention, and is doing very well. West Germany has the same level of government spending as Canada, certainly a greater degree of government direction of the economy, and it, too, is doing quite well.

If these facts and figures have only confused you, you are in good company. The world is changing so fast and so unpredictably, it is almost impossible to have a thorough understanding of the global situation.

How, then, can Canada expect a future of economic prosperity without sacrificing its democratic ideals? What would be the role for business in achieving such a future? What new strategic management skills need business learn? Should the government provide leadership and direction? Can there be greater co-operation, consultation, and consensus between business and government, as in Japan and West Germany? How might business and government develop a greater appreciation for the growing interdependencies of the global economy?

These are among the challenging questions facing Canadian business and government leaders today. In the following pages, we will examine some of the factors that have created these situations.

THE STRATEGIC PROBLEM FOR BUSINESS AND GOVERNMENT

The amount of interaction between business and government has risen considerably in recent years. Business, to its credit, has exhibited growing concern about government's increasing role in economic affairs. However, the private sector remains reluctant to spend more money on the political process involved in shaping the role of government. It sees this as a long-term investment with no clear short-term benefits.

Business leaders may recognize that non-business interest groups are becoming more politicized, with greater success in getting their issues onto government's agenda. Yet, the private sector continues to be very reactive in nature, communicating its concerns to government *after* it discovers a threat, rather than before, by using the political process. In fact, most firms have no policy on political involvement, which underscores the low priority this subject has for business. Another distancing factor is management's disinterest in encouraging grass-roots political involvement among employees.

Therefore, the primary challenge for Canadian business lies not in managing its traditional tasks of production, marketing, or finance, but in relating individual firms to their ever-changing environments. Business must become particularly concerned about such non-economic factors as government policy, environmental uncertainty, global economics, and public pressure groups. As Figure 1-4 illustrates, business has evolved from a determinant economic system to a responsive social system.

This may at times require business to defend its very legitimacy in a mixed economy in which government apparently holds the upper hand. Managers will once again have to demonstrate convincingly to the electorate, through compassion and superior economic performance, that the "public interest" is indeed being well served by industry and commerce. Above all, this must be accomplished while working with government on an ongoing, proactive basis. Nothing will be gained by ignoring or working against government today. Business must adapt to this reality, as it must to free trade and other environmental changes.

To do this within a public forum, however, will not be easy. Beginning in the 1960s and continuing throughout the next two decades, public expectations of business rose dramatically. During the 1970s and 1980s, business was increasingly viewed by the public with suspicion. Both its size, its sheer economic power, and its ability to slow the rate of innovation were contributing factors to this attitude. Business could refuse to expand capacity at times to create much-needed employment; it deliberately inflated prices when improved productivity reduced production costs. In the public's mind, as well, business polluted cities and destroyed the environment. Business' interests were no longer blindly endorsed by the electorate as being in their own.

As a result, government's economic involvement with business has increased in a way not always to business' liking. Regulations now affect almost everything; e.g., hazardous product labelling, foreign investment control, language requirements in Quebec, pollution abatement, and so on. Public enterprise plugs market gaps to produce goods and services. Some firms have even been nationalized to better serve the public's interest.

In effect, the price system no longer directs the Canadian economy; instead, society's value system does — one which measures success other than just by profit. Social values are important to government today, and are eventually reflected in its policy. Public policy planners now concentrate on the net, as well as the gross, benefits of new business plans, proposals, investment, and requests.

Figure 1-4

The Firm as a Determinant Economic System

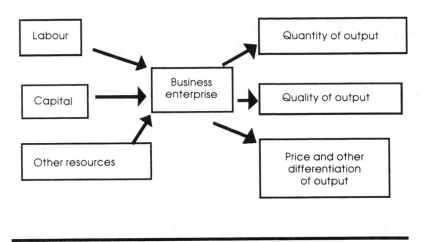

The Firm as a Responsive Social System

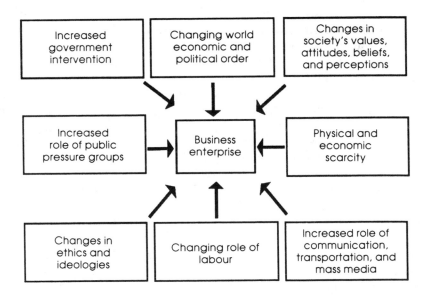

Source: Based upon a concept found in R.A. Buchholz *et. al. Management Response to Public Issues.* 2nd ed. Toronto: Prentice Hall, 1989.

The question of whether or not business has a corporate social responsibility is no longer debatable. Such arguments are akin to closing the barn doors after the horses have escaped. The voters have decided that business *does* have a social responsibility regarding job satisfaction, environmental protection, pay equity, community participation, and moral and ethical issues. The public looks to government, regardless of political stripe, to enforce this belief.

Why did this change occur in the public's attitude toward business? Some anti-business sentiment, sociologists would argue, is the result of Canada's inherent Judaeo-Christian suspicion of materialism. To many, there are higher callings than selling wares and accumulating wealth.

However, there is another reason. At the same time the public was becoming critical of business' behaviour, and government had begun encroaching on the private sector, business overtly started asking government for help. The economics of doing business were becoming more unfavourable to the risk-averse Canadian private sector. Therefore, government was asked for investment incentives, duty remissions, quota protection, loan guarantees, supply and price management mechanisms, and financial bailouts. Personal income tax rates—not corporate income tax rates—rose to cover these government expenditures. A new form of income redistribution was created: from the personal income taxpayer to the corporate income taxpayer, who often paid no tax at all!

Business is obviously reluctant to mobilize itself politically because there is no real advantage in doing so; in all probability, there is a great disadvantage. This is exemplified in a passage from a Sherlock Holmes story in which the intrepid detective described to his stalwart companion-in-arms, Dr. Watson, the unusual behaviour of a watchdog at the scene of a nocturnal murder. It was committed, as it turned out, by the dog's owner.

> Dr. Watson: Is there any point to which you would wish to show my attention?
> Sherlock Holmes: To the curious incident of the dog in the night-time.
> Dr. Watson: The dog did nothing in the night-time.
> Sherlock Holmes: That was the curious incident.

(Dogs do not bark at or bite the hand that feeds them.)

Where does government stand with all of this? Both business and government in Canada share the belief that it is in everyone's interest for Canada's economy to prosper and grow. Government obviously needs the tax revenue generated by economic growth to pay for all the social programs demanded by the electorate. Therefore, the Canadian government would be unlikely to stimulate competition through antitrust legislation and litigation, as in the United States. What's wrong with oligopolies, anyway, especially when one's small domestic market cannot support profitable and competitive businesses in many industries?

However, if you ask representatives of business and government to rank such economic issues as controlling inflation, providing full employment, stimulating real economic growth, reducing regional income disparities, and controlling foreign investment and ownership, you will receive many different opinions. *Although business and government agree on the ends, they disagree substantially on the means—and therein lies the strategic problem for business and government in Canada today.*

The ball is in business' court. The whole business-government issue is no longer a matter of garnering short-term benefits and assistance. It is now an issue of legitimacy and competence. Management must learn to better understand the players and processes of the public policy machine, the social, economic, and political goals of government, and the potential role of the private sector in government's formulation of macro-economic policies within this changed environment. To accomplish this, management must reorganize its corporate structures and allocate resources, no matter how scarce, to this vital task. It must also concentrate on the long-term survival of the firm, its industry, and the entire private sector, rather than on short-term profits, quarterly returns, and annual growth rates.

Above all, business management must be consistent, both in language and behaviour. Its credibility suffers immensely when it first cries for less government intervention and defends "free enterprise," then accepts government subsidies, tax breaks, and "corporate welfare."

Both public scrutiny of business, and business' growing dependency on government, have increased business-government interaction in frequency, if not in effectiveness. Yet, a wedge has been driven between business and government, of which we have seen only the thin edge. The government relations function for business has become a crucial, if under-utilized, function of corporate management.

Business is used to competing with other businesses in Canada. Now, it must get used to competing under a free trade regime with the United States, and in a freer trade environment worldwide. The challenge remains for business to effectively compete with other legitimate interests to establish a solid position on government's agenda. Ironically, it must also learn how to compete with government itself in the marketplace.

IMPLICATIONS FOR MANAGEMENT

Successfully managing a business enterprise today requires an understanding of several environmental variables. These include technology, government, social values, demographics, organized labour, international competition, shifting trade relations, and the ability to adapt to change. In traditional graduate management education, business strategy or policy is a solution to a problem. The problem usually arises when a product or technology is mismatched with the market—a situation almost always precipitated by external change. The solution lies in adjusting that "fit" or developing a whole new interface.

Today, however, the business problem is as much a mismatch between its mission and its socio-political-economic environments as with the marketplace. Therefore, business' approach to strategy formulation, implementation, and management must change accordingly. Business must try to understand government and society just as it understands its markets, products, and technology. The strategic question for business today should no longer be, "What is our role in society and how do we survive?" Unfortunately, management education and practice remain primarily market- oriented.

There is no denying the need for planning as resources become scarce everywhere and as the Western world's economic hegemony diminishes. Therefore, business-government relations today must be managed strategically for the long-term economic survival of both the firm and the country.

Given the environmental uncertainty of doing business anywhere in the world today, and given government's pervasive role in Canadian society, improving business-government relations can best be illustrated (as in Figure 1-5) by an open-system model of change. This is responsive to environmental changes, is cyclical in nature, and is chock-full of interdependencies.

Government thrives because people want more of what it provides. Government in Canada has also grown partly because business has wanted it to grow. Today, Canada and the world continue to change. For example, the United States is a declining economic power. This decline may be temporary or permanent, but either way Canada has linked its future with that of the United States—as the Free Trade Agreement testifies.

What role will Canada play in tomorrow's world economy? How long can this nation export its natural inheritance, while remaining grossly self-*in*sufficient in manufactured and high-technology goods and services?

What role should business take in plotting Canada's future? What is the role of a chief executive officer? What responsibility should government take? How can business and government co-operate for the benefit of all Canadians, given the overwhelming odds against this happening?

Admittedly, this chapter has offered more questions than answers. However, without a clear view of the problems and questions to be faced, the next chapters would be far less meaningful.

The management of business-government relations is the greatest challenge to both business and government leaders today—whether in day-to-day management of the Canadian political economy, or in bravely facing the new world together. *It is no longer adequate to just strive to do things right. Today management, whether private or public, must strive to do the right things.*

Figure 1-5

The Business-Government Relationship within an Open-System Framework

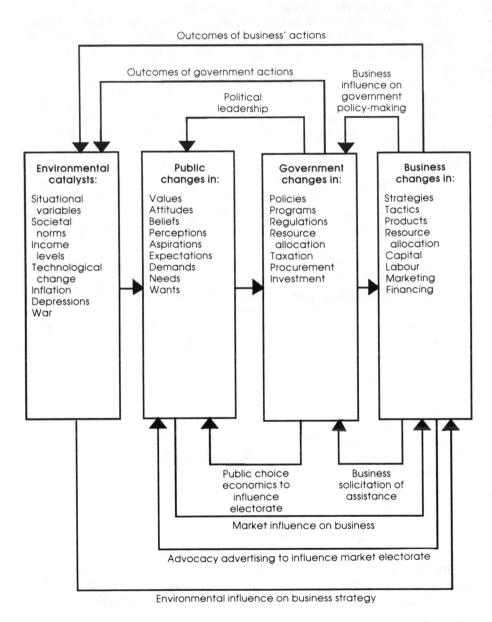

Source: Based upon a concept found in N.H. Jaesby. *Corporate Power and Social Responsibility.* New York: Macmillan, 1973.

SUGGESTED FURTHER READINGS

Ansoff, I.H. "The Changing Shape of the Strategic Problem," as in D.E. Schendel and C.W. Hofer, eds. *Strategic Management.* Boston: Little, Brown & Co. Inc., 1979, 30-44.

Banner, David K. *Business and Society: Canadian Issues.* Toronto: McGraw-Hill, 1979.

Bell, Daniel. *The Coming of the Post-Industrial Society.* New York: Basic Books, 1973.

Caldwell, G.T. *Corporate Planning in Canada: An Overview.* Ottawa: The Conference Board of Canada, 1985.

Danielson, Christen. "Business and Politics: Toward a Theory Beyond Capitalism, Plato and Marx." *California Management Review,* 21 (Spring 1979), 17-25.

Drucker, Peter F. *The Age of Discontinuity.* New York: Harper and Row, 1969.

Galbraith, J.K. *Economics and the Public Purpose.* Boston: Houghton- Mifflin, 1973.

————. *The New Industrial State.* Boston: Houghton-Mifflin, 1971.

Gilder, George. *Wealth and Poverty.* New York: Basic Books, 1981.

Keynes, J.M. *The General Theory of Employment, Interest and Money.* New York: Harcourt, Brace, 1965.

King, William L. Mackenzie. *Industry and Humanity.* Toronto: University of Toronto Press, 1919, 1973.

Murray, V.V., ed. *Theories of Business-Government Relations.* Toronto: Trans-Canada Press, 1985.

Murray, V.V. and C.J. McMillan. "Business-Government Relations in Canada: A Conceptual Map," *Canadian Public Administration,* 26 (Winter 1983), 591-609.

Schumpeter, Joseph A. *Capitalism, Socialism and Democracy.* New York: Harper and Row, 1942, 1946, 1949.

Smith, Adam. *An Inquiry Into the Nature and Causes of the Wealth of Nations.* New York: Modern Library, 1937.

Statistics Canada Publications.

Trebuss, A. Susanna. *Defining the Strategic Environment: An Analysis of Organizational Perspectives.* Ottawa: The Conference Board of Canada, 1981.

CHAPTER 2
A BRIEF HISTORICAL BACKGROUND

In Canada, you are reminded of government every day. It parades itself before you. It is not content to be servant, but will be master.

Henry David Thoreau, 1817-1862

Many historians, political scientists, and sociologists have concentrated on Canada's business-government relationship as affected by the country's economic development, social order, and cultural confusion. The one common thread through all these studies has been the ease with which the state was accepted, and at times even solicited, by the private sector as an economic partner—often a senior one. Canada's economic history clearly shows the reciprocal, almost symbiotic relationship between public and private sectors. Thus have national and private economic goals been achieved.

Because Canada has remained an open and relatively small economy, the United States has historically had significant potential influence on this country's pattern of economic development. Therefore, both political and business elites throughout Canada's history have regularly co-operated to develop a healthy, independent economic and political entity. In fact, businesses have frequently and consciously sought protection from American economic dominance. Consequently, the Canadian economic culture is different from the American economic culture against which Canadians often, and inappropriately, compare themselves. The government has always dominated the Canadian economy.

As Prime Minister Pierre Elliott Trudeau so succinctly noted in a 1976 speech to the Canadian Club in Ottawa:

The free market system, in the true sense of that phrase, does not exist in Canada . . . the fact is that for over a hundred years, since the government stimulated the building of the CPR by giving it Crown land, we have not had a free market in Canada, but a mixed economy—a mixture of private enterprise and public enterprise. . . . Moreover, it has been with the support and encouragement of the business community that the government has continued to enter the marketplace to promote growth and stability. Among many examples are the creation of the Canadian Wheat Board, the negotiating of the Canada-United States Auto Pact and the government's heavy investment in Syncrude.

19

THE EARLY YEARS: NATION-BUILDING OR EMPIRE-BUILDING?

Of course, the roots of Canadian business-government relations germinated long before the United States was a mighty economic power or Pierre Trudeau was Prime Minister.

The much-heralded fur trade, for example, was a state-created monopoly. If not for the Crown's 1670 chartering and protection of the Hudson's Bay Company, and the colonial governing elites' involvement with the fur trade, so much wealth would never have been available to build the commercial empires which succeeded the fur trade.

Concurrently, the Canadian timber trade was a state-franchised oligopoly, again based upon the lease and/or sale of Crown land to geographically franchised monopolies. These seldom, if ever, had the inconvenience of competition imposed upon them. In fact, there was a succession of staple traders, each encouraged and protected by government. Each was dependent upon a more advanced, external economy for financing and markets; each business was an oligopoly or monopoly.

Some historians believe that this reliance upon exporting staples and importing foreign investment has kept Canada in a permanent state of colonialism. Others would argue that it was the only way such a geographically dispersed, thinly populated nation could have survived, let alone grow to be a member of the First World (OECD). However, the facts remain: government intervention and business success worked hand in hand to build Canada.

Back in the seventeenth and eighteenth centuries, it was quite common to find Canada's founders, or their heirs, directing their conglomerates of monopolies and trading houses, sitting in the legislatures, and advising the heads of state as members of Cabinet. The local conservative merchant banks and insurance companies, which did their small part to finance and insure the trade of fish, furs, timber, and grain were also owned by mercantilist-politicians. Seldom was a loan directly advanced to the manufacturing industry or to agriculture.

"Conflict of interest" was a concept yet to be advanced. There was no shame in being a merchant, banker, landowner, canal builder, and politician, all at the same time. Such was the closeness of business and government then; the public purse hung from the waistcoat of business.

In 1826, the St. Lawrence canal system was begun. Even into the present, the system has been an example of a publicly financed work. It was undertaken and is still operated to reduce transportation time, to lower costs, and to benefit the coffers of Canadian commerce.

Confederation, and Canada's evolution from a scattering of colonial autocracies to a unified, pluralist democracy, did nothing to change this business-government relationship. As Prime Minister Trudeau earlier indicated, the building of the Canadian Pacific Railway (CPR) was actually a joint venture between the private and public sectors. Sir John A. Macdonald's National Policy of 1879 was one of tariffs and quotas. It was intended to build domestic industry by assuring it the growing Canadian market and protecting its independence from the United States.

Typical of the omnipresent businessmen-politicians of that era was Sir George-Étienne Cartier, a Father of Confederation and Quebec Lieutenant to Prime Minister Sir John A. Macdonald. Cartier's grandfather was a classic mercantilist, or intermediary in the flow of goods and services. He traded in fish, wheat, and salt; his father used the family fortune to establish the Bank of Montreal with Peter McGill of McGill University fame. Cartier himself was also intimately involved with the Grand Trunk syndicate, while serving as Sir John A.'s second-in-command.[3] His rhetoric underscores his beliefs: "In order that institutions may be stable and work harmoniously, there must be a power of resistance to the democratic element."

As one of the French-Canadian elite, Cartier, along with Sir John A. Macdonald, would begin to accommodate the French-English elite in Canada. He also represented the elite accommodation of business and government.

A typical example of someone on the other side of the business-government fence (a very low, un-intimidating fence) was Donald Smith, later to become Lord Strathcona. Both preceding and following Confederation, he owned, controlled, or was a major shareholder in both the Hudson's Bay Company and its chief rival and eventual partner, the North-West Company. He also held shares in the Bank of Montreal, the Grand Trunk Railway, and the Canadian Pacific Railway. Strathcona also happened to own most of the land designated for the CPR and the urban settlements along its route, as well as most of the arable western land that the CPR would open up to settlers!

Canadian politicians and businessmen were quite willing to use the state to control and develop the economy in the name of nation-building, and to defy the lure of the south. If these well-meaning public servants and entrepreneurs happened to enrich themselves along the way and acquire their own personal financial empires, such was the reward for public-mindedness. National goals were met, and personal wealth was accumulated. What a business-government relationship!

Another result of this interrelationship of Canadian merchant capital, British financial capital, mercantilistic zeal, and a sympathetic political establishment was the dearth of indigenous Canadian industrial capital and entrepreneurship. However, that could always be imported from the United States — for a price. Canada had everything it needed to drive a

---

[3] Sir John A. Macdonald was later President of the Manufacturers Life Assurance Company.

ribbon of steel across the northern half of the continent: money, labour, raw materials, land. All it needed was know-how. It was no accident that William Van Horne, an American engineer, became responsible for the construction of the CPR.

The National Policy of 1879 may have protected Canadian industry, but it also invited American industry to jump the tariff barriers and set up branch plants in Canada. These were of adequate size to serve Canada's small domestic market with neither mandate nor capacity to export. Macdonald's plan did create industry—American branch plant industry. Thus the growth of Canadian industrial entrepreneurism was further hindered, a situation that continues today. True free-enterprisers would never have allowed such government "protection." They would have fought to the finish and died an honourable, glorious death.

The Canadian mercantilists of the nineteenth century were, in fact, the forebears of the service sector, now the largest single employing sector of our modern economy. More important, Canadian business has continued to solicit and receive government intervention and protection throughout the twentieth century.

THE EVOLUTION OF A BUSINESS-NATION

Canada's reliance upon its primary industries at the expense of its secondary (manufacturing) industries is no longer news to most Canadians. The preoccupation with the fur trade first by the French and then by British settlers represented the first and second commercial empires in Canada. The preoccupation with fish, grain, pulp and paper, minerals, and fossil fuels over the past century represents the third successful commercial empire in Canada. Each of these empires has been commercially, not industrially based, and has been subservient in one form or another to a foreign, more advanced economy, whether French, British, or American.

In effect, Canada still is a colony. With respect to industry, Canada is underdeveloped. As George Brown, one Father of Confederation, said as the new Dominion of Canada set its expansionist eyes on borders eastward, westward, and northward: "If Canada acquires this territory it will rise in a few years from a position of a small and weak province to be the greatest colony any country has ever possessed." History has proven George Brown right, although not in the way he would have hoped.

Colonialism implies that someone benefits from the exploitation of another. Therefore, being in an almost permanent colonial state is not all bad; at least the elites of the economies involved benefit. During the French regime—the first commercial empire of the North—native Canadians were exploited for their furs and the *coureurs de bois* were exploited for their labour, while the Montreal merchants grew rich.

With the Treaty of Paris in 1763, the French gave the British a virtual

monopoly in Canada. This, combined with Britain's established monopoly in the North-West, laid the foundation for modern-day Canadian
business. Almost a century later, in 1844, the pattern of Canada's market
structure was cast with the merger of the two largest land companies in the
nation: the Canadian Company of Upper Canada, owned by Father of
Confederation John Galt, and the British American Land Company of
Lower Canada, owned by Peter McGill and George Moffat. Ironically, the
new interlocked board of directors of the merged company also represented a large portion of the Executive Councils, or Cabinets, of these two
provinces. This particular arrangement became known as the *Family
Compact,* or *Château Clique*—the new elite of the second commercial
empire of the North.

Business life was similar in the Maritimes. The merchant class had
acquired wealth during the War of 1812, importing American goods and
selling them to Britain, and importing British West Indian goods and
selling them to the United States. This elite, led by Joseph Cunard,
virtually controlled the timber, banking, shipping, and shipbuilding industries in Atlantic Canada.

Overall, there was low capital investment in pre-Confederation Canada, which relied almost solely upon labour-intensive harvesting of natural resources for its income. Local merchant capitalists, who dominated the
business scene, were financed by British bankers, thus insuring that more
money was sent to the mother country than remained in local coffers. As
time passed, Canadian merchants pooled their capital into their own
banks. It was natural for Canadian bankers, controlled by the land, fur,
shipping, and timber companies, to allocate most of their loan capital to
those involved in the trading of fish, fur, grain, and timber. Such investments were short- term and obviously with minimum risk. This was not so
of agricultural or industrial development, which received very little in the
way of loans.

During the late 1700s and early 1800s, Britain and the United States
were beginning to invest in their own countries' industrial production.
Growth of their respective manufacturing industries and saturation of
their domestic markets required Britain and the U.S. to find new markets
for exports, and new and greater sources of raw materials. Canada offered
both.

In 1854, a fundamental shift in Canadian economic dependency began
taking place. Canada initiated a policy of reciprocity (what we would
today call, "free trade") with the United States to develop this potential for
trade. Railroads such as the Grand Trunk were built to penetrate the
American midwest market and reach the ice-free ports of the East Coast.
Americans built railroads and the Erie Canal across New York State to
access Canadian raw materials and transport American manufactured
goods to Canadian markets. Shippers of both countries soon preferred to
use the American transportation network, since it was shorter and cheaper.

Canadian business leaders began to look to the United States for financial opportunities and away from their parent, Great Britain.

In due course, however, the Grand Trunk and other Canadian railroads faced bankruptcy. Fortunately, John Galt, Minister of Revenue for the colony of Canada, was a member of the Grand Trunk Board. He proceeded to raise tariffs to protect his railroad; the United States retaliated, and reciprocity was scuttled. Canadian business-government relations were alive and well.

As the Union forces of the North emerged successful from the American Civil War in 1865, British investors in Canada, fearing Canadian annexation, clamoured for government protection of their assets. Canadian merchant capitalists also feared that, unless they were unified and protected, they would soon become American citizens. Sir John A. Macdonald and his allies provided the answer: political union of the British North American colonies and a tariff wall around the new dominion. As Macdonald argued:

> There are national considerations . . . that rise far higher than the mere question of trade advantage; there is prestige, national status, national dominion . . . and no great nation has ever arisen whose policy was Free Trade.

Thus was born the third commercial empire of the North—a mercantilist empire characterized by a strong and interventionist state, state protection of big business, tariff barriers, subsidies, and a positive trade balance. Strong corporate, elitist linkages were forged among merchant capitalists, landowners, financiers, transportation czars, and government leaders. The CPR replaced the Hudson's Bay Company as the favoured state-chartered monopoly. Tariff barriers protected small Canadian businesses, attracted foreign industrial capital (which was scarce in Canada), and discouraged potential emigrants from seeking opportunities elsewhere.

Macdonald could not have said it better when, in 1878, he cried:

> We have no manufacturers here. We have no work-people; our work-people have gone off to the United States . . . these Canadian artisans are adding to the strength, to the power, and to the wealth of a foreign nation instead of adding to ours. Our work-people in this country, on the other hand, are suffering from want of employment. . . . If these men cannot find an opportunity in their own country to develop the skill and genius with which God has gifted them, they will go to a country where their abilities can be employed, as they have gone from Canada to the United States. If Canada had had a judicious system of taxation, they would be toiling and doing well in their own country.

Merchant capitalists grew richer without having to spend their own dollars; the state made sure of that.

THE HALCYON DAYS OF C. D. HOWE: COME AND GONE

The Great Depression of the 1930s stimulated government intervention in the economy on an unprecedented scale. Keynesian economics, emphasizing government deficit spending in times of scarcity, took firm hold of the public policy fraternity. Unfortunately, most government policymakers soon forgot the other half of Keynes' prescription: for governments to save during times of economic prosperity!

After the Depression, World War II produced a skilled federal bureaucracy reasonably in tune with, and partly recruited from, the business community. Businessmen, as "dollar-a-year-men," were conscripted into many of the major government positions under the leadership of American immigrant Clarence Decatur (C.D.) Howe.

C. D. Howe was in many ways the reincarnation of the nineteenth-century mercantilist. He was a self-made millionaire from the grain trade and the consulting business, was blessed with sound intuition, and was a recognized leader of the national business community. He was also a minister of the Crown and a popular leader of the Liberal Party of Canada (until 1984, the dominant one in Canada). Business' interest was solidly in the forefront of public policy.

During the war, the federal government's economic policy increasingly reflected the influence of Keynes, and its budget became the major tool of economic reform. Business-government relations were considered by both sides to be very good and very important. Everyone agreed on the one clear, overriding objective—winning the war.

Under Howe's leadership, the Canadian GNP increased from $5.6 billion in 1939 to $11.9 billion in 1945. During the war, Canada was the fourth-largest Allied supplier of military goods and services. This industrial expansion was attained through Howe's generous loans, grants, tax write-offs, and accelerated depreciation. Canadian industry emerged from the war with world-class facilities fully financed by untaxed war profits. These firms had been primarily engaged in manufacturing small items to foreign design specifications and assembling off-line manufactured parts.

Postwar business-government relations continued to be good. Although the 1945 White Paper on Employment and Reconstruction, a product of the public service, was a large step towards government direction of the economy, the business community generally accepted it. Government supported economic expansion, particularly in the basic industries, and semi-annual meetings were held for business and government economists. Fearing a postwar depression, the government extended its "temporary war-time measures" of assistance to business every year into the 1950s. Business, of course, did its share to co-operate. In fact, for over a decade after the war, Canada was regarded as one of the best countries in the world in which to invest.

Also after the war, Howe sold off many of the Crown corporations he had created for the war effort. He retained his strong belief in the concept of Canadian public enterprise, however, keeping Polymer Corporation Ltd. (the forerunner of Polysar) and Eldorado Mines (Eldorado Nuclear). He also protected the trans-national monopoly of Trans-Canada Airlines (Air Canada).

Prime Minister William Lyon Mackenzie King had delegated so much authority to Howe during the 1940s and early 1950s that national economic and industrial policy had become his personal jurisdiction. If Sir John A. Macdonald had been the architect of the Dominion of Canada, C. D. Howe was the contractor who built it!

After the war, as in Confederation-era Canada, Howe's wartime "dollar-a-year-men" returned to the head offices of corporate Canada. They used their knowledge, contacts, and expertise to build and expand their empires and create huge fortunes. The epitome of these was E. P. Taylor, who amassed his empire under the name, Argus Corporation.

Howe's greatest asset was his two-way channel of information from the boardrooms to the Cabinet table and back. His greatest skills were in intelligence-gathering and organization—and organize he did. Howe created the public enterprises to supply the Canadian war effort when the private sector could not respond quickly enough. He also helped put together the consortia that built the St. Lawrence Seaway and the Trans-Canada natural gas pipeline, and he encouraged the harvesting of Canada's vast natural resources—all, of course, with heavy government assistance.

Howe was the champion of megaprojects. He sincerely believed that the Canadian economy needed at least one megaproject on the go at all times. C. D. Howe did not believe in a competition policy just for the sake of having one. The key to Canadian prosperity, he believed, was low-cost, high-efficiency manufacturing. This meant large, workable business conglomerates with internal economies of scale, often oligopolies or monopolies, to offset the nation's natural dis-economies of scale.

Above all, Howe believed in Keynesian economics. He urged Canadians to believe that, by carefully balancing government fiscal and monetary policies, economic growth would continue in perpetuity. The unabashedly pro-business Howe introduced to Parliament the 1948 White Paper on Employment and Income, the blueprint for Keynesian countercyclical government budgeting and government intervention.

To say the least, C. D. Howe was an enigma. He believed in private initiative; he believed in government protection of public initiative; he believed in government initiative. He certainly believed in the personal accumulation of power. Howe was conceptual and abstract in his thinking, yet he was pragmatic in his actions. Above all, he was typical of the era; he was truly "Canadian."

It was Howe who helped keep Mackenzie King in power longer than any other prime minister in the history of the British empire. But, in 1957, it was Howe who was largely responsible for his government's downfall under Prime Minister Louis St. Laurent.

That year, the Liberals were defeated by the western populist Progressive Conservative leader, John Diefenbaker. The new prime minister decried the immorality of big business, big government, and the United States' collusion to build the Trans-Canada Pipeline. Howe, who had represented big business and big government, was also personal friends with American cabinet members and Texas oilmen supporting the project.

The Canadian electorate chose Diefenbaker's nationalistic rhetoric over Howe's continentalist pragmatism. Observers noted a gradual worsening of business-government relations with Diefenbaker's election. The process was rapidly accelerated under the successive Liberal governments of Lester Pearson and Pierre Trudeau.

One of Howe's projects, or "children of the war," was A. V. Roe Co. (Avro), a manufacturer of warplanes for the Pacific theatre. Avro made its mark in the world of aviation with the production of its conventional jet fighter, the CF100 *Canuck.* With its cost-plus defence contracts and aircraft manufacturing profits, Avro purchased control of Atlantic Canada's steel and coal interests and diversified into a true conglomerate. As the *Canuck* aged, Avro unveiled plans for a successor—a supersonic, all-weather, state-of-the-art jet interceptor, the CF105 *Arrow.*

Cost projection overruns of 800% soon led to the Liberal government's secret plan to scrap the *Arrow* after the 1957 election, but the Liberals lost to the Progressive Conservatives. When Prime Minister Diefenbaker cancelled production of the *Arrow,* 14 000 jobs were lost at the Malton, Ontario, plant alone. Research engineers emigrated in droves to the United States, where a growing space program beckoned.

Prime Minister Diefenbaker's fortunes declined steadily thereafter, as did the state of business-government relations. Yet, they should not have. The Progressive Conservative government's 1960 budget guaranteed that business would be pre-eminent among the growing number of pressure groups appealing to government for intervention. By re-introducing accelerated depreciation, investment tax credits, exemptions, and depletion allowances, government hoped to accelerate investment and economic growth and to postpone the feared postwar recession. Excise taxes, customs duties, and tariff rates were also increased to bolster government revenue to offset lost tax revenue. However, one effect of stimulating Canadian manufacturing and decreasing a reliance on imports would be to negate the increase in nominal import tax rates. Business won again; private investment was again underwritten by an unwitting public.

C. D. Howe died in 1960 and was succeeded by Winnipeg economist Mitchell Sharp, who was both intellectual and personable. Sharp, too, had origins in the grain trade. He eventually became Howe's speechwriter, and rose to become Deputy Minister of Trade and Commerce. He eventually ran for Parliament, and was appointed to, among other posts, Minister of

Industry, Trade and Commerce and Secretary of State for External Affairs. However, business-government relations were not the same as under Howe.

Later, under Pearson and Trudeau, decision-making in Ottawa changed. It became collegial, centralized, and rationalized. Strong ministers were replaced with strong Cabinet committees; strong departments and their mandarins were replaced by strong central agencies—a new, inaccessible cabal accountable only to the prime minister.

Yet, as political economist, former cabinet minister, and successful businessman Eric Kierans noted:

> For the life of me, I cannot understand the hostility of the business community to the Trudeau government. It cannot be on the basis of what the federal government has done, for literally big business has never had it so good. With the exception of the United Kingdom, I doubt that any nation in the world has given its Corporate 1000 a more handsome gift package of subsidies, tax allowances, two-year write-offs, deductibility of merger costs, cheap loans, export credits and insurance than our present Trudeau government. If this be socialism, business should cry for more.

Ironically, these centralizing trends have not been undone by Progressive Conservative Prime Minister Brian Mulroney, former president of the American-owned Iron Ore Company of Canada and self-described ideological ally of neo-conservatives Ronald Reagan and Margaret Thatcher. In fact, since Mulroney first took office in 1984, there is strong evidence that rule- by-central-agency has become a given. Every minister in his government has been instructed to hire a chief of staff to co-ordinate the interaction among the minister, the minister's department, the minister's constituency, and the central agencies.

However, despite business' growing dissatisfaction with government, the two most significant reforms of the Canadian tax system since the 1930's Depression came from Liberal Finance Minister E. J. Benson in 1971, and Progressive Conservative Finance Minister Michael Wilson in 1988. These offered more provisions for big business to get bigger at the expense of the individual taxpayer.

From the 1960s through the 1980s, Canada experienced the birth and rapid growth of social security programs, federal-provincial transfer payments to finance them, social and economic regulations of every kind, and higher taxation to pay for all this. Canada also felt the effects of double-digit inflation and unemployment, despite Keynesian interventions to control these. Due to government's overwhelming complexity today in both decision-making and program delivery, it is inconceivable to return to the halcyon days of C. D. Howe and the older, much simpler methods of business-government accommodation. The days of C. D. Howe are over—never to return. But does it really matter?

IMPLICATIONS FOR MANAGEMENT

David Lewis, the former leader of the New Democratic Party (NDP), attacked Canada's "corporate welfare bums" in the 1968 federal election. But Lewis' targets for denunciation were not recent phenomena. Canada did not embark upon the road to a symbiosis of big business and big government with Prime Minister Mulroney's election in 1984. Nor did it begin with C. D. Howe during the 1940s and 1950s; nor with the National Policy of 1879.

In fact, it began with the chartering of the Hudson's Bay Company in 1670. Since then, the government of Canada has been very supportive of business—particularly big business. It was true back in the days when Canada's national politicians were also Canada's business leaders, and when business' favourite son, C. D. Howe, was also controller of government policy levers. It remains true today. Canada has never looked back— nor ahead—until the signing of the Canada-U.S. Free Trade Agreement on January 2, 1988.

Government's continuing economic support of business in this country has not eased the environment in which these two forces have co-existed. Misunderstandings and conflict abound. The tide of events influencing business-government relations has been running in the wrong direction. Of course, business people still work with government, but many are unhappy about its type of leadership. Nor has communication been as productive as might have been hoped. New initiatives have been tried and found wanting. Government has sought to legitimize labour organizations, whether or not they truly represented their sectors of society, or were interested in participating.

With rare exceptions, the intimacy and obvious linkages between business and government of the 1950s, let alone of the nineteenth century, no longer exist. The few exceptions are challenged by charges of conflict-of- interest. In fact, business-government interaction today is very formal, with government acquiring information and advice through advisory boards and sectoral committees. Business offers its opinion when testifying before committees of the House of Commons or before royal commissions. One no longer "talks" to the deputy minister responsible for "whatever the industry- related ministry is called this week." Now industry-related policy decisions are taken by a committee of Cabinet advised by a general secretariat in the Privy Council Office.

Business' rhetoric criticizing government's intervention is both useless and hypocritical. Nor does the public buy it—or government's rhetoric against big business. Both sides could better spend their time and energy reconstructing the linkages which have been broken—ironically, often as a result of government's trying to operate in a more businesslike manner.

It is true that the federal government still solicits advice about business' needs at budget time, so appropriate changes to various tax statutes can be made. But is that enough? Can government alone construct the economic climate necessary for Canada to successfully compete with the rest of the world? Can government alone forge the alliances which will best serve this nation's interest in waging that war? Can government alone carve out a niche for Canada within the global marketplace, after the dust of economic conflagration has settled? Most likely not. Business must be heard in Ottawa again, as it was ever so briefly in the shaping of Canada's negotiating position prior to signing the Canada-U.S. Free Trade Agreement.

As celebrated political scientist Professor Alexander Brady has professed: "The role of the state in the economic life of Canada is really the modern history of Canada." There is no denying or escaping that fact. The only difference between today and the 1860s is that the Canadian mixed economy of Macdonald's era was business-dominated; today, government dominates it. Business must learn to live with this reality as best it can. Government and its economic intervention are not going to disappear overnight.

SUGGESTED FURTHER READINGS

Aitken, H.J.G. "Defensive Expansionism: The State and Economic Growth in Canada" as in W. T. Easterbrooke and M. H. Watkins, eds. *Approaches to Canadian Economic History*. Toronto: McClelland & Stewart, 1967.

_____. "Government and Business in Canada: An Interpretation." *Business History Review*, 38 (1964), 4-21.

Berton, Pierre. *The Last Spike*. Toronto: McClelland & Stewart, 1971.

_____. *The National Dream*. Toronto: McClelland & Stewart, 1970.

Bliss, M. *Northern Enterprise: Five Centuries of Canadian Business*. Toronto: McClelland & Stewart, 1987.

Bothwell, R., and William Kilbourn. *C.D. Howe: A Biography*. Toronto: McClelland & Stewart, 1979.

Bothwell, Robert et al. *Canada Since 1945*. Toronto: University of Toronto Press, 1981.

Brady, Alexander. "The State and Economic Life in Canada" as in K.J. Rea and J.T. McLeod. *Business and Government in Canada: Selected Readings*, 2nd ed. Toronto: Methuen, 1976.

Creighton, D.G. *The Commercial Empire of the St. Lawrence*. Toronto: Macmillan, 1970.

_____. *The Empire of the St. Lawrence*. Toronto: Macmillan, 1956.

Innis, H.A. *Essays in Canadian Economic History*. Toronto: University of Toronto Press, 1956.

_____. *The Fur Trade in Canada*. Toronto: University of Toronto Press, 1930.

_____. *Problems of Staple Production in Canada*. Toronto: Ryerson, 1933.

Lower, A. *Canadians in the Making*. Toronto: Macmillan, 1959.

Marr, William L. and D. G. Paterson. *Canada: An Economic History*. Toronto: Gage Publishing Limited, 1980.

Naylor, R.T. *The History of Canadian Business 1867-1914*. 2 vols. Toronto: James Lorimer and Company, 1972, 1973.

_____. "The Rise and Fall of the Third Commercial Empire of the St. Lawrence," as in Gary Teeple, ed. *Capitalism and the National Quest in Canada*. Toronto: University of Toronto Press, 1972.

Nelles, H.V. *The Politics of Development*. Toronto: Macmillan, 1973.

Traves, T. *The State and Enterprise*. Toronto: University of Toronto Press, 1979.

CHAPTER

3 ENVIRONMENTAL FRAMEWORK

He blunted us.
We had no shape.
Because he never took sides,
And no sides,
Because he never allowed them to take shape.

F.R. Scott, 1899-1985

Having briefly surveyed the history of Canadian business-government relations, the questions which arise are: Why do Canadians elect governments which directly interfere with the economy? Why has Canada chosen the collectivist path of Tory conservatism rather than the individualistic route of liberalism? Why do both national parties, lacking any distinct ideologies but straddling the political centre together, support state intervention, state social security, and state protection of production and the owners of capital? Moreover, why does business not object philosophically to the growth of government?

THE CANADIAN INHERITANCE

The answers lie in a paraphrase of R. MacGregor Dawson, dean of Canadian government studies in the early 1900s. Professor Dawson maintained that if an individual's personality, traits, and characteristics were predetermined both genetically and through socialization, a nation's culture could form the same way. It would be affected by the heredity of its charter groups and its environment, including such situational variables as geography, climate, natural transportation networks, and human immigrations.

Canada's tendency towards an organic polity is thus deeply rooted in a lack of revolutionary tradition and a high tolerance for state intervention by the nation's founding, or charter, groups. Both "Tory" British loyalists, fleeing the republican anarchy of the United States, and pre-French Revolution francophone settlers, easily accepted a paternalistic state supporting their major economic institutions. *Thus, the early political, corporate, bureaucratic, and landed elites of our nation cast the mould for business-government relations for centuries to come—elitist, cooperative, and even collusive at times.*

For this reason, contradiction is the norm in Canadian politics and economics. The Conservative government of Prime Minister R.B. Bennett created the state media consortium of the Canadian Broadcasting Corporation (CBC). Similarly, the Progressive Conservative government of Prime Minister Brian Mulroney attempted to trim federal expenses by "privatizing" selected Crown corporations, (just as the Liberals did after the war), while defending Canada's need to retain control of a state-owned national airline.

In the mid-1980s, Conservative Energy Minister Pat Carney told the House of Commons that the price of oil would not be lowered, nor would Petro-Canada, the country's state-owned oil conglomerate, be sold. These tax and operating revenues, she stated, help pay for a universal health insurance system, post-secondary education, and pensions. This is not right-wing ideology; this is Canadian pragmatism. (As is today's debt-ridden government's talk about selling Petro-Canada.)

Initially, the concerns of our United Empire Loyalist and French-Canadian ancestors centred around protecting their beliefs and identities from the political, economic, and cultural expansionism of the United States. Never could they have realized the impact that their preserved values would have on modern-day Canada. The British North America Act, 1867, Canada's first constitutional document, included the Tory Loyalist values of social stability, hierarchy, order, and collective social action. These were manifested in the Act by the words, "peace, Order and good Government"—in stark contrast to the American Constitution's guarantee of individual rights to "life, liberty, and the pursuit of happiness."

The differences are clear. The United States was symbolized by Wyatt Earp—sometimes marshall, sometimes killer—his brothers and Doc Holliday shooting it out with the Clanton Gang at the O.K. Corral for control of the territory. Canada, on the other hand, was symbolized by stiff and proper Superintendent James Walsh (who?) of the North West Mounted Police, leading the exiled American Indian chief, Sitting Bull, to a peaceful new home north of the border. The American cowboy *tamed* the Wild West; the North West Mounted Police *settled* the Canadian West.

That is not to say that, in Canada, individualistic roots are trampled underfoot by a state monolith. Canadians are very individualistic. However, they temper their individualism with compassion for those in Canada less fortunate than themselves, who cannot exercise their rights as freely or as demonstratively. They manifest this compassion through the electoral and state policy apparatus.

With respect to business, there has never been a dogmatic, universal, liberal, free-enterprise spirit in Canada, as there is in the United States. Canada's founding fathers were immune to liberalism and capitalism, and to a large degree, so are their descendants.

These two founding nations produced the mercantilists of Canada's past and the Keynesian capitalists of Canada's present. Most illustrative of this influence is corporate concentration. As American industry consolidated in the late 1800s and reduced the level of competition in many industries, the United States government implemented a series of antitrust laws and regulations. It hoped to break up monopolies and oligopolies and restore a semblance of unfettered competition.

In contrast, as Canada's industry consolidated during the late 1800s and the level of competition was reduced, the Canadian government did nothing. Thus, the state tacitly acknowledged and protected economic concentration in this country.

Historically, Canada has been, and still is, a public enterprise country, where business and government elites together direct and co-ordinate the economy. This has always been the case, and probably always will be. As a result of this heritage, Canadians are, above all, pragmatic. Many critics say Canada has no national ideology because of this. They are wrong. Canada's ideology *is* pragmatism.

AN ECONOMIC CULTURE

Most social critics today, influenced by American hegemony, equate a society's cultural identity with its economic system. As a result, critics often mistakenly accuse Canada of not having a discernible cultural identity, since it has no distinguishable economy. Canadians appear to the uncritical and untrained eye as well-mannered Americans.

In fact, however, Canada's unique economic system is responsible for this nation's particular cultural identity. In keeping with the critic's form of analysis, the Canadian cultural identity *does* reflect its economic system. Both are grounded in two aspects of modern economic life. While not unique to Canada in form, they are certainly unique to Canada in the zeal and effectiveness with which each is applied: public enterprise and regional economic redistribution.

As evidenced earlier, Canadian public enterprise had its beginnings in the chartering of staple monopolies and the building of transportation and communication infrastructures for the growing Canadian economy. The latter commenced with the building of the Lachine Canal in 1821 along the St. Lawrence River to facilitate ease of passage for staple-bearing ships. Since then, public enterprise has provided the main stimulus to build a modern nation-state. Locks and canals, railways, public utilities, broadcasting, airlines, petroleum processing and marketing, and hundreds of other businesses have all worn the Crown in the name of uniting this vast land as Canada grew from sea, to sea, to sea.

For a labyrinth of political, economic, and cultural reasons, regional redistribution has equally been a force in this nation's building. The federal government has sought to keep geographically, socially, and economically disparate regions unified and as equal as possible in their standards of living, levels of health care, rates of employment, and opportunities for higher education. To facilitate regional equity, it has devised a number of complex financing arrangements and policy instruments. These have often been implemented through provincial agencies.

Canada's polity is continually reinforced by its *confederal* form of government. This is often erroneously labelled and compared to the *federal* form of government practised in the United States and elsewhere. A *confederation* by definition is a union of formerly independent political entities. It possesses a national government, as well as provincial or state governments. The national government is a first among equals, similar to the principle of the prime minister and his fellow ministers of the Crown in Cabinet. A *federation* is also a union, but clearly sets the national government supreme above the subordinate stable governments. In reality, the balance of power in a confederation fluctuates over time, despite a written constitution, often because of judicial or legislative interpretations.

Canada appears federal in nature when the national government is strong vis-a-vis the provinces collectively, as during the Government of Prime Minister Trudeau. It is in practice quite confederal when the national government is weaker vis-a-vis the provinces collectively, as it is said to be today. Curiously, Sir John A. Macdonald's first preference was for a *unitary* form of union and government, as in the United Kingdom, where there would have been no provincial governments.

Thus it is that Canada *does* have a cultural identity, grounded in the principles of public enterprise and regional parity, and complemented by the neo-corporatist values of state direction of the economy, and state respect for and protection of private property.

IMPLICATIONS FOR MANAGEMENT

Canadians are a collectivist, politically pragmatic people strongly influenced by, but largely ignorant of, their past (remember Superintendent Walsh?). This is true of both the average individual's general historical awareness of Canada's roots, and of business' and governments' understanding of their beginnings in this country. Few Canadians truly understand the framework within which business-government relations were cast long ago and have operated ever since.

Most Canadians are also unaware of the historical, cultural, and socioeconomic differences between Canada and the United States. For one thing, despite government protection of its *cultural industries* (including broadcasting, publishing, and the arts), Canadians are bombarded daily with modern American "culture." Second, and more important, Canada's social system and its novelties are less apparent to the naked eye and uninformed mind than are those of the United States.

Canadians have become masters in distributing wealth, whether as mercantilists or as enterprising, socially conscious public officials torn between liberalism's equality of opportunity and socialism's equality of condition. Such traits are well hidden in the superficial constructs of a western economy. Canada's roots in eighteenth-century Toryism have made twentieth-century democratic socialism quite acceptable—even by business—in many aspects of daily Canadian life. Business has even accepted publicly owned corporations which fill voids where private enterprise would not risk financial ruin in a country with a population so widely and thinly dispersed.

Canada exhibits traditional views which can only be retained through slowly evolving social change. Revolution quickly kills old traditions and creates new ones. This is not to say that Canadians have not and are not changing; of course they are. For example, the government's inability during the 1970s to curb rising inflation and unemployment severely undercut public confidence in, and traditional deference to, government.

The Canadian experience has revealed a high tolerance for diversity and a capacity to incorporate social change with relative ease. However, the changes are incremental and slow in evolving.

Business managers in this country must remember that environmental influences are not always variables that can be internalized and controlled. They are fundamental to the very being of business and must be dealt with by chief executive officers head-on, with unblinkered vision, open minds, and all the negotiating and navigational skills they can muster. Of course, business can influence, and even control to some degree, its environment through advertising, vertical integration, cartelization, or other means. However, there are very real limits to what even the largest corporation can do, given the momentum of the Canadian political juggernaut.

If anything, Canada is a practical country founded by practical people. Necessity has truly been the mother of invention, whether it be public enterprise to supply public goods or regional income redistribution to overcome industrial and commercial disparities.

These characteristics also represent the price Canada pays for independence, success in the world, and the unique benefits of a Canadian way of life. Canada's economy is definitely a public economy; Canada's culture, a public culture. The retaining of private property, promoting of state collectivism, and resolving of the conflict between the two are achieved through a process of elite accommodation.

Canadians have chosen to compete less against each other than against the odds of building a world-class country and economy. They both fear and envy the United States, where geographically such a feat was considered illogical and impossible. Canadians are not second-rate Americans. They are first-rate Canadians—a nation of creative, determined survivors.

Today Canada faces its greatest challenge since Confederation: surviving in a rapidly changing world economy in which the competitive advantages of yesterday will become the millstones of tomorrow. Business and government also face their greatest challenge: they must act in harmony as they have never done before. Only thus can they meet this external threat of global proportions when pressures are pulling them apart, and when public esteem for both institutions has waned significantly.

To do this, as noted economist and adviser James Gillies has advocated for some time, business and government must forge a truly "Canadian" approach to future interactions. For business, the economic imperative of long-term survival is identical to that of the Americans, Japanese, or British. All must maintain an adequate competitive advantage over existing and potential rivals, and continually strive to produce an optimal balance among their environment, goals, strategies, structure, performance measures, and control and reward systems.

However, the political imperative of Canadian business is significantly different from its foreign counterparts to warrant an unprecedented approach to business-government relations. Not only has the Canadian government accommodated the economic needs of business throughout history, but Canadian business has been expected to provide the means by which to achieve government objectives. These include such areas as regional employment, security of domestic supply, and interprovincial equity in prices and services. Of course, government has helped, but this co-agency of business and government is far more integral to the Canadian socio-economic system than to the American system.

Canada's past must be the basis for its future, particularly with respect to business-government relations. This implies a uniquely Canadian approach to a uniquely Canadian problematic relationship. To this end, the nation must move forward.

SUGGESTED FURTHER READINGS

Bell, D.V.J. and L.J. Tepperman. *The Roots of Disunity: A Look at the Canadian Political Culture.* Toronto: McClelland and Stewart, 1979.

Blair, R.S. and J.T. McLeod, eds. *The Canadian Political Tradition: Basic Readings.* Toronto: Methuen, 1987.

Grant, George. *Lament for a Nation.* Toronto: McClelland & Stewart, 1965.

Hardin, Herschel. *A Nation Unaware: The Canadian Economic Culture.* Vancouver: J.J. Douglas, 1974.

Hartz, L. *The Liberal Tradition in America.* New York: Harper and Row, 1963.

Horowitz, G. "Conservatism, Liberalism and Socialism in Canada: An Interpretation." *Canadian Journal of Economics and Political Science*, 32:2 (1966), 143-171.

Kierans, Eric. *The Corporate Challenge to Government.* The Walter L. Gordon Lecture Series, 1976-1977, Volume I.

Lindblom, Charles E. *Politics and Markets: The World's Political-Economic Systems.* New York: Basic Books, 1977 (especially Chapter 13).

Macpherson, C.B. *The Real World of Democracy.* Toronto: CBC Learning Systems, 1976.

Rea, K.J. and N. Wiseman, eds. *Government and Enterprise in Canada.* Toronto: Methuen, 1985.

Stewart, W. *True Blue: The Loyalist Legend.* Toronto: Collins, 1985.

THE PLAYERS

Having now developed an appreciation for the historical and cultural underpinnings of Canadian business-government relations, let us examine the nature of the key players—business and government. The next four chapters will show how Canada's past has shaped the respective roles and structures of business and the state, and how these in turn influence their interrelationships.

CHAPTER 4

BUSINESS IN CANADA

Markets are not created by God, nature, or economic forces but by businessmen.

Peter F. Drucker, 1909–

What legacy remains from Canada's three original commercial empires? How have they helped shape Canada's present business community?

First, staples continue to be the basis of Canada's largely service-oriented economy. Natural resources are generally sent from west to east, while manufactured goods flow from east to west. Ontario produces 54% of all manufactured goods and 57% of all technology-intensive exports. Toronto has become the commercial, financial, and trading capital of the nation, amassing its wealth from the natural resources of the rest of the country.

Generally speaking, economies today are divided into three sectors, each of which is subdivided into a number of industries. The three economic sectors are: primary (agriculture, fishing, mining, oil and gas, and forestry); secondary (manufacturing, processing, and construction); and tertiary (wholesale/retail trade, finance, insurance, real estate, government services, transportation, communications, and utilities).

In 1867, about 50% of Canada's GDP was in the primary sector; 30% was in the tertiary sector, and only 20% was in the secondary sector. By the early 1900s, those figures had changed to 40%, 30%, and 30% respectively. Today, less than 10% of Canada's GDP is from the primary sector; secondary industry now accounts for little more than 25%; and the tertiary sector, including all government administration, accounts for over 65% of the GDP.

Over 70% of Canada's employment today is in the service sector, with less than 7% in agriculture and resources. This may be one reason why Canada's overall productivity has not increased dramatically of late, since most productivity-improving technology is used by the primary and secondary sectors. However, government is well aware of the service sector's importance to employment. American hotel magnate J. Willard Marriott, when opening his 161st hotel worldwide in Toronto in 1986, noted with envy the launch's enthusiastic reception from both provincial and regional governments.

43

In the U.S., a governor will fly to Japan immediately if there is a chance of getting an electronics plant in his state to employ 200 people; but propose to build a hotel, which will employ 600 people, and you get practically no response and certainly little incentive . . . Tourism is the main employer in 35 of our states, but our state and federal governments don't recognize it as an industry like they do here in Canada.

Tourism is Ontario's second largest industry. It employs more than 70 000 people in Metropolitan Toronto alone, and adds $1.7 billion to the area's economy. Yet the Americans recognize that although service industries are labour-intensive, it is manufacturing that creates wealth, not hotels.

Second, there is a high degree of economic concentration within Canada today. This is particularly true of the insurance, transportation, brewing and distilling, natural resource, and merchandise trading industries. Increasingly, leaders of these industries are committing to foreign investment, thus becoming multinational corporations (MNCs). They have done so rather than support growth in their own country's secondary sector of manufacturing, processing, and construction.

Third, although Canada possesses a healthy supply of its own capital, foreign investment continues to pour into the country, while interest and dividend payments pour out. Today, the vast majority of foreign direct investment funds flow to and from the United States. Canada's economic metropole is no longer Great Britain, but the United States. Some would argue that American political influence is evident as well.

Fourth, Canada continues its tradition as a trading nation. As recently as 1988, with the signing of the Canada-U.S. Free Trade Agreement, Canada reaffirmed this focus. From Confederation to World War I, Canada imported manufactured goods from the United States and exported resources to Britain. However, by the outbreak of World War II, Canada had become much more reliant upon the United States as both a source of manufactured goods, and a market for raw materials. As Figure 4-1 shows, about 75% of all Canadian trade today is with the United States.

Fifth, Canada has a very fragmented industrial relations system, with only about 30% of labour unionized. Active government involvement in social welfare has pre-empted the development of a strong, unified, politically active labour movement. However, Canada's labour costs are high because of both minimum-wage legislation and pro-labour industrial relations legislation.

Canada also has a chronically high rate of unemployment, primarily because of a reliance upon seasonally operated resource industries such as fishing and logging. The temporarily unemployed are supported by government- financed schemes, in turn financed by taxation. This ultimately increases the costs of operating a Canadian business.

Finally, Canada has a very strong state which, except for labour rights, is

Figure 4-1

Trade by Geographic Region–Canada, 1987

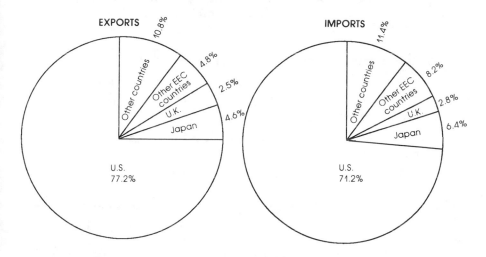

Source: "Trade by Geographic Region, 1987", Catalogue No. 65-0018, Statistics Canada. Reproduced with the permission of the Minister of Supply and Services Canada, 1990.

both pro-business and pro-mercantilist. Canada's business community has grown, first through outside financial interests and later supported by a paternalistic state defending it from an expansionist United States.

Canada is, in effect, a business-nation: a country founded by business, and developed to further business' interests, all in the public interest. If the Fathers of Confederation were alive today, they probably would be pleased with the results of their initiatives; their objectives of a sovereign state with a mercantilist economy have been well met. Of course, some Canadians are not as pleased with the current state of affairs as would be the Founding Fathers.

ECONOMIC CONCENTRATION

Canada has a highly concentrated economy. In 1978, the Royal Commission on Corporate Concentration discovered that the volume of sales for the top 100 companies was equal to that of the rest of corporate Canada. More significantly, 1/8 of 1% of all registered Canadian corporations controlled 58% of all Canada's private assets, produced 30% of all goods and services, and received 39% of total corporate profits. Since then, that figure has not changed.

The author's 1984 survey of the top 500 firms in Canada further revealed that 75% were in industries where the top four firms serviced 50% or more of their respective markets.

According to economic theory, the ownership of assets will be more concentrated than average within an economy in general, or a particular industry, when:

1. there is a sustained economic downturn;
2. an industry has reached maturity and real growth is negligible;
3. economies of scale are both desirable and achievable for the industry's long-term survival as competition intensifies;
4. tariffs are used to protect domestic industry in a small domestic market; and/or
5. there is no government legislation to prevent it.

In Canada's case, explanations (3), (4), and (5) apply in almost all cases historically; explanation (2) applies in some cases; explanation (1) applies occasionally.

Observant students of capitalism will readily admit that economic concentration is a natural objective for free market forces to pursue. Predator capitalists will attempt to diminish competition and increase their profitability through mergers and acquisitions. Monopolies or oligopolies make it much easier to control one's market.

In this sense, Canada is even more "capitalistic" (or at least, a more mature version) than the United States. Thanks to a Tory-corporatist heritage, there has been little government interference in the concentration of wealth in the hands of a few. Canada has a "competition policy" which advocates a "reasonable" degree of competition for the economy. As a result, the rankings of Canada's largest companies usually change slowly. Few large firms ever go bankrupt. The United States, in contrast, has "antitrust" statutes which enable the government of that country to dismantle business giants such as Standard Oil and A.T. & T.

The disadvantage of economic concentration is simple: there is an inefficient allocation of economic resources. This results from the "waste" inherent in the "excess" profits from those companies that dominate an industry's production and ownership.

Historically, *aggregate economic concentration*—the percentage of economic activity accounted for by the very largest firms (usually four)—is lower today in Canada than it was at the turn of the century. In fact, it declined from 1923 to 1966, remained about the same for the period 1966 to 1975, and has slowly increased since then. Furthermore, the average size of Canada's 100 largest non-financial, or 25 largest financial, firms is much smaller than their counterparts in other major industrialized countries. Yet Canadian aggregate concentration by assets is generally much higher than elsewhere, and about twice that in the United States.

However, Canada's level of *industrial* or *market concentration*—that within a particular industry—has been steadily increasing, particularly in the secondary sector, since 1948. Major booms occurred in the 1948-1954 postwar period of C.D. Howe, and more recently during the 1980s. Today Canada's degree of industrial concentration is generally much greater than that found in the United States.

On a global scale, most Canadian firms may seem small and inefficient, but within the home market, they are giants! Top Canadian firms are only 20% the size of their American counterparts, and serve a domestic market only 10% the size. Only five Canadian corporations rank in the world's Top 100: General Motors of Canada Ltd., Bell Canada Enterprises Inc., Ford Motor Company of Canada, Canadian Pacific Ltd., and George Weston Ltd. Yet, General Motors is 100% American-owned and Ford is 97% American-owned. Weston's is 58% owned by the Weston family. The only Canadian-owned companies with widely distributed ownership to make the Top 100 are Canadian Pacific and BCE.

However, the actual level of concentration may be even greater than statistics show, given the level of private and family ownership of Canadian assets, and a fluid definition of "control" (as opposed to outright ownership) of a firm. This effect is probably magnified by interlocking boards of directors, the relationship between holding companies and their subsidiaries, creditor relationships, pension fund investment strategies, public enterprise and state ownership of assets, and the personal influence of key individuals.

Holding companies and multi-divisional conglomerates have enabled 361 of the largest Canadian companies to maintain operating linkages with 4 944 other companies. The most important linkage of all, however, was through their boards of directors—a vast network of interconnecting points consisting of even fewer individuals. Members of a firm's board often include members of rival boards, its suppliers, major buyers, legal counsel, and most important, its bankers. Such formal contacts have helped to stifle "destructive" competition, improve financing capacity, improve communications within the industry, and lessen the overall risk of doing business.

Up until the 1980s the trend was in the concentration of ownership of assets, and not in control of sales. In fact, concentration on the basis of sales has dropped slightly over the last two decades as conglomerates diversified into unrelated product areas. On the basis of assets, 80% of the Toronto Stock Exchange 300 (TSE 300) is owned privately, compared to 20% of Standard and Poor's 500 in the United States. *Nine families control 46% of the value of the TSE 300!* The only obvious exclusions from these tightly held holdings were the banks, steel companies, Canadian Pacific, and BCE—all widely held stocks.

The 25 largest companies in Canada were owned by 32 families and 5 corporate conglomerates. In turn, *these 25 firms* (as compared to 100 firms in the U.S.) *owned 30% of Canada's almost $500 billion worth of non-financial assets— this in a country in which there are over 400 000 incorporated businesses!* Out of the 100 leading firms by assets in Canada, 25 were family-controlled, 25 were controlled by conglomerates, 25 were foreign-owned and 25 were state enterprises. In fact, only 25 of the 500 largest companies in Canada had a wide distribution of ownership, as compared to 425 out of 500 in the United States.

These statistics for Canada do not include companies in which families/individuals may own only 20-30% of the equity but exert *de facto* control. Some of these families are household names to most Canadians. They are led by the Reichmann family with a net worth of $9 billion, and K.C. Irving and his family at $8 billion (as compared to the richest American, Sam Walton of Walmart fame, reportedly worth only US $2.8 billion). Following them are Lord Thomson and his family at $6.4 billion, the two Bronfman families with $2.4 billion and $1.6 billion respectively, and the Eaton and Weston families at $1 billion apiece. Then there are the non-billionaires who round out the top ten: Ted Rogers, Robert Campeau, and Michael G. DeGroote.

Whether the above are household names or not, the companies they control surely are. For example, Lord Thomson owns The Bay, Simpsons, Zellers, Markborough Properties, Thomson Travel, and more than 300 newspapers in the English-speaking world, including *The Globe and Mail.* The Reichmanns own, among others, Olympia and York, Abitibi-Price, Consumers Gas, Gulf Canada Resources, and Block Brothers Industries, and control 24% of the Campeau empire. The "poorer" Bronfman cousins—Edward and Peter, who were left out of the Seagram inheritance—landed on their feet owning: Brascan Ltd., John Labatt, Noranda, Hees International Bancorp Inc., London Life Insurance, Royal Trustco, Royal LePage, Trizec, Bramalea, the Toronto Blue Jays, and more. Probably the farthest-flung empire is that of W. Galen Weston. His nearly 1 000 companies in a dozen countries include: Loblaw Companies Ltd., Weston Bakeries Ltd., Bowes Company, Donlands Dairy Company Ltd., Wm. Neilson Ltd., Eddy Paper Company Ltd., British Columbia Packers Ltd., National Tea Company, Holt Renfrew, and Fortnum & Mason.

Of course, as mentioned earlier, two management-controlled conglomerates are not privately owned and are equally powerful: BCE Inc. and Canadian Pacific. BCE's holdings include: Northern Telecom, Bell Canada, Telesat Canada, Memotec Data, the former Dome Canada, Teleglobe Canada, New-Tel Enterprises, Bruncor, Maritime Telephone and Telegraph, the former Daon Development, and TransCanada Pipelines. Canadian Pacific Inc. owns, among many others: AMCA International, Syracuse China, CP Hotels, Marathon Realty, CP Steamships, Soo Line, Arion Insurance, CP Express and Transport, CPR, CIP, Laidlaw Transportation, CP Telecommunications, and Great Lakes Forest Products. And these are only the tips of the mammoth commercial icebergs!

Figure 4-2 Selected Industries and their Respective Concentration Ratios, 1970 and 1980

INDUSTRY/PRODUCT	CR$_4$ * 1980	1970
Tobacco products	99.6%	96.9%
Breweries	99.0	94.0
Motor vehicles	93.7	93.3
Aluminum rolling, casting	88.1	89.6
Iron mines	86.7	76.8
Railway rolling stock	85.3	79.2
Fabric gloves	82.7	67.4
Biscuits	79.9	68.1
Iron and steel mills	77.9	76.2
Major appliances	77.0	62.8
Stone products	25.0	22.2
Logging	21.4	20.8
Children's clothing	21.0	13.1
Men's clothing	20.6	12.0
Commercial printing	18.2	17.1
Dental labs	14.8	19.5
Plastics fabricating	10.1	16.2
Misc. machinery and equipment	8.3	16.1
Machine shops	6.4	7.2
Women's clothing	6.4	8.0

* Percentage of shipments from the four largest enterprises

Economists would use a *concentration ratio* to describe the phenomenon of economic concentration. Most common is the CR$_4$. This indicates the weighted average percentage of the total production of a particular industry by the four largest companies in that industry. A *strong oligopoly* is said to exist when the four largest producers within an industry control more than 40% of their market. A *weak oligopoly* exists when the CR$_4$ is between 20% and 40%.

When the four largest producers within an industry account for less than 20% of total industry sales within their market, *effective competition* is said to exist. For example, in 1980 the CR$_4$ for tobacco products was 0.996. This tells us that the four largest tobacco companies produced 99.6% of the total in that industry (see Figure 4-2).

The industry concentration ratio for agriculture, on the other hand, is extremely low. This reflects the small, fragmented, family orientation of farming and the competitive nature of a commodity market structure. Another reason for the lack of large American-style agriculture-business in Canada is the reluctance of Canadian banks to give the high-risk, long-term loans necessary to aggregate farming interests. However, agriculture is largely cartelized on the supply side, where federal or provincial marketing boards can set quotas. Supply management affects such products as eggs, broiler chickens, turkeys, milk, most fruit and vegetables, and wheat.

About one-half of all manufacturing sub-industries have a CR_4 of 0.75 because of oligopoly market structures. The other half has very low concentration ratios. As Figure 4-2 depicts, in general, the higher the technology-based, value-added component of the product, the higher the concentration ratio. The more labour-intensive a segment, the lower its CR_4.

Despite recent attempts at deregulation, Canada still has duopolies in national air and rail transportation, as well as in TV networks. Government-owned or franchised monopolies provide telecommunications, electric energy, and natural gas distribution.

On the other hand, concentration in the retail and wholesale sectors is generally low. That is changing rapidly, however, as the impact of specialty chains headed by Dylex and the Grafton Group makes their presence known. Similarly, within a particular product line, strong market control usually belongs to one or two companies. For example, Storkcraft makes 66% of all baby cribs sold in Canada; 75% of all baby food sold is made by Heinz. Kraft sells 65% of all cheese eaten in Canada; 35% of all detergent purchases are of Proctor and Gamble's Tide, while 65% of all disposable lighters sold are by Bic.

As to services, Budget and Tilden handle 63% of all car rentals; Southam and Thomson combined produce 50% of all newspapers read in Canada, and The Toronto Stock Exchange performs 74% of all stock trades.

Overall economic concentration in Canada is largely the result of three major periods of merger and acquisition since the turn of the century. 1909 to 1912 saw a shake-out in the steel, cement, and automobile industries worldwide, resulting in the formation of the oligopolies now common to those industries. From 1925 to 1930, the processing industries such as pulp and paper, food products, and chemicals became much more concentrated through takeovers and expansion. And most recently, the retail, land development, and resource industries were allowed to become heavily concentrated through mergers and takeovers between 1974 and 1984.

It was during this latest period that the giants of Canadian industry got involved. Abitibi merged with Price; Consumers Gas merged with Home Oil and then acquired Hiram Walker; Olympia and York took over Abitibi-Price, Consumers-Home-Hiram Walker,[4] Block Brothers, Brinco, and got a share of Trizec. The Hudson's Bay Company acquired Zellers, Simpsons, and Markborough Properties, only to be acquired along with F.P. Publications by the Thomson family. Petro-Canada gobbled up Petrofina Canada, Pacific Petroleum, and BP Canada. Peter and Edward Bronfman acquired Brascan, which through its subsidiary, Brascade Resources, acquired Noranda Mines, which had already acquired MacMillan Bloedel.

---

[4] In 1986 the Reichmanns sold Hiram Walker-Gooderham & Worts to Allied Lyons PLC of Britain for $2.6 billion.

From 1974 to 1984 a staggering 4 685 corporate takeovers were re-corded—largely made possible by pension funds.[5] The total price: $235 billion—an amount equal to the national debt! Of that amount, only 6% or $14 billion left the country.

Today, Canada is in the throes of another takeover binge. As a result of deregulation in the financial sector, the major banks are each acquiring a major stock brokerage firm. Hot on the banks' heels were Nova Corporation's takeover of former Crown corporation Polysar Energy and Chemical Corporation, and Dofasco Inc.'s purchase of Algoma Steel Corporation from CP Ltd.

Three other already heavily concentrated industries also saw their ranks thinned during the week of January 16, 1989. Texaco Canada was absorbed by Imperial Oil Ltd., Wardair was acquired by Canadian Airlines International (itself a recently acquired subsidiary of Pacific Western Airlines), and the Molson Companies' brewing operations merged with those of Australian-owned Carling O'Keefe.[6]

What does all this economic concentration mean for Canada? Is it good or bad for the consumer? for the nation?

Certainly, there are drawbacks to a highly concentrated economy, an environment of oligopolistic industries, and a country where government lacks initiative to force the private sector to compete. For one, there will be higher and more stable prices than in a more competitive situation. If prices do change, they usually go in one direction—up. Economists call this *price leadership*: one firm within an industry decides to increase or lower prices, and the others swiftly follow. There may or may not be collusion involved; it just becomes accepted behaviour that the others will follow. Stelco has done this for years in the steel industry; Canadian General Electric (CGE)—now Black and Decker— does this in the small household appliance trade.

As demand exceeds industry capacity, price leadership keeps new entrants out. The price leader, because of its size and its inherent economies of scale, will keep the price below a monopoly price level. It will also resist natural inflationary pressures to increase it, so that the leader and its few rivals can keep the lion's share of the industry in their own hands.

In the resource industry, this is taken to an extreme where enormous

---

[5] The top ten pension funds in 1987 had a total asset base of $38.24 billion of which $26.97 billion was invested by public sector employee groups.

[6] Ironically, the Chief Executive Officer of Molson's is Marshall (Micky) Cohen, who as Deputy Minister of Energy, Mines and Resources introduced the Trudeau Government's National Energy Policy. This was designed to significantly raise the federal government's share of equity in the oil and gas industry. His rationale for the Molson-Carling merger was to develop economies of scale so as to better compete with the American beer giants, Anheuser-Busch and Miller, under the Canada-United States free trade regime. Wardair, however, was left penniless while facing major costs for fleet replacement and expansion. The partial deregulation of the airline industry lowered fares and forced Wardair to operate at un-economic margins.

barriers to entry and economies of scale exist. These arise from the control of the supply of raw materials and vertical integration. In resources, there is usually one very dominant firm, such as Alcan in aluminium and Inco in nickel.

When ownership of assets is concentrated in the hands of a few, with no specific firm dominant, and when products are homogeneous, a behaviour called *conscious parallelism* can also develop. Prices are never cut for fear of a devastating price war, and prices are seldom increased because of buyer resistance. When prices are increased, they rise simultaneously and to the same level because of their almost identical cost function. Such is the case of the oil companies and most industrial products. The results give the appearance of collusion, but are really the outcome of mutual interdependencies. Collusion is seldom necessary.

Finally, a common criticism levelled at big business is that economic concentration inhibits new job creation. Supposedly, the small, independent business sector, not big business, creates employment. However, in Canada such is not completely the case. Between 1974 and 1982, small business generated 55% of all new jobs, while big business (employing 500 or more workers and usually part of an oligopoly) accounted for 40% of new employment opportunities. Overall, the effects of concentration for Canadians are:

• higher, yet more stable prices than under a more competitive regime;
• lower rates of entry, with less selection;
• excess capacity;
• slower rates of adapting technological innovation than in a more competitive situation; and
• gradually upward shifting cost curves following this inefficiency and lack of competition.

Yet, what does government do? Canada has had a competition policy of various sorts since 1889, but over 50% of its prosecutions occurred after 1970. Why? Originally the Competition Act was part of the Criminal Code. It is now part of the Civil Code, making prosecution and the burden of evidence to prove guilt a lot easier. However, even though litigation has gone up, convictions remain few and penalties light. Furthermore, the entire service sector was excluded from the Act until 1976.

Canada's competition policy has always been little more than a grinning, toothless paper tiger. Business has successfully argued that stiffer anti-trust regulations are not "in the public interest," and government has agreed. For big business in today's competitive world, it is either grow or die.

FOREIGN DIRECT INVESTMENT, OWNERSHIP, AND CONTROL

No other major industrialized nation in the world has the level of foreign direct investment, ownership, and control that Canada has. Foreign ownership of Canadian business peaked in 1973 at 37% of assets. By 1985, it had dropped to 29%.

According to the 1981 census, foreigners controlled or owned 50% of all manufacturing businesses in Canada, 44% of the oil and natural gas industry, and 46% of mining and smelting interests. Figure 4-3 gives a breakdown by selected industry of foreign ownership in 1985 as compared to 1975.

Before World War I, Britain was the major source of foreign capital and ownership in Canada. In 1900, for instance, 85% of all foreign investment in Canada came from Britain in the form of portfolio investment; a full 90% of British capital in Canada was invested in Canadian securities. Of particular appeal were government bonds, non-voting shares of banks and companies with monopoly or oligopolistic market control, and short-term loans. Thus Canada had the best of both worlds—foreign investment and domestic control.

Today, the proportion of foreign ownership of Canada's economy is about the same as it was in 1900. However, instead of Britain's 85% involvement, the United States accounts for 60% of total foreign investment today. Although the Statute of Westminster of 1931 formally severed Canada's last colonial ties to Britain, Americans accounted for 54% of foreign investment in Canada as early as 1926.

Most American investment is in Canadian branch plants as common voting equity or foreign direct investment (FDI). Today, Canada pays for its foreign investment by losing some control over its private sector. Originally, branch plants were built to produce and sell to the Canadian market without having to pay import tariffs. Since tariffs did not generally apply to "parts," most American branch plants were simply assembly operations, importing parts for assembly from elsewhere. As a result, these branch plants today are small, since they are to serve only the Canadian domestic market. For the most part, they are in southern Ontario to minimize shipping costs from the United States' industrial heartland. Today, however, there is very little correlation between tariff protection and American FDI, as indicated in Figure 4-4.

In 1978, the Royal Commission on Corporate Concentration revealed that foreign interests owned or controlled $100 billion worth of assets in Canada. Almost 75% of that was American-owned, a percentage first reached in 1959. It has remained stable at this level ever since. Of that $75 billion, almost 60% was invested in secondary manufacturing, 30% in oil and gas production, and 10% in the mining industry. Clearly, American capital has filled the gap left by the lack of Canadian industrial capital. In fact, over the past decade, nine Canadian businesses have been sold to foreign investors, each worth over $100 million (see Figure 4-5).

Historically, there has been a strong, positive correlation between FDI and concentration within the Canadian economy. The level of FDI is high

Figure 4-3

Foreign Ownership of Selected Industries, 1975 and 1985

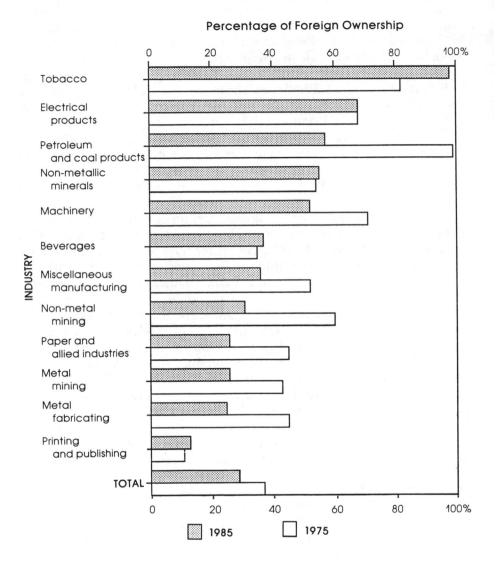

Percentage of Foreign Ownership

INDUSTRY

Tobacco
Electrical products
Petroleum and coal products
Non-metallic minerals
Machinery
Beverages
Miscellaneous manufacturing
Non-metal mining
Paper and allied industries
Metal mining
Metal fabricating
Printing and publishing
TOTAL

1985   1975

Source: "Corporations and Labour Union Returns Division," Statistics Canada. Reproduced with permission of the Minister of Supply and Services Canada, 1990.

Figure 4-4

Tariff Protection and Foreign Direct Investment

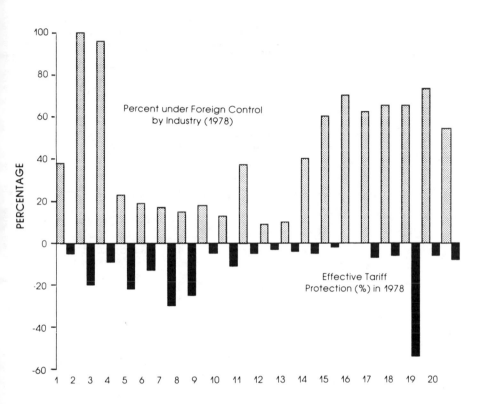

Industry

1. Food & beverage	11. Printing & publishing
2. Tobacco	12. Primary metals
3. Rubber	13. Metal fabricating
4. Leather	14. Machinery
5. Textile mills	15. Transportation equipment
6. Knitting mills	16. Electrical products
7. Clothing	17. Nonmetallic minerals
8. Wood	18. Petroleum & coal
9. Furniture	19. Chemicals
10. Paper & allied	20 Misc. manufacturing

Sources: *Corporate and Labour Unions Report*, 1985, Statistics Canada. Reproduced with the permission of the Minister of Supply and Services Canada, 1990.

Figure 4-5

Major Foreign Takeovers, 1979-1989

YEAR	ACQUISITION	NEW OWNER
1979	Canadian Superior Oil Ltd.	Superior Oil Co. (U.S.A.)
1985	Mitel Corp.	British Telecom (U.K.)
1986	Hiram-Walker Gooderham and Worts	Allied Lyons PLC (U.K.)
	Continental Bank	Lloyds Bank (U.K.)
	deHavilland Aircraft of Canada	Boeing Co. (U.S.A.)
1987	Cadillac Fairview Corp.	JMB Realty Corp. (U.S.A.)
	British Columbia Forest Products Ltd.	Fletcher Challenge Ltd. (New Zealand)
	Carling-O'Keefe Ltd.	Elders IXL Ltd. (Australia)
	Versatile Farm Equipment Corp.	Ford Motor Co. (U.S.A.)
1989	Consolidated-Bathurst	Stone Container (U.S.A.)

in industries with both high concentration ratios and moderate-to-high barriers to entry, such as producers of automobiles, tobacco products, office equipment, petrochemicals, and pharmaceuticals. Americans in particular own a large proportion of these capital-intensive manufacturing interests and non-renewable resource industries—the latter being Canada's historical competitive advantage. However, there is no valid evidence to suggest that FDI has added significantly to the high levels of economic concentration in this country.

Conversely, less FDI exists in industries with lower levels of ownership concentration. In fact, foreign investors (particularly Americans) are divesting themselves of assets and operations in unconcentrated industries. This is a result of the unacceptably low profit margins and intensifying domestic and international competition. Industries such as those producing clothing, beverages, furniture, and leather goods, as well as construction, retail, and wholesale merchandising—all heavily labour- intensive— have now become targets for foreign *divestment.*

Thanks to government policy and regulation, a low level of FDI is also found in industries of "national strategic significance," such as public utilities, transportation, communications, financial institutions, and broadcasting. Therefore, Canada has developed sufficient competitive advantages in these areas to acquire a solid foothold in world markets.

In 1987, 190 of the top 500 corporations in Canada were at least 50% foreign-owned. Of these, 139 were completely foreign-owned. Another 15 of the top 500 were foreign-controlled.[7] Of these 205 companies (40% of Canada's top 500 corporations) 116 were American-owned or controlled.

Is FDI good or bad for Canada? As might be expected, there are advantages and disadvantages, depending on one's personal and political perspective. On the plus side, many argue that FDI provides:

- technology otherwise not available;
- management skills different or superior to our own;
- much-needed industrial capital, either through initial investment or re-investment of earnings;
- improved productivity through economies of scale;
- industrial growth;
- new markets for domestic goods and services;
- employment;
- more competition;
- more selection/better quality; and
- a higher standard of living.

Those who argue against FDI cite that it:

- restricts the amount of research and development (R&D) done in Canada, therefore decreasing Canadian innovativeness;
- retards even further Canadian industrial entrepreneurism;
- reduces Canada's exporting/trading capacity;
- reduces the opportunity to upgrade raw materials before exporting;
- increases the outflow of capital from the country in interest, principle, and dividend payments;
- infringes upon Canada's political sovereignty, since many multinationals place their home country's laws above those of their host country;
- reduces Canadian control over the Canadian economy;
- takes employment away from Canadians;
- reduces Canada's independent identity;
- forces consumers to pay higher prices while bearing much of the risk of foreign-owned business, while the rewards of doing business in Canada are exported;

---

[7] 20-49% ownership of voting equity representing the largest single block.

- reduces Canada's real income and economic growth;
- reduces Canadian participation in the economy; and
- impedes government from formulating and implementing economic and social policies designed in Canada's best interests.

Although the debate over FDI's advantages and disadvantages has raged on-again, off-again over the past 25 years, two truths have emerged from a number of studies. *First,* FDI has had no real effect on R&D or technological development in Canada. If Canadian investors owned the enterprises now in foreign hands, there is little evidence that they would have either the economies of scale or the retained earnings to conduct the same level of research and development as that of multinationals in their home countries. What little R&D does occur in Canada's foreign-owned or controlled multinational corporations probably equals what domestic companies could afford, given comparable Canadian spending patterns in this area. On the whole, foreign subsidiaries have contributed as much or more to new technology development in their industries as have their Canadian-owned competitors. The notable exceptions are such stars of Canadian R&D as Northern Telecom Ltd. and Spar Aerospace. American investors of sizeable R&D funds in Canada are IBM Canada Ltd., Digital Equipment of Canada Ltd., Unisys Canada Inc., and Litton Systems Canada Ltd.

The *second* emergent fact about FDI is that Canadian-owned companies are estimated to be 19% less productive than foreign-owned or controlled subsidiaries. This is a direct result of the availability of capital to foreign multinational corporations. Other factors are production and marketing economies of scale, lower costs, advantages in production and information technology, and transfer pricing and internal trade capabilities.

What has government's response been to foreign ownership and foreign control of Canadian business? Imperceptible. From 1974 to 1984, only 11% of all foreign investment proposals were denied. This, during the most nationalistic period of government screening of foreign investment! The Canadian government, regardless of political stripe, has accepted FDI as inevitable in a small, yet advanced, open economy where mercantilists have always prevailed over industrialists. An impressive 95% of foreign investments approved by government have been "compatible with national industrial and economic policies".[8]

The irony of the foreign investment issue is that FDI by Canadian companies abroad between 1973 and 1985 grew faster than did FDI in Canada (see Figure 4-6). At the end of 1987, however, the country still had a FDI deficit: Canada's stock of direct investment abroad totalled $60 billion, while FDI in Canada totalled $103 billion.

---

[8] This topic is further explored in Chapter 12.

Figure 4-6

Growth in Direct Investment

Canadian FDI abroad grew as Canada's weighted average manufacturing capacity utilization rate reached 81.7% by 1987. Eight of the 22 major secondary industries were posting rates of 90% or better. Growth like this demands either increased capital spending, diversification, or acquisition. The largest Canadian takeovers in the past decade include Campeau Corporation's ill-fated $5 billion purchase of New York-based Allied Stores, and Seagram's $3 billion controlling interest in duPont Nemours. Eight other Canadian acquisitions fell within the $500 million to $1 billion range; seven of them involved American firms. In fact, by the end of the 1980s, Canadian companies were investing in the U.S. a third of the amount that American interests were investing in Canada. This is a remarkable figure, given that the U.S. market is ten times bigger than Canada's.

Foreign investment also changed form during the 1980s. Before the mid 1970s, half of foreign investment was direct; the other half was portfolio. By 1985, however, FDI had dropped to only 28% of total outside investment, while 72% was now debt. The servicing of this foreign debt explains to a large extent Canada's growing trade deficit in services.

SUGGESTED FURTHER READINGS

Bertrand, R. *Canada's Oil Monopoly.* Toronto: James Lorimer Publishers, 1981.
Bliss, Michael. *A Living Profit.* Toronto: McClelland & Stewart, 1974.
Crane, D. *Controlling Interest.* Toronto: McClelland & Stewart, 1982.
The Financial Post 500. Toronto: The Financial Post Company (latest issue).
Levitt, K. *Silent Surrender.* Toronto: Macmillan, 1970.
Report of the Royal Commission on Corporate Concentration. Ottawa: Supply and Services Canada, March, 1978.

CHAPTER
5 THE MYTH OF A BUSINESS IDEOLOGY

> Here's the rule, for bargains: "Do other men, for they would
> do you." That's the true business precept.
>
> Charles John Muffam Dickens, 1812–1870

Any business-government relationship consists of social, political, economic, legal, and technological connections. The nature of these linkages reflects the prevailing ideology of a given business environment, and vice-versa. There are four such ideologies, each producing different connections between business and government: *libertarianism (or liberalism)*, *egalitarianism (or socialism)*, *environmentalism/humanism*, and *corporatism*.

Libertarians believe in the maximum freedom of the individual, in competition, and in government being limited to the courts, defence, and law enforcement. *Egalitarians* believe in economic and social equality among people within a society with state direction of economic affairs. *Environmentalists/humanists* seek to preserve the physical environment and promote the quality of human life above all else. This would obviously require close co-operation between business and government, and the responsible use of private property. *Corporatists* seek optimal economic growth, economic efficiency, and a high standard of living. Government would support the private sector by fostering efficiency and setting policies for economic growth to achieve this high standard of living.

Panitch further defined corporatism as "a socio-political structure in which different centralized, hierarchical organizations interact and co-operate harmoniously at an elite level, and together control the masses."[9] Government in a corporatist state strongly urges private enterprise toward four goals: order, unity, nationalism, and "economic success." Many regard corporatism as an integral quality of a post-industrial, anti-liberal, neo-mercantilist state.

Part I of this book described an existing pattern of elitist mutual co-operation in Canada. The state has strongly emphasized corporatism's first three goals; consequently, the nation exhibits strong anti-liberalist tendencies. However, Canada does not fit the definition completely. Therefore, it is said to be a *neo-corporatist* state.

---

[9] Leo Panitch, *The Canadian State: Political Economy and Political Power.* Toronto: University of Toronto Press, 1977, p. 66.

Potential relationships between business and government can also be categorized a different way using three models: *elite accommodation, market,* or *business ecology.*

The *elite accommodation,* or *dominance,* model is pyramid-shaped, depicting society as a hierarchy. Business and government elites create a privileged establishment which dominates the pyramid. Those with a Marxist orientation maintain that the state acts as the executive committee of the ruling class; thus, the business elite uses government for its own ends. Following this line of thought, economist John Kenneth Galbraith gave "socialism" an entirely new meaning in a 1980 interview with *The London Free Press*:

> Modern socialism comes not from socialists and not from liberal econo-
> mists. Socialism comes when the heads of troubled corporations, pushed by
> unions, and urged by bankers, go to governments to be bailed out.

On the other hand, corporatists maintain that a dominant government elite uses private property to further its social goals, such as full employment. Galbraith contends that the business elite has become increasingly dominated by professional managers who are not owners of capital, and the government elite influenced by decision-makers who have not been elected. The collusion between these two elites has created a *technostructure*, as Galbraith terms it. This dominates the whole of society and attempts to maintain a benign and stable environment for itself.

The *market,* or *market-capitalism*, model conceived by Adam Smith in 1776 and refined by David Ricardo in 1817, regards business as being at arms-length with social forces, and focuses on economic forces affecting the market. The market is seen as a self-contained system which buffers business from non-market, environmental forces such as church and interest groups. In this model, business managers concentrate on such market goals as profit, efficiency, and economic growth. Government, not business, ministers to social needs. The key elements of the market model are private property, economic incentives (the profit motive), a free market system, and political and economic freedom. These obviously hold strong appeal for libertarians.

Finally, the *business ecology,* or *systems,* model is concerned with the interrelationship of all the institutions and forces within the business environment. According to Steiner and Steiner, firms are driven by a wide range of economic factors, as well as socio-political demands from government, pressure groups, and individuals. Business is oriented towards self-preservation, maintaining its boundaries and increasing its control over forces acting upon it. In response to the cultural, economic, environmental, individual, political, social, and technological demands business makes on its environment, society makes new demands. It also chooses to increase or decrease its support of business, depending upon management's actions. Environmentalists/humanists would work most effectively within a business ecology model.

ORIGINS OF THE BUSINESS IDEOLOGY

Business philosophy in Canada can best be understood by comparing it with parallel development in the United States—a country with similar antecedents and with whom we conduct 75% or so of our trade. Some of the first American entrepreneurs believed that anyone could achieve economic success through hard work, thrift, prudence, foresight, and patriotism. They believed that government was inherently evil, to be limited to protecting life and property, administering justice, and defending the nation. Government intervention in the economy was considered a violation of "natural laws" which controlled the marketplace, resulting in lower output and less efficient production and distribution.

This early American business elite also considered government expensive, wasteful, inefficient, and prone to attract inferior workers. Government expenses were considered burdens on producers and consumers that diverted resources from better use; i.e., producing goods, services, and wealth. Government could best promote competition, they believed, by allowing the natural forces of supply and demand to operate freely. These leaders of industry and commerce were also generally opposed to subsidies and tariffs, although many did favour protecting their own industries. With this sole exception, these early capitalists were libertarians and followed the market model.

The above philosophy often is referred to as *the business ideology*—a clear statement of the ideals held by a business community.

CHALLENGES TO THE BUSINESS IDEOLOGY

The study of Canadian business-government relations reveals four premises which challenge the above ideology:

1. Competition in the marketplace is the preferred means to make business activities consistent with community need. Government involvement in business activities is justified only if there is a deficiency in the marketplace. In this case, government agencies take action: (a) to strengthen competition, such as by requiring a divestiture; or (b) to correct marketplace deficiencies by regulation, taxation/subsidization, or government ownership.

2. There is and will continue to be a high level of government involvement in business. Government is now and will continue to be a primary force in business decision-making. It is therefore vital that business managers learn how to work effectively with government to resolve business-government conflicts.

3. Business has a legitimate role in the government decision-making process. Government needs feedback from business and other interest groups regarding the legislative and regulatory processes.

These groups can provide information and even initiate legislation, as well as find ways to solve social problems.

4. Co-operation among business, government, and labour is necessary to solve major national problems. Indeed, co-operation may be the key to coping with most of Canada's major public policy problems. In addition, as Japan and Western Europe enjoy a postwar economic renaissance, international competition for world resources and markets has intensified. Canada's ability to compete will require effective working relations among business, government, and labour.

Today's business ideology has actually been very responsive to changes in the business environment during the twentieth century. The traditional view of business as a stable, predictable economic institution has changed. Business is now regarded as a more complicated economic and socio-political institution within a turbulent, rapidly changing environment.

A NEW MANAGERIAL IDEOLOGY

Business ideology in Canada is different from that of the United States for a fundamental reason, again rooted in their two respective pasts. The United States made a clean break from Britain in the late eighteenth century, whereas Canada preferred to remain within the British sphere of security well into the twentieth century. Americans in business had to take risks, and because of their revolutionary past were more inclined to do so. Canadians have remained risk-averse—a notion antithetical to a liberal, capitalist philosophy of doing business.

Modern business ideology is actually a *managerial ideology*. As large corporations grew even larger, management became separated from ownership, and it became practical for managers to accept Keynesian economics. Resisting government intervention proved futile. It therefore made more sense to manage the situation than to continue to crusade for what was past. Over time, this separation created a professional managerial class which has accepted this modern managerial ideology. Today, many chief executives may affirm the virtues of, but do not necessarily practise, the liberal market model.

BUSINESS AND GOVERNMENT

In Canada, today's well-educated, professionally trained manager is really no different from that of a hundred years ago. Both generations have recognized that Adam Smith's theory of capitalism was simply an intellectual construct to describe the nineteenth century's Industrial Revolution. The "natural laws" and organization of economic society into private property and competitive markets were really analytical tools, not laws. Therefore, Canadian business has no discernible ideology. The current business-government relationship in Canada is actually a mixture of many shifting ideologies and perspectives. Consequently, each set of interactions—economic, social, technological, legal, and political—may lack ideological focus or at times be at cross-purposes. In fact, the whole business-government relationship may be unclear.

Due to this fluctuating ideological base, the nature of the relationship between business and government tends to change with prevailing conditions. In some situations, government actions may dominate business operations; in others, business may heavily influence the activities of government. Many contend that Canada's government is controlled by big business. Others hold that the public sector so dominates the economic activities of Canadian business enterprises that they are no longer competitive, either at home or abroad.

Some see the business-government relationship as adversarial, with business jealously guarding its territory from outside interference, claiming that any intrusion into market affairs could cause inefficiencies. Others argue that government is the unco-operative party, making arbitrary decisions that waste resources. Still others warn that it is actually better to keep business and government as adversaries, lest solidarity result in a tyrannical government-industrial complex.

In short, the business community holds no fundamental belief in the virtues of competition in Canada. Economic and political powers need not be separated for the good of free enterprise; in fact, Canadian business generally believes in the exact opposite. The business community has no strong anti-combine policies similar to those in the United States; nor is there a natural constituency for private enterprise in this country. Competition is viewed as a destructive force to be avoided, not a constructive force to be sought.

This lack of a free-enterprise ideology among the Canadian business community was highlighted in the mid-1980s by Peter Pocklington, Alberta businessman and one-time aspiring leader of the Progressive Conservative Party. Pocklington requested government assistance to save his commercial empire from the heavy debt incurred from bad investments, high interest rates, and Alberta's economic bust. Pocklington, a verbal proponent of free enterprise, managed to salvage most of his businesses by selling off his personal assets in 1982 to 1983, and accepting a $31 million helping hand from the Alberta Treasury Branches in 1984.

Once tasted, however, government largesse became addictive. In July, 1987, Pocklington accepted a $100 million line of credit from the Treasury Branches for his Palm Dairies Ltd. operations; it was extended another $55 million in March, 1988. At that time, Pocklington also accepted a $12 million loan for his meat-packing company, Gainers Inc. In any other circumstances, this would qualify as a corporate "bailout." For Pocklington, despite his libertarian mantle, it was good business.

Business is largely ambivalent towards business-government relations.

It wants to be free of government when it is doing well, and helped by government when it is doing poorly. For example, many firms in the 1960s and 1970s advocated international free trade policies. In the recessionary early 1980s, many of these firms wanted to retain, if not increase, tariff barriers to keep foreign goods from displacing domestic ones. Today, managers tend to regard government as a necessary evil.

Just as capitalism is now regarded as more theory than fact, an identifiable business ideology in Canada is more myth than reality.

IDEOLOGY AND FREE TRADE

Today, Canadian business has become complacent. If a large firm faces bankruptcy due to its own inefficiencies, lack of strategic vision, and/or market forces, government will be there to assist (for as much and as long as it can), to save those jobs.

But soon, government will not be able to help. Renewable resources are being harvested faster than they can be replenished. Reserves of non-renewable resources are becoming scarce within Canada, while world supply exceeds demand; inefficient manufacturing firms—even whole industries—shakily face free trade with the United States; the huge tertiary sector of Canada distributes wealth— it does not create it; and labour productivity is declining just when productivity is vital to compete in an essentially non-technological economy.

The century-old National Policy has protected inefficient Canadian manufacturers by maintaining a tariff barrier to imports. FDI has built branch plants in Canada to jump that barrier. As free trade completely removes it, neither domestic nor foreign-owned secondary manufacturing industries will be protected. Success within a non-competitive environment does not herald success in a freer, much more competitive climate. Free trade is not about ideology; it is about Canadian manufacturing interests competing in tougher times. These times will require capital investment, rationalization, specialization, economies of scale, and a strong desire to win.

Certainly, Canada will export more of its finite supply of resources. There will even be competition in most segments of the service sector. However, in an age of leveraged buyouts, successful Canadian resource and service firms will become prime candidates for takeover—both domestic and foreign. FDI in manufacturing, on the other hand, may decline as free trade makes it cheaper to export to Canadian buyers, rather than produce in Canada. Also to be expected are a few high-technology winners.

Overall, though, free trade does not promise less FDI or reduced economic concentration. If anything, probably the reverse is in store. History has shown that foreign investors have greater confidence in Canada's governments, social institutions, and resources than do Canadian business leaders.

Canada's corporate form of capitalism—oligopoly capitalism and administered pricing—is not competitive capitalism. Free trade, however, is *all about* competition.

IMPLICATIONS FOR MANAGEMENT

This chapter has shown that neither the general Canadian business community nor "big business" displays the characteristics of classical, competitive free enterprise in which talented individuals seek and develop opportunities to secure wealth and status. The virtues of competition do not form the fundamental beliefs of Canada's private sector. This fact, combined with socially accepted, large-scale government economic intervention to restrict potential entrants from joining the capitalist class, has put producer interests above those of the consumer.

Canada is clearly void of a free-enterprise ideology. Simply observe the record of high tariffs, high levels of industrial and aggregate concentration, high levels of FDI, foreign ownership and foreign control of industry, production inefficiencies, and business' continuing solicitation of government assistance.

One observer has actually defined a *Canadian entrepreneur* as "one who pushes his way to the front of the line to get a government subsidy." In truth, however, government's role in a classical free market situation is to help people become rich. In Canada, it appears that government's role is to protect those who are rich and to subsidize those who are not.

Business leaders will obviously publicly defend the merits of free enterprise, if only to retain their air of legitimacy in the eyes of their stakeholders. However, their actions—which restrict trade, invite "appropriate" government intervention, and contradict market theory—do not support their rhetoric. While bemoaning the level of concentration in industries with which they have to deal, they will strive vigorously to rationalize assets, capacity, and ownership within their own industries.

Does it really matter that Canadians are not really free enterprisers? Business is successful enough, and provides Canadians with one of the highest standards of living in the world. What should business management be doing differently? Why?

How should government policy-makers respond? What should the role of government be in economic affairs? Why?

The remainder of this book should offer some insights into the above questions—and their answers. As to the "why's," the answer is simple. Canada's past cannot become its future if it wishes to retain a preferred standard of living. The forces of change will not allow the status quo to be maintained if long-term economic survival is Canada's goal.

Yet Canada's history of growth—through business and government working closely together to accomplish their goals—is the key to achieving a better future. After all, Canadian economic policy has always been pragmatic. Similarly, Canadian business has been pragmatic when dealing with government, its rivals, and its public. However, business has forfeited its former role in shaping the public interest by accepting the will of a more aggressive, ideologically driven government over the past twenty years.

Changing ideologies will not solve the problem, however. Canadian business need not launch a defence of free enterprise; the Canadian public would never buy it. It is obvious that the Reichmanns, Campeau, and Canadian Pacific have moved into the United States *not* because Canada's government is socialist or anti-business, but because their abilities to grow in Canada were limited.

Canadian business must return to its pragmatic roots. Big business does much of its trade with government; it depends upon a publicly financed infrastructure. Business often goes to government for working capital in times of trouble; in return, the private sector must now act in the public interest to regain a privileged position in society.

Why is this so crucial today? Primarily, it is because business management in Canada lacks the global perspective necessary to survive in an increasingly integrated global marketplace. Although foreign trade accounts for nearly one-third of both Canada's GDP and Canadian employment, the nation's international business expertise is minimal. There are exceptions, but generally the skills demonstrated by Canada's business managers do not meet the standards required for international trade. Most success stories of Canadian exporters have had a helping hand from the federal government's trade commissioner service. However, government cannot do it all; nor can it move quickly enough.

Business alone is not at fault. Of the fifty business schools in Canada, only four have a required course in international business. A few have required courses in an area known as the "environmental framework" of business. Some schools have business-government courses; none are yet required for graduation. Disturbingly few institutions have placed a high priority on these subjects.

If business and government are two solitudes, then academe is a third. Now, greater co-operation and improved understanding are needed among business, government, and the academic world. Business' needs must be met; but first, business should recognize its inexperience in negotiating successful business strategies within a freer global environment.

The dynamics of the world market will no longer allow business in Canada to retain its privileged position. If the functions of management are to plan, organize, direct, and control, then Canadian business managers must learn to plan in an era of uncertainty; to organize to achieve their objectives; to make things happen; to provide leadership that will influence government and labour to accept this challenge and work with business, not against it.

Managers must also recognize the necessity of real-time, integrated information systems and performance measurement systems, so that corporate bureaucracies can shift in midstream when results do not match expectations. Mergers and acquisitions may provide growth for a firm, but they usually do nothing for the economy as a whole. Canada needs growth in the production of those goods the world demands.

If financial security and growth have indeed replaced short-term profitability as the goals of Canadian business, then global competitiveness is the only means to achieve these ends. Resources will not provide long-term growth and services, but will only reinforce the status quo.

Yet, business needs help to reach its goals. The tried but true bureaucratic symbiosis of business and government is ripe for revival to face a new challenge. If C.D. Howe was right in saying Canada always needs one megaproject on the go to remain prosperous, then here is the golden opportunity.

Canadian business can no longer afford to remain complacent. Today, business and the public share one compelling interest: economic and political survival!

SUGGESTED FURTHER READINGS

Andrain, C.F. *Politics and Economic Policy in Western Democracies.* Cambridge, Mass.: Dubury Press, 1980.

Aupperle, K.E. et al. "An Empirical Examination of the Relationship Between Corporate Social Responsibility and Profitability." *Academy of Management Journal,* Vol. 28, no. 2, 1985, 446-463.

Bell, Daniel. *Cultural Contradictions of Capitalism.* New York: Basic Books, 1976.

Friedman, Milton. "The Social Responsibility of Business is to Increase Its Profits." *The New York Times Magazine,* 13 September, 1970: 33+.

Galbraith, J.K. *Economics and the Public Purpose.* Boston: Houghton-Mifflin, 1973.

———. *The New Industrial State.* Boston: Houghton-Mifflin, 1971.

Kristol, Irving. *Two Cheers for Capitalism.* New York: Basic Books, 1978.

Panitch, Leo. *The Canadian State: Political Economy and Political Power.* Toronto: University of Toronto Press, 1977.

———. "The Development of Corporatism in Liberal Democracies." *Comparative Political Studies,* Vol. 10, no. 1, 1973, 61-90.

Post, James E. *Corporate Behavior and Social Change.* Reston, Va.: Reston Publishing, 1978.

Preston, Lee E., ed. *Research in Corporate and Social Performance and Policy.* 4 vols. Greenwich, Ct.: JAI Books, 1978-82.

Report of the Royal Commission on the Economic Union and Development Prospects of Canada. Ottawa: Supply and Services Canada, 1985.

Stanbury, W.T. *Business Interests and the Reform of Canadian Competition Policy, 1971-1975.* Toronto: Methuen Publications, 1977.

Steiner, G.A. and J.F. *Business, Government and Society: A Managerial Perspective.* 4th ed. New York: Random House, 1985.

CHAPTER

6 GOVERNMENT IN CANADA

The important thing for government is not to do things which individuals are doing already, and to do them a little better or a little worse; but to do those things which at present are not done at all.

Lord John Maynard Keynes, 1883-1946

The natural progress of things is for liberty to yield and government to gain ground.

Thomas Jefferson, 1743-1826

Prior to the twentieth century, classical economists such as Adam Smith and David Ricardo believed that the role of government was to do what the market could not do for itself: to determine, arbitrate, and enforce the rules of the free-enterprise game.

During the Industrial Revolution of the 1800s, governments of capitalist democracies delegated to business the responsibility for developing and managing the economy. Government's priority was to "take care of business." The resultant economic growth would then help government attain its social policy goals, such as full employment. This would be achieved through "mutual adjustments" within a traditional bargaining process. Such is the case no longer in capitalist democracies, and certainly not in Canada.

GOVERNMENT INTERVENTION: ALL IN THE PUBLIC INTEREST

Adam Smith, the "prophet of capitalism," anticipated the deterioration of market capitalism once the pursuit of wealth began to conflict with the purposes and prerequisites of the system. Wealthy capitalists would obstruct the very economic mechanisms which had enabled them to succeed, thus preventing any of their wealth from falling into the hands of new entrants.

Competition begat concentration, rather than sustained competition. Economic progress, although democratically demanded, was not democratically achieved. As natural resources predictably dwindled, and as economic resources were increasingly owned by a few, government

71

extended its influence over business. It chose to do this by a number of economic and social means, including:

- fiscal policy
- monetary policy
- subsidies
- the promotion of exports
- guaranteed loans
- the procurement of goods and services
- joint ventures
- the regulation of price and/or entry
- direct competition through state enterprise
- the regulation of disclosure, trade, labour, health and safety practices
- environmental protection
- minimum wage legislation
- the restriction of political involvement

Some of the above have been beneficial to business; others have been burdensome and costly.

The growth of the Canadian state and its interventions received strong impetus from the 1879 National Policy of tariff and non-tariff barriers—a state initiative planned and introduced fifty years or so before the impact of Keynesian intervention was realized in Canadian economic life.

Since World War II, business, too, has spurred the growth of government in Canada. Both federal and provincial policies toward business have slowly moved away from tariff protection and taxation policy, and toward transferring income from the public to the private sector. This shift helped advance such public policy goals as regional economic expansion, employment, exports, and industrial rationalization.

Today, Canada is one of the most Keynesian countries in the world. In fact, it is the epitome of John Kenneth Galbraith's "new industrial state," with high levels of corporate concentration, no real antitrust legislation, no free enterprise ethic *per se*, and government solutions to economic problems. The federal government has been quick to assist the private sector when it was confronted with economic crises and dysfunction.

Why has government intervened? Because it has been in the "public interest" to do so. What, then, *is* the public interest—and by whose interpretation?

Ideally, the *public interest* can be defined as the combining, weighing, and balancing of many special interests with those universal interests shared by the vast majority, such as fairness and equity. However, on a practical basis, the "public interest" often reflects whatever special interest wins government's support. In truth, the "public interest" depends upon where you sit.

For example, the government performs direct economic regulation "in the public interest" to protect consumers from destructive competition, fraud, unsafe goods and services, or monopoly prices and profits. The prime beneficiaries, though, are the producers with their economic rents, oligopolies, and "polite" competition. Because regulation is promoted as "in the public interest," it is difficult to remove, even if it really only benefits a specific interest.

Government may also act in the public interest to address the unintended, usually negative impact of an individual's or group's actions upon others, such as pollution, littering, or traffic congestion. The wide- ranging government interventions in the marketplace are also intended to provide—or ensure that the private sector provides — certain "public goods." These include social security, education, defence, health care, telecommunications, utilities, and transportation.

Why must it be the state that intervenes? Primarily, because most members of the public are self-utility maximizers, following the dictates of public choice economics. Government, theoretically, can take a longer, societal view and assure that more people gain than lose. It can also, by redistribution or compromise, guarantee that the winners will compensate the losers.

The brokerage of special interests into a national public interest is no longer the responsibility of the elected official, but of the appointed official — the public servant— operating within his or her own world of public choice economics. However, except where public servants have been given complete discretionary authority, the appointed official's interpretation of the public interest is almost always accredited to a political master.

Ultimately, the appropriateness of all forms of government intervention "in the public interest" will be value judgments based on personal standards of legitimacy, expediency, and morality. However, it is seldom the public's judgment.

FINANCING THE STATE

With the advance of neo-conservatism in western industrialized societies, the increasing involvement of the state has been seriously questioned. There has already been public—and political—resistance in many countries to the high level and intensity of state participation in the economy.

On the whole, however, this has not been the case in Canada. This country has become, and remains, a government-centred society. Unlike in the United States, only a modest amount of serious debate has arisen about the appropriate role for, and the growth of, the public sector. Canada has put a higher priority on reforming and making more accountable its government structures and processes.

Despite a Conservative government in Ottawa, Canadian federal government expenses totalled almost $120 billion in 1987 (see Figure 6-1), representing 21.5% of the country's GDP. In contrast, only $44 billion, or 18% of the GDP, was spent in 1978. The most significant increases were in

Figure 6-1

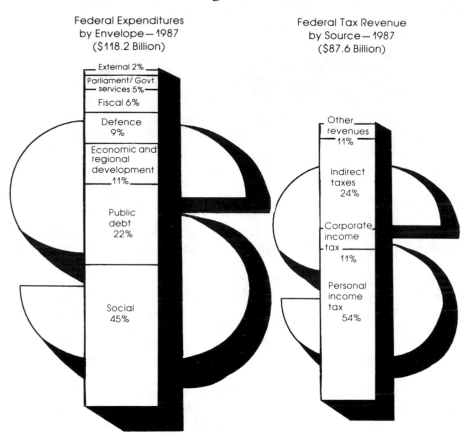

Federal Expenditures
by Envelope—1987
($118.2 Billion)

- External 2%
- Parliament/Govt. services 5%
- Fiscal 6%
- Defence 9%
- Economic and regional development 11%
- Public debt 22%
- Social 45%

Federal Tax Revenue
by Source—1987
($87.6 Billion)

- Other revenues 11%
- Indirect taxes 24%
- Corporate income tax 11%
- Personal income tax 54%

Source: Public Accounts of Canada, 1987

financing the national debt, funding statutory programs, entitlements, and transfer payments such as medicare, the Canada Pension Plan, unemployment insurance, and defence. The Library of Parliament shows that federal subsidies and assistance payments to business over the past decades have grown faster than social program spending. Further, the Finance Department reveals that between 1970 and 1989, corporations carried less and less of the tax burden, despite tax reforms to achieve the opposite result.[10]

Of that $120 billion worth of expenditures, 74% was paid for by tax revenues, over one-half of which was personal income tax (see Figure 6-1). The remainder was paid for by government borrowing. The so-called

---

[10] Corporate tax as a percentage of federal government revenues peaked at 26% in the mid 1970s and dropped to approximately 11% by the end of the 1980s.

"federal deficit" climbed from $5.5 billion in 1978 to almost $27 billion in 1987, totalling 80% of all Canadian public-sector indebtedness.

As alarming as this may sound, one must put it in the proper perspective. Between 1965 and 1985, the Canadian economy grew at a compound, real, annual rate of approximately 4%. Simultaneously, private capital formation grew at a slightly healthier pace of 5%: the rich got richer. Federal expenditures rose 6% per year in real terms—at 150% the rate of the economy as a whole. However, federal revenues barely kept up with general economic growth and grew at an annual rate of just under 4%. As a result, the net federal debt grew by almost 3% annually. Almost all that debt was accumulated between 1975 and 1985![11]

In 1977, the federal government owed 10% of its debt to non-Canadians. By 1987, that figure had climbed to 15.9%. By 1988, it had jumped to 19%.

The weakness in Canada's borrowing abroad, in particular, is its subsequent use of these funds to sustain government spending on goods and services. Much of this has been in the form of transfer payments that are simply consumed, rather than on items that will increase the country's net economic well-being. Unlike private-sector investment, which produces an income stream, government-incurred debt produces no income and is not self- liquidating. Thus, government programs designed to raise Canada's standard of living are actually reducing it!

Debt accumulated for such spending must be serviced one of two ways. First, it can be paid out of current domestic output and export earnings, which lowers standards immediately. This works only until the next recession hits, when tax revenues decline and the cost of borrowing goes up. The second alternative is more foreign borrowing, higher taxes, or an increased money supply, all of which will lower living standards in the future.[12] Look at Latin America, for example, and how its foreign debt load has crippled a number of economies. Canada's government has gone abroad because its domestic capital markets are already saturated with government debt instruments.

As a strictly financial matter, the remedy to the federal government's deficit is obvious; the course of action straightforward. Before the next economic downturn, when export earnings drop and interest rates climb,

---

[11] Remember, the Liberals kept their 1972 campaign promise just in time for the 1974 election. They indexed the Canada Pension Plan and other social programs so that entitlement expenditures followed the spiral of inflation, and also de-indexed the personal income tax system, thus guaranteeing less from the federal government's major source of revenue.

[12] A third alternative is to follow Irving Fisher's 1935 prescription of borrowing from the Bank of Canada at 0.5% and requiring the chartered banks to maintain 100% reserves for demand deposits. However, the first rule of public regulation is that the regulator tends to be captured by the regulated industry. In every country except Switzerland and Japan, perhaps, the public's bank—the central bank—serves the private banks' interests more than those of the public.

as much of the debt as possible should be paid off. But there are signs the economy is already slowing down.

As a political matter, the best that any government can do is inch toward fiscal reform. Despite government rhetoric, big spending is still on tap in Ottawa. The Macdonald Commission's survey of public opinion polls during the mid 1980s clearly showed that the public is not willing to have social programs — the most costly — cut or cancelled. Government waste in management was its target.

In September, 1984 Deputy Prime Minister Erik Nielsen was appointed by the Prime Minister to chair the Task Force on Program Review. This held the mandate to review all government programs except defence and foreign aid, and to recommend ways of improving service to the public and reducing costs of program delivery. The Task Force concluded that many government programs subsidized activity and not results, and that the public service lacked the tools and incentives to control costs. Yet it only recommended that less than 8% of the 1 000 programs reviewed be terminated, privatized, or devolved to the provincial governments. After 19 months of work, the Task Force's 15 000-page report received only twenty hours of scrutiny by committees of the House of Commons. Nielsen left the federal Cabinet in 1986 under the cloud of failed good intentions.

The Nielsen Task Force failed primarily because the government was unwilling to challenge the legitimacy of vested interests held by the beneficiaries of government programs.

By definition, government is inefficient, largely since it does what business cannot do profitably or will not do because of the economic risk. Therefore, government really has no deficit. The federal budget is balanced; unfortunately, however, 26% of Canada's operating expenses is funded by short and long-term borrowing.

To its credit, the federal government has tried to control its spending. But government is not a single entity. Its budgets are the temporary culmination of multiple processes and competitions for funds. Federal budgeting has been best characterized as a game between spenders and guardians. Lower-level officials have little or no spending discretion. The middle-manager tries to meet all objectives within a budget while satisfying the requirements of Treasury Board. The "spenders" are the deputy ministers, who manage departmental resources. They are pitted against the "guardians" (also spenders in their own right) such as Finance, Treasury Board, and the Privy Council Office, who make the system work to meet the government's priorities.

Meta-budgeting—responding to or anticipating changes in the world economy and other countries' budgets—has eliminated much of the discretion in federal budgeting. The most complex attempt to improve management of federal government resources was the top-down, program-budgeting process used in Ottawa until 1989. Known as the Policy

Expenditure Management System (PEMS), it was devised by the Privy Council Office under Prime Minister Trudeau and first used by Prime Minister Clark. Quite simply, the Cabinet was divided into seven policy fields: External Affairs, Defence, Social Affairs, Economic and Regional Development, Parliamentary and Government Services, Fiscal Arrangements, and Public Debt. These covered all departments, agencies, and other financial obligations of the federal government (refer back to Figure 6-1).

Each year in late summer, the Planning and Priorities Committee of Cabinet decided the government's spending level for the next five years. It then allocated funds to each of the seven policy fields, or *envelopes*. One envelope might receive a greater increase than another, reflecting changing government spending priorities. A committee of Cabinet, representing each envelope, then distributed that envelope's resources in early winter among its departments, agencies, and programs. Individual departmental increases could vary within and across envelopes. In early summer, the departments then prepared their estimates, or budgets, along with requests for additional funding beyond their allocation limit. These were sent on to Treasury Board and the Privy Council Office for review, revision, and approval. The Minister of Finance then prepared his Budget Speech eighteen months or so after the process commenced.

PEMS returned control over government spending to the politicians. Priorities and spending limits were set before budgets were drafted. It may not have been a rational budgeting system, but it was "workably rational," considering that it was a political process first and foremost. If nothing else, it forced managers to reallocate scarce resources.[13] PEMS returned control over government spending to the politicians. Priorities and spending limits were set before budgets were drafted.

However, PEMS was based on an assumption of a steadily rising supply of funds. In January, 1989 Prime Minister Mulroney and Finance Minister Wilson finally realized that this assumption was no longer valid. When funds had gotten tighter back in 1987, too many ministers had gone to Cabinet for money, where forty politicians found it difficult to collectively say "no" to new spending.

Bartering for money works when there is money for which to barter; when there is not, the system becomes meaningless. As a result, the Prime Minister abolished the envelopes and assigned a rejuvenated Treasury Board control over existing programs. He then gave the responsibility for new spending to the Priorities and Planning Committee of Cabinet, and created a new "executive committee" of Cabinet called the Expenditure Review Committee. This body would identify programs to be terminated and money to be saved.

---

[13] The best example of this was the Ministry of Transport (MOT). Over the years, MOT underwent significant reconfiguration with a host of new programs and projects—but at great expense to itself. It gave up a lot to get on with its departmental priorities.

As with PEMS, the tough part of this process is still left up to the politician, who must match revenue with expenditure. In this age, where demands on government increase faster than economic output, the alternatives are to cut programs, raise taxes, or borrow money. However, budget cuts are generally unrealistic for politicians, since over 80% of government expenses are salaries, wages, and benefits. Another 5% is for prepaid expenses such as rent, retrofitting of assets, and defence procurement contracts.

A government budget is an expenditure budget: each expenditure item is specified. However, revenue (taxes, tariffs, user fees, Crown corporation dividends) is reported in an aggregate form as the Consolidated Revenue Fund. Universality, equity, and fairness in government policies override any incentive for cost recovery or net budgeting. Therefore, program budgets seldom balance; department budgets seldom balance; only the overall budget balances, thanks to debt borrowing.

Ottawa plays a highly sophisticated level of budget gamesmanship. Federal bureaucrats are, above all, human, displaying human frailties encouraged by this environment. Public servants are budget maximizers. Since salaries for senior managers are lower than those of their counterparts in the private sector, government employees seek other rewards, such as information, "perks" (some of the most lavish executive offices are in Ottawa), and empire-building. Ottawa's mandarins are *lapsophobics*— they spend every penny of their annual budgets to justify increased funding in the following year.

Finally, when talking about financing the state and managing the public purse, remember Wagner's Law:

> As per capita income increases in industrialized countries, the public sectors in those countries will increase in relative importance; but as per capita incomes decline in real terms or the rate of increase in per capita incomes declines, the public sectors will continue to grow.

Or, as Pogo more succinctly put it: "I have seen the enemy and he is us!"

GOVERNMENT STRUCTURE AND THE POLICY-MAKING PROCESS

To influence government policy, in whatever direction, for whatever purpose, we must clearly understand how government operates. It is not as simple as most would believe. Canada is a constitutional monarchy with a parliamentary form of government. The federal government is comprised of three branches: the executive branch (Prime Minister, Cabinet, and public service), the legislative branch (House of Commons and Senate), and the judicial branch (Supreme Court of Canada and Federal Court of Canada). The judiciary operates at arms' length of both Parliament and the executive branch.

Inherent in the concept of Parliament are the two principles of *representative government* and *responsible government*. Representative government means that the people of Canada elect their governors to a legislative assembly, the House of Commons. Responsible government implies that the Cabinet, including the Prime Minister, sit and are responsible to that legislative assembly. The political party winning a plurality of seats forms the government, with the leader of that party becoming Prime Minister.

Cabinet ministers are appointed and hold their offices "at the pleasure of the Prime Minister." There are ministers with portfolio (heads of traditional line departments with vertical constituencies, such as Agriculture and Labour); ministers without portfolio (Cabinet spokesmen for particular issues, usually with no departmental staff); and ministers of state (Canada's version of junior ministers who perform a staff function or oversee part of a larger department). Some ministers with portfolio have horizontal, co-ordinative functions (Justice, External Affairs), or head up central agencies (Treasury Board, Finance) or co-ordinative, administrative departments (Revenue, Public Works, and Supply and Services).

Canadian cabinets operate under the principle of collective responsibility or cabinet solidarity; ministers never publicly disagree with government policy. Legislation and regulations generally emerge from committees of Cabinet, assisted by the public service and then introduced by a Cabinet minister in the House of Commons for Parliamentary review and debate. In most cases, the latter is more ritual than substantive policy-making. Only recently have committees of the House of Commons been empowered to review issues other than those brought to the House by the Government. However, the funds given these committees are inadequate for their new formal responsibilities; thus, little investigation has transpired to date.

In such a system, the Prime Minister has an inordinate amount of power. A strong-willed prime minister with firm control of his party and a clear majority in the House is, for all intents and purposes today, the Government. The only sure check against tyranny is the formal executive or head of state—the Queen of Canada—as represented by the Governor-General. The Governor-General has the formal power to dissolve Parliament, appoint governments, and call elections. Rarely have any of these been done against the will of the Prime Minister.

Most regulations, guidelines, policies, and programs used to implement Parliamentary legislation appear as *orders-in-council*. These are executive fiats of the Cabinet and, due to their scope and technicality, are drafted by the public service.

In this system, the key to attaining political power is votes. One of the main keys to garnering at least a plurality of votes is the promise of economic prosperity, reflected primarily by full employment. However, the key to power within government is the information by which one can shape, create, or derail policy. Those with information have power. Those with power make policy. Revenue is a distant concern compared to votes, jobs, and information. (For more about the power of information, see Chapters 9 and 10).

Figure 6-2 shows a traditional, if skeletal, view of the structure of the government of Canada. It also identifies four overlapping policy levels within this framework. Departmental policy is normally administered by directors-general and their subordinates. Yet departmental policy is produced by not just ministers and their deputies, but by assistant deputy ministers, directors-general, and sometimes even directors. Departmental priorities are set by ministers, who consult with their deputies.

Long-term government priorities are set by the 19-member Priorities and Planning Committee (P&P) of the 39-member Cabinet. This *inner cabinet* is supported by a *shadow committee* of deputy ministers headed by the Clerk of the Privy Council. P&P chooses its priorities from among those departmentally sponsored policy initiatives that won approval from their respective policy-area committee of Cabinet, and fit in with the political imperatives of the Prime Minister.

Spending for existing programs is controlled by the statutory six-member Treasury Board; all new spending must be approved by P&P, chaired by the Prime Minister. The Operations Committee of Cabinet (Ops) sets the weekly agendas for both P&P and Cabinet (see Figure 6-3). Ops is chaired by the Deputy Prime Minister, who is also vice-chairman of P&P. The Deputy Prime Minister is also the vice-chairman of the eight-member Expenditure Review Committee (the Prime Minister is the nominal chairman). This committee is commissioned to eliminate those programs that fail to serve the government's highest priorities.

The Prime Minister's Office (PMO), personally appointed by the Prime Minister, provides the head of government with clerical, media relations, party relations, and constituency relations support. It is also the Prime Minister's major source of political advice. It is partisan, politically oriented, yet operationally sensitive. The PMO's staff of one hundred or so is headed by a chief of staff, considered to be the closest person to the Prime Minister.

The Privy Council Office (PCO), comprised of career public servants, and traditionally the secretariat for Cabinet and its committees, has evolved to become the "department" of the Prime Minister. Two hundred and fifty staff members offer a full array of policy advice, and attempt to co-ordinate government policy and action. The PCO is non-partisan, operationally oriented, yet politically sensitive. It prepares discussion papers for Cabinet under the Prime Minister's direction, and writes or critiques departmentally generated memoranda to Cabinet. These memoranda are secret. They synthesize policy advice and recommendations and shape statutes, regulations, and government policy.

The head of the PCO is the Clerk of the Privy Council/Secretary to the Cabinet, who also chairs the Committee of Deputy Ministers and recommends deputy minister appointees to the Prime Minister. The Clerk is

Figure 6-2

Management Organization of the Government of Canada

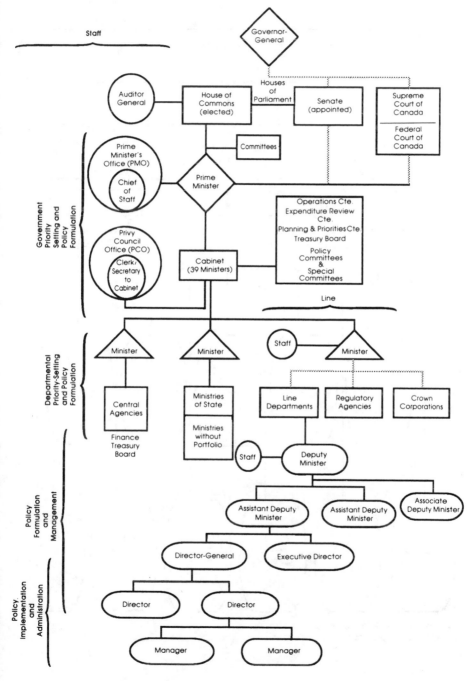

Figure 6.3

The Federal Cabinet
(number of members in parentheses)

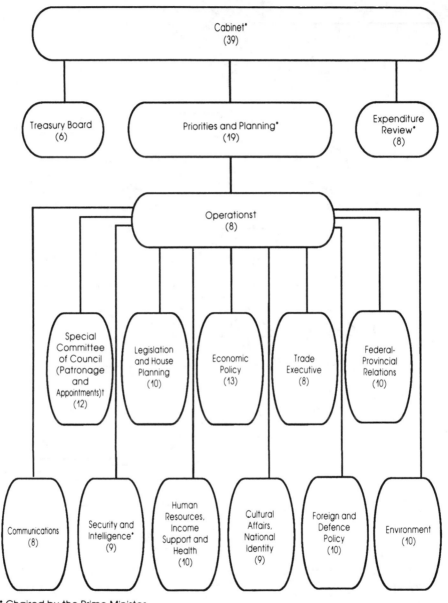

* Chaired by the Prime Minister
† Chaired by the Deputy Prime Minister

arguably the most powerful person in government, except for the Prime Minister.

The PMO, PCO, the Treasury Board Secretariat, and the Ministry of Finance comprise *the Central Agencies* of the federal government. These departments are responsible for co-ordinating policy, allocating resources among competing government interests, and generally managing the policy process. The Agencies have evolved from simply providing advice, to making decisions, to actually controlling the decision-making process. While line departments give politicians technical data to make technical decisions, the Agencies provide the information politicians need to make political decisions. Further, the Privy Council Office and Treasury Board Secretariat provide many of the fast-tracking senior management super-stars in the federal government. These tend to be better educated than their peers, ambitious, loyal to the process of government, and have little or no business experience.

The days of swashbuckling Cabinet ministers who dominated their departments and policy areas are long gone. Cabinet ministers today are marketers of government policy. In a majority government, government policy is usually the Prime Minister's policy. Canadians live at a time when the most important decisions are imposed on them by officials who need not face the consequences of those decisions. They are political admin-istrators as much as they are policy advisers.

Where is the true power in the government of Canada? Constitu-tionally, it is in Parliament, which under a majority government means the Prime Minister. Politically, it is with the leader of the governing party — the Prime Minister. Managerially, it is Cabinet — the executive branch of government — the members of which owe their appointments to the Prime Minister.

The Prime Minister, however, is hardly accessible. Even cabinet minis-ters must make distant appointments to see him. In fact, ministers not on the P&P, Operations, or Expenditure Review committees of Cabinet must wait in line like everyone else.

How, then, is policy made at the national level? The size and complex-ity of government prevent it from operating as a single entity. There are, however, obvious patterns of policy-making in Ottawa that represent the government's decision-making process.

Before government entertains a public policy issue, a demand for action must be heard, whether from an interest group, a private individual, a Cabinet minister, backbenchers, or the public service. Increasingly, though, modern survey technology has helped the executive branch of government, especially the ever-growing PMO, to monitor public con-cerns and determine the country's political agenda. Today, this process is ultimately controlled by the Prime Minister and the Operations Commit-tee of Cabinet, chaired by the Deputy Minister.

If the government wishes an issue to just go away, a Task Force or Royal Commission may be appointed to study it into oblivion. If the government is unsure what to do, it will issue a Green Paper for public debate.

Once an agenda item is selected for action, the public service is instructed to develop specific proposals. These are sent to the appropriate Cabinet Committee for review. At this time, the PCO will either adapt these ideas into a more manageable form for the politicians (thus influencing the discussion through their editorializing), be asked to provide other options, relate the proposal to overall government priorities and existing programs, and/or negotiate with provincial officials, if necessary. At this time, the PMO will inform the Committee of the political ramifications of its proposal and give the Prime Minister's position, if one exists.

The Cabinet Committee will then report to Cabinet as a whole, where the proposed policy will be approved, amended, or rejected. Cabinet's action is then documented in a Record of Decision, of which the Prime Minister is the final arbiter. Cabinet, through the Prime Minister, will then inform the Government party's caucus and introduce the policy. It may take either the form of legislation to be passed in the House (a mere formality in a majority government situation), or an Order-In-Council (or Cabinet fiat) under existing legislation. The final statute or regulation will then be implemented and administered by the bureaucracy.

In short, *policy-making is controlled and directed by the political executive and bureaucracy.* It is hardly a creative process, as creativity emanates only from policy decisions made at the very top, such as the Constitution Act, 1982 or the Canada-United States Free Trade Agreement, 1988. The federal government's policy-making process is at best the resolution of conflict, the result of a bargaining process, and incremental political change. The question for business is when and where to try to influence that process: at the issue identification stage, the policy formulation stage, or the Parliamentary debate stage? The answer to this question will depend on which policy instrument the government chooses.

INSTRUMENTS OF GOVERNMENT POLICY

Before an issue becomes part of government's policy agenda, there will be a gestation period characterized by cultural change or structural, social change. Only when a specific change challenges beliefs, values, or material wealth so drastically that "winners" and "losers" will result, does a phenomenon become a public issue. Groups will then mobilize, costs will be itemized in the media, and the public awareness level will be raised. Only then will an issue be politicized and government action demanded "in the public interest."

There are many types of policies available to government. American political scientist T.J. Lowi offers the definitive categorization of four public policy types:

- *Distributive*: benefits are solicited by and awarded to specific persons or groups, while costs are distributed equally to the general population (e.g., tariffs, business subsidies, export incentives);
- *Regulatory*: economic and/or social behaviour of individuals or organizations is directly modified by sanction (e.g., environmental protection, price controls, control of entry);
- *Redistributive*: wealth is indirectly transferred from one segment of a population to another (e.g., progressive income taxation, medicare, subsidized housing);
- *Constituent*: state management is facilitated; establishes the "rules of the game." Benefits and costs are widely dispersed (e.g., monetary policy, fiscal policy, enabling legislation for special-purpose bodies).

Lowi argues that each policy type reflects a particular type of politics, policy arena, and set of public demands. *Distributive* policies are usually chosen when government responds to the needs of a single interest group or coalition of interest groups, using general government revenues as funding. *Regulatory* policies are the outcome of conflict between two parties, whether producer and consumer or two segments of the business community. The problems in resolving the conflict are passed on to ill-defined, special-purpose bodies, thus eliminating the need for politicians to act further. *Redistributive* policies, too, are usually the outcome of conflict between certain parties. Both regulatory and redistributive policies create winners and losers, further stimulating special interest groups to organize. *Constituent* policies are at best the compromises resulting from competing points of view within the government structure, as much as they are responses to the demands of the political environment. The development of these policies is an ongoing process, only interrupted by economic or social crises, or less often by a philosophical change in the government's executive.

The type of government action chosen fully depends on the type of problem it is to address. Whether or not the political executive deals with the issue legislatively or through an Order-In-Council is unimportant. These are merely the vehicles by which decisions are transmitted. The crucial factor is to understand and appreciate the wide gamut of measures government can use to implement a decision or policy (see Figure 6-4).

Factors which shape government's choice of policy instrument include (a) deciding how much coercion will be necessary to change behaviour; (b) identifying who will benefit, and who will pay the costs; (c) deciding which publics must be considered; (d) establishing whether the market deficiency or social problem is real or perceived, and (e) assessing how urgent the need is for government to be seen to be doing something.

Government's options are numerous if it intends to change private behaviour. It can lead by example; rely upon generally accepted, self-enforcing conventions (such as traffic signals); regulate; license; ration; charge user fees; prohibit outright; or nationalize private assets. If the

Figure 6-4
Instruments of Government Policy

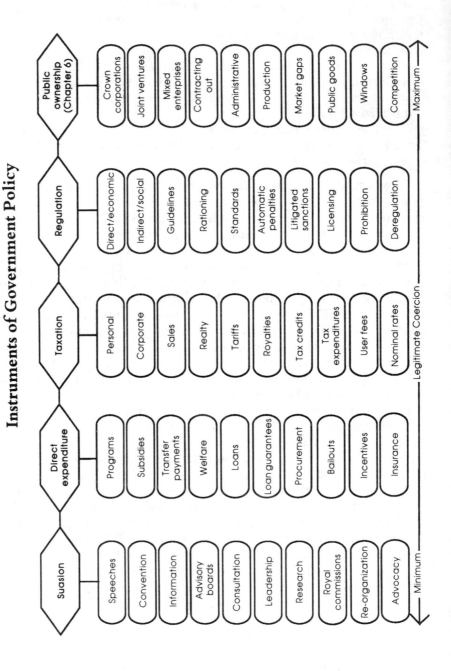

intent is to provide public goods or services such as street lighting, fire protection, or telecommunications, government either will do so directly (Crown corporations), contract-out with an external party, command the private sector to do so (regulation), or give the private sector the means to do so profitably (incentives).

Inevitably, the problem of compliance arises. Minimal fines for pollution violations, for instance, are seen by some corporations as fees to pollute. Parking tickets have a similar effect. Desired outcomes are not always achieved; behaviour is not always modified. *Even when there is full compliance, outcomes do not always equate with objectives.*

The choice of policy instrument and the type of policy will also determine whether government must push legislation through Parliament, or can use an Order-In-Council to deal with the problem under existing legislation. Similarly, government's choice will determine the structure and systems needed to carry out its decision.

A good example of this contingency approach to choosing government policy is the manner in which the federal government has treated FDI over the years. Basically, government has two choices to respond to the Canadian public's concern over the level of FDI in the country: *performance regulation or nationalization.* Performance regulation is designed to increase Canadian control over foreign-owned/controlled companies. This ensures that the company's net benefits contribute to the national economic well-being. The nationalization approach simply increases Canadian ownership. It offers no guarantee that Canadian business or government ownership will contribute any more than foreign companies would to the nation's welfare.

In 1957, a Royal Commission headed by Walter Gordon (a rare member of both the business and government elites), recommended that government increase its ownership of key industries in response to growing American ownership of Canadian assets. The government of Canada responded in the early 1960s by negotiating the Canada-United States Automotive Agreement (Auto Pact), which increased the American-owned companies' production levels and expenditures in Canada. The Auto Pact was a form of performance regulation.

In 1966, the government developed its *Guidelines of Good Corporate Citizenship* to increase the benefits of foreign enterprise to Canadians. They were largely ignored by the private sector. Persuasion clearly was not going to work.

In 1968, Mel Watkins, a member of the New Democratic Party's left-wing "Waffle," University of Toronto economist, and consultant to the Privy Council Office headed up a task force to assess the causes and consequences of FDI and to make policy recommendations. He called for a clear strategy whereby a new central agency could regulate the performance of foreign-owned companies in Canada. Shortly thereafter, successive Trudeau governments created more state enterprise than Canada had ever seen to counterbalance the American presence. This culminated in Petro-Canada in 1975, as well as the Canada Development Corporation (CDC). *Obviously, there need not be any connection between government studies and government action. Similarly, the policy pendulum swings with rhythmic regularity.*

The whole issue of FDI was finally addressed by the Foreign Investment Review Agency (FIRA). This body was charged with screening and approving all foreign acquisitions, transfers, and establishment of firms in Canada. From 1974-1984, 89% of all applications to FIRA were approved—a much higher rate than those of its counterparts in the United States, Netherlands, West Germany, France, Britain, Spain, Norway, Sweden, Finland, Austria, Japan, Australia, or New Zealand. FIRA, under Prime Minister Mulroney, has been repackaged as Investment Canada—a more positive, investment-attracting *nom de guerre* but with an identical mandate, contrary to public belief.

All of these government actions were taken "in the public interest," reflective of public opinion. This despite the fact that foreign-owned subsidiaries are 19% more productive than domestic competitors, and that foreign subsidiaries develop at least as much technology in Canada as do Canadian companies.

If the costs of FDI truly outweigh the benefits, government can either nationalize foreign-owned assets or better regulate their performance. If there are net benefits to foreign direct investment, then what? Either way, government must be seen to be doing something. It is simply a question of how coercive it wants to be—and how effective.

ECONOMIC REGULATION (AND DEREGULATION)

Canadians spend an inordinate amount of time preoccupied with death and taxes. Yet, a third, equally pervasive phenomenon has received much less attention: regulation. One-third of all federal and provincial legislation is regulatory in nature; over 55% of private economic activity is subject to regulation. About half of all regulated activity is in the transportation field alone. When regulation does receive attention, it centres around two themes: there is too much regulation — or there is too little.

To date, no one agrees on the optimal level of regulation, how to deregulate, or how to reform regulatory regimes. Worse still, there is little understanding of the cumulative effects of increasing regulation. Many theorists believe that ultimately there must be diminishing cost/benefit returns for a marginal rise in the level of regulation. However, few researchers have tackled the problem of how to measure the costs and benefits of regulation.

Business in Canada has generally adapted well to existing regulation, but dreads the cost of compliance future regulations might require. There is also general disagreement about the value of the level of discretion most special-purpose bodies (regulatory agencies) possess. The vagueness of enabling legislation—embodying the terms of reference for regulatory bodies—permits these agencies to regulate on a case-by-case basis, a controversial practice.

Most agree, however, that there is redundancy in existing regulation. Overlapping regulations or their absence entirely may be blamed on the division of powers between the national and provincial governments. Regulations across the ten provinces are often inconsistent, proving costly to business. Overlapping may exist within a single jurisdiction because of multiple regulations and regulatory agencies.

Interestingly, business in Canada generally does not support deregulation *per se*. It dislikes the uncertainty involved in a change of rules. Business usually demands *better* regulation based on equity, not efficiency.

Regulation is intended to alter the behaviour of individuals in the private sector. *Direct, or economic, regulation* tries to alter the private sector's economic behaviour. It is usually industry-specific and controls price levels, rates of return, entry, exit, and/or output. Economic regulation is almost always administered by a regulatory body or agency.

On the other hand, *indirect, or social, regulation* may not be industry-specific, and is designed to modify the social behaviour of the private sector. Areas covered include health and safety, environmental protection, fairness and equity in the workplace, consumer protection, and social and cultural values. Social regulation is as often administered by a government line department as it is by a regulatory agency. Most new regulations since 1970 have been social regulations.

Although some regulations may be intended to protect the consumer, it is ironic that most economic regulation is requested by industry and supplied in turn by government.

The impact of economic regulation can be measured in a number of ways. First, there are measurable direct costs of both providing and enforcing regulation. An estimated 2% of the federal budget and 6% of its labour force are allocated to regulatory matters.

Second, there are indirect costs, including production inefficiencies, lags in adopting technological innovation, and mis-allocation of resources. In a protected environment, there is also less impetus to remain competitive.

Third, economic regulation has winners and losers. Although the net effect upon national income is zero, income is redistributed within society. New "rights" and entitlements are created with regulation, and are threatened with deregulation. In most cases of economic regulation, wealth is transferred from the consumer to the producer. This results in higher prices, which reflect higher operating costs due to inefficiencies and the higher capitalized costs of entry into a regulated industry.

Fourth, benefits accruing to certain parties are hard to measure, yet economic rents and capital gains upon exiting can be estimated in cases of economic regulation. However, it is harder to measure the values of less pollution, fewer deaths, reduced discrimination, and new employment opportunities from social regulation.

What are the effects of economic regulation?

1. Prices are usually higher and more stable.[14]
2. Multi-part pricing is practised.
3. Quantities produced can be increased or decreased.
4. Demand can be shifted upwards or downwards.
5. Costs are usually higher.
6. Producers tend to be price-searchers rather than price-takers.
7. There tend to be fewer firms in an industry due to closed or restricted entry and/or exit.
8. Firms tend to be larger than in an unregulated market of similar size.
9. Profits tend to be higher.
10. Monopoly rents are accrued.

The objective of economic regulation is ostensibly to protect the consumer from the effects of "destructive competition" (poor quality, excess capacity, price-fixing, price wars, and withheld supply). The outcome, however, is the protection of the producer from the effects of destructive competition (lower profits, greater instability, shake-outs, and fluctuating demand). *Little wonder that business demands to be regulated more often than not, and abhors the idea of deregulation!*

In Canada, government has also initiated its fair share of regulation in the "public interest," justifying it as follows:

1. Market failure is the usual excuse for government-initiated regulation: (a) to prevent or control natural monopolies; (b) to protect the consumer; (c) to prevent or ease negative results of private activity, such as pollution; and (d) to provide for the disclosure of information.

2. Government also wishes to redistribute income to a limited extent and sometimes uses regulation to do it.

3. Social and cultural objectives are also met through regulation at times: (a) Public goods, such as transportation, are provided to peripheral communities because of regulation and the internal subsidization it supports; (b) Canadian ownership is increased in key sectors. (A nation is built and its identity protected.)

4. Finally, regulation is a great means by which government can be seen to be doing something when the public demands it. ("Taxation by regulation" gets votes!)

---

[14] A 1983 study by Statistics Canada showed that regulated prices do not respond to changes in market conditions as quickly as non-regulated prices. This is one reason it takes longer for inflation in Canada to come down than in the United States.

Special purpose bodies (SPBs) or *Statutory Regulatory Agencies (SRAs)* have a distinct purpose in all of this. Regulation is intended to create equity and fairness. SPBs relieve ministers of direct accountability in politically sensitive areas. For instance, most would agree that property rights should not be a political issue, but are a quasi-judicial matter. While not appropriate for departmental staff to handle, they do not warrant the costs of the courtroom, either. Often specialized technical expertise is required and can only be obtained by setting up a new agency.

For this reason, SPBs usually are not accountable to a minister. They are even able to enact "subordinate legislation" or regulations which might counter Cabinet or Parliament's intentions. For this reason, their often discretionary decisions can *sometimes* be appealed to the Federal Court of Canada, the Supreme Court of Canada, or even to the Cabinet.

The major disadvantage of SPBs lies in the *captive agency theory.* Simply put, when an industry is first regulated, its regulators need the industry's co-operation to garner the information required to do their job. Over time, politicians lose interest in the SPB; the SPB's semi-judicial process becomes bureaucratic and the SPB gradually becomes more concerned with equity than policy. As a result, the SPB becomes preoccupied with protecting its industry from the effects of outside competition, rather than with the effects of the industry on the marketplace and the consumer. Thus, the SPB becomes a "captive" of the industry. Business and government become *partners.*

Marketing boards are SPBs that enact a particular type of economic regulation: that which sanctions and supports cartels. Marketing boards inflate prices, close entry, and restrict output. Profits of large, efficient producers increase dramatically. Profits of small, inefficient producers rise only slightly. Additional capital gains are realized when excess profits are capitalized in the market value of the licence required to enter the industry. Therefore, early entrants benefit more than late entrants.

Today, as world prices for most commodities drop and exports decline, excess capacity is created. Marketing boards often end up having to purchase surpluses from producers. However, the call is not to abolish marketing boards, but to *better regulate* them! Economic regulation demonstrates well the concept of *Pareto optimality:* it always makes one person, or one class of persons, better off at the expense of someone else. This tradeoff is generally acceptable if ultimately in the public interest. But is it?

Some would counter that *deregulation* is in the public's best interest. During the early 1980s, Liberal Minister of Transport Lloyd Axworthy proposed to deregulate the transportation sector, including the airline industry. Government-owned Air Canada opposed it, fearing competition on routes it had monopolized for decades, as well as the ensuing reduction of prices. Privately owned, much smaller Canadian Pacific Airlines (CPAir) was in favour. Eventually, CPAir convinced Air Canada that an orderly phasing-in of deregulation was good for them both. Deregulation of routes (entry) and prices began, and a host of small regional carriers entered the low end of the market. Pacific Western Airlines (PWA), a privatized Alberta Crown corporation, and Wardair began to challenge Air Canada's industry leadership. Prices plunged and competition intensified, requiring new, more efficient aircraft with which to compete. Capital costs and corporate debts soared, and soon small carriers were being acquired by Air Canada, CPAir, and PWA. CPAir (now Canadian Airlines International) was bought by PWA, and Max Ward sold Wardair to PWA before Wardair crumbled under the weight of its debt.

As a result of deregulation in the airline industry, concentration is greater and prices higher than before. Ironically, one of the big losers was CPAir (not to mention the public). Yet, this experience could have been foretold if the American venture into deregulation several years earlier had been better understood. (Or maybe the ultimate outcomes of deregulation were very well understood.) Regulation had held prices below the level of a natural cartel, yet above the level of free competition. Total deregulation would likely have eliminated all competition. Now Canada has once again a natural oligopoly in airline transportation. If the American example is followed full circle, the industry will soon be calling for better regulation.

Regulation is a tool of modern mercantilism. Regulations would not be proposed if someone important did not want them. Therefore, regulations transcend democratic political ideologies. An industry will only change its support for a regulation if changing conditions in the industry or market make that regulation disadvantageous.

Regulation creates other vested interests, as well, particularly those of the regulators. A proposal to do away with regulation means a loss of employment to those who regulate. Yet, the only sure constant is change. Industries have life cycles: some long, some short, some rejuvenative. But none is static. The burning question is whether there is any normative justification for regulation. For some industries, regulation is as much an anachronism as are labour unions; for others, it is the key to survival.

NEW ROLE FOR THE JUDICIARY

In 1982, with the advent of the Constitution Act and The Charter of Rights and Freedoms, rights which were previously taken for granted (and in effect were only privileges under a constitutional monarchy) were guaranteed. Today, if individual rights are violated, the victim can ask the courts for retribution. Even if federal, provincial, or municipal laws violate most individual rights, with certain exceptions of national security, etc., the courts can now "strike down" those laws as unconstitutional. *Parliament is no longer supreme.*

This is important for business because, in legal matters, the courts treat corporations as people. Firms now have rights which government cannot violate. Technically, companies could even challenge advertising restrictions under the fundamental right of freedom of speech. Inter- provincial trade barriers could be also challenged under the right to earn a living in any province. One could also defend one's right to as prompt a regulatory hearing as one could expect for a court trial or public trial.

Of course, every guaranteed right and freedom is "subject to such reasonable limits as can be demonstrably justified." Here, then, is where the interpretative, discretionary, and veto powers of the Supreme Court of Canada come into play.

The Charter is Canada's final, formal recognition that the United States is its model, not Britain. Protecting basic civil rights in a written constitution is an American phenomenon. Thus, we can expect Canadian interest groups to follow more America's pattern, rather than Britain's. Public court challenges of government actions will promote pressure group interests, mobilize public opinion, and perhaps even help restrain government.

Business should watch and learn. If Canada's system does evolve in this manner, a new window of opportunity for business will open. Business will have a legal avenue by which to reassert its claim as the engine of the economy deserving of a special place on the public agenda.

IMPLICATIONS FOR MANAGEMENT

In the *public choice* model of economic decision-making, politicians and bureaucrats alike generally attain personal goals through the promotion of public policies ostensibly designed for another purpose. In particular, government tends to select policies which will benefit *marginal voters*— those groups, whether geographical or conceptual, to be won by narrow margins. Also attractive are well-organized, politically active interest groups. Costs of these policies will be dispersed as widely as possible over the remaining voters. Government will exaggerate the benefits of the policies and downplay their costs, which will be imposed early in a government's term of office. The benefits are released prior to elections.

Pareto optimality, where the greatest benefit is enjoyed by the greatest number, will remain an ideal in a pluralistic economy such as Canada's. Here, varied interest groups will vie for scarce resources and politicians will adopt a planning horizon as far away as the next election. Although the structure and players of the ten provincial and hundreds of regional and local governments are different, the principles are the same. Public choice economics is here to stay.

But that is not all bad for business. The private sector needs only to learn and apply the techniques already used by successful public pressure groups to win with government. Because business has more to offer, it can uniquely contribute to the formulation of national economic policy. This would be good for business, and if done well, could be good for Canada.

Business must try to side-step the trap into which most Canadians have fallen—that of "letting government do it." It must be willing to forgo some of government's largesse to achieve a more dynamic economy less burdened by government borrowing. Government itself will not take the initiative to forge a Brave New Canada if it means being turned out of office.

Business must also be willing to demonstrate to all Canadians that it can do without some assets the government has offered in the past. Government must get back to "governing" and business must get back to "creating wealth." This is probably as unappealing to one as it is to the other. It also will require skills not yet mastered and knowledge not yet acquired by business. But now is the time to learn—and to do.

The policy-making process in Ottawa is not impermeable or hostile to outsiders. It just needs to be understood in its proper context and worked with accordingly (more on this in Chapter 9). Remember, though, the "bottom line" to government is equity, redistribution, efficiency, information, revenue, jobs, and votes — all rolled into one.

To quote Prime Minister Trudeau in a 1981 pre-budget speech:

> I am not asking individual Canadians or individual companies to play the role of self-sacrificing heroes. I am asking the nation itself to come to its senses and act collectively to fight the enemy which is wounding us all. Principally, that means supporting our efforts to restrain the growth of government spending.

A decade has passed since that plea was issued. Government continues to grow, and business is now the only institution that might help government slow down this growth. As an economic entity, it is of top priority for Canada to get on with competing in the global marketplace. Therefore, it is in the public's interest, as well.

SUGGESTED FURTHER READINGS

Allison, Graham T. *Essence of Decision: Explaining the Cuban Missile Crisis.* Boston: Little, Brown & Co., 1971.

Campbell, Colin. *Governments Under Stress: Political Executives and Key Bureaucrats in Washington, London & Ottawa.* Toronto: University of Toronto Press, 1983.

Campbell, Colin and George Szablowski. *The Superbureaucrats: Structure and Behaviour in Central Agencies.* Toronto: Macmillan, 1979.

Doern, G.B. and R.W. Phidd. *Canadian Public Policy: Ideas, Structure, Process.* Toronto: Methuen, 1983.

Downs, A. *An Economic Theory of Democracy.* New York: Harper Brothers, 1957.

————. *Inside Bureaucracy.* Boston: Little, Brown & Co., 1967.

Easton, David. *A System Analysis of Political Life.* New York: John Wiley and Sons Inc., 1965.

Edelman, Murray. *The Symbolic Uses of Politics.* Chicago: University of Illinois Press, 1980.

French, Richard D. and Van Loon, Richard J., *How Ottawa Decides: Planning and Industrial Policy-Making 1968-1983.* 2nd ed. Toronto: James Lorimer & Co., 1984.

Jordan, William A. "Producer Protection, Prior Market Structure and the Effects of Government Regulation." *The Journal of Law and Economics.* XV:1, 151-176.

Kernaghan, W.D.K., ed. *Public Administration in Canada: Selected Readings.* 5th ed. Toronto: Methuen, 1985.

Kernaghan, W.D.K. and D. Siegel. *Public Administration in Canada: A Text.* Toronto: Methuen, 1987.

Lamontagne, Maurice. "The Role of Government" as in K.J. Rea and J.T. McLeod. *Business and Government in Canada: Selected Readings.* 2nd ed. Toronto: Methuen, 1976, 67-8.

Landes, R.G. *The Canadian Polity: A Comparative Introduction.* 2nd ed. Toronto: Prentice-Hall Canada Inc., 1987.

Law Reform Commission of Canada, Working Paper 51. *Policy Implementation, Compliance and Administrative Law.* Ottawa: Law Reform Commission of Canada, 1986.

Lermer, George, ed. *Probing Leviathan: An Investigation of Government in the Economy.* Toronto: The Fraser Institute, 1984.

Lindblom, C.E. "The Science of Muddling Through." *Public Administration Review.* XIX: 79-88.

Lowi, T.J. "American Business, Public Policy, Case Studies and Political Theory." *World Politics.* Vol. 16, no. 4 (1964), 688+.

————. "The State in Politics: The Relation Between Policy and Administration." In R.G. Noll, ed. *Regulatory Policy and the Social Sciences.* Berkeley: University of California Press, 1985.

Osbaldeston, G.F. *Keeping Deputy Ministers Accountable.* Toronto: McGraw-Hill Ryerson, 1989.

Pal, L.A. *Public Policy Analysis: An Introduction.* Toronto: Methuen, 1987.

Trebilcock, M.J. *et al. The Choice of Governing Instrument.* Ottawa: Supply and Services Canada, 1982.

_____ *et al. The Political Economy of Bailouts.* Vol. 1. Toronto: Ontario Economic Council, 1985.

Wilson, H.T. *Political Management: Redefining the Public Sphere.* Berlin: Walter de Gruter, 1985.

CHAPTER 7

CROWN CORPORATIONS: CANADIAN PUBLIC ENTERPRISE

Government, even in its best state, is but a necessary evil; in its worst state, an intolerable one.

Thomas Paine, 1737–1809

Throughout the historical development of the Canadian economy, there has evolved a "Canadian public enterprise culture" with great "entrepreneurial zest."[15] In fact, Canada's greatest managerial strength has been in public enterprise. Given Canada's geographic enormity, sparse population, inhospitable climate, and mercantilist capital base, commercially oriented Crown corporations[16] were a natural means by which government could intervene in the economy "to bind the nation (together), to develop and market its resources, and to retain some measure of the profits and rents."[17]

The omnipresence of public enterprise in Canada is best exhibited by a glance at the *Financial Post 500.* Of the top 50 firms in Canada ranked by revenue, eight were Crown corporations; seven of the top 50 financial institutions were state-owned. Ranked by employees, state enterprises accounted for six out of the top 50; ranked by capital spending, 11 out of the top 50 were Crown corporations. In fact, altogether, Crown corporations numbered 43 out of the top 500 Canadian industrial firms. Even after the latest spate of privatization, there remained in Canada over 400 federal and 200 provincial Crown corporations. These accounted for 15% of corporate assets in the country, 30% of all fixed assets, 25% of all net fixed assets, and 11% of the GNP.[18]

---

[15] Herschel Hardin. *A Nation Unaware: The Canadian Economic Culture.* Vancouver: J.J. Douglas, 1974, Ch. 5 and 6.

[16] "Crown corporations," "public enterprise," and "state enterprise" can be used interchangeably.

[17] Tom Kierans, "Commercial Crowns," *Policy Options,* 5:6 (November 1984), p. 27.

[18] The top ten federal Crown corporations account for 90% of federal Crown assets. These are: Petro-Canada, with $5.2 billion revenue in 1986—1987, CNR ($4.8 billion), Canadian Wheat Board ($3.1 billion), Canada Post ($3.0 billion), Bank of Canada ($2.0 billion), Royal Canadian Mint ($1.0 billion), Canadian Mortgage and Housing Corp. ($0.9 billion), Canadian Commercial Corp. ($0.8 billion) and VIA Rail ($0.7 billion). Only Canada Post, CMHC and VIA lost money.

Adding to the confusion surrounding the role of government in Canada, however, is the changing behaviour of public enterprise. Given the background on business and government in Canada, the advent of Crown corporations is not surprising. However, many observers are puzzled by increasing evidence that public enterprise in Canada is often more concerned about getting a competitive rate of return on its investment than about the political imperative given to it by the Government of the day. Also, like many private sector enterprises, Crown corporations have exhibited social responsibility only when required to stabilize their task environments, to routinize their procedures, or to escape from politics and surprise intervention; in short, to stay in business.

IN THE BEGINNING . . .

I know of no difference in the machinery of government in the old and new world that strikes a European more forcibly than the apparently undue importance which the business of constructing public works appears to occupy in American [Canadian] legislation. . . . The provision which in Europe, the state makes for the protection of its citizens against foreign enemies, is in America required for . . . the 'war with the wilderness'. The defence of an important fortress, or the maintenance of a sufficient army or navy in exposed spots, is not more a matter of common concern to the European, than is the construction of the great communications to the American [Canadian] settler; and the state, very naturally, takes on itself the making of the works, which are a matter of concern to all alike.[19]

Historically in Canada, public enterprise has arisen where there was little other prospect for profit. In the past, it was found predominantly in the transportation, communications, and utilities industries. As early as 1821, the government of Lower Canada built and operated the Lachine Canal as a "public work" to assist the fur trade of the Hudson's Bay Company.

Over the decades, little ideological resistance has greeted public ownership of assets and state operation of enterprise. No right-wing party has campaigned against public enterprise. Government ownership of railroads, airlines, electric power companies, the grain trade, and so on has always been a fact of Canadian political life. In fact, it was the Conservative government of R. B. Bennett that established the Canadian Radio Broadcasting Commission (predecessor of the CBC).

Canada may lack the industrial entrepreneurism of the United States, having inherited its financial entrepreneurism from Britain. But Canada's unique version of entrepreneurism is reflected in the zeal with which public enterprise has been applied as a public policy instrument in this country.

According to Borins, nowhere was this pragmatism more evident than

---

[19] Lord Durham. *Report on the Affairs of North America*, 1839.

in the rapid growth of public enterprise under the leadership of pro-business C. D. Howe during World War II. At that time, the overriding national goal was to win the war. Business-government co-operation was essential to this effort and the Liberal government found any form of "institutional innovation" justified. National security and security of supply were essential, and government needed a means to co-ordinate private activity with public policy; it needed a "window on the industry." Where regulation would not produce the desired results quickly enough, Crown corporations were used. It was as simple as that.

Some Crown corporations were incorporated to actually produce wartime goods and services, such as Eldorado Mining and Refining (1944) Ltd., Quebec Shipyards Ltd., Victory Aircraft Ltd., Small Arms Ltd., and Polymer Corporation Ltd. There were insufficient numbers of wartime suppliers, and capacity needed to be increased dramatically and rapidly. Some suppliers were monopolies in the interests of security (Eldorado); other were "yardstick competitors" to monitor private companies and increase capacity (Victory).

Joint ventures with the private sector were equally common. Ambitious middle-managers were recruited from the private sector; hoping for exclusive postwar opportunities, they performed meritoriously. It was clear that the private sector must produce, or the public sector would. Even private assets could be nationalized, if necessary. However, it was war; business trusted government, and government did not hesitate to act. History shows that Canada's public corporate suppliers of wartime needs enabled it to become the fourth-largest Allied supplier of war goods.

Other Crown corporations were created as simply administrative agencies. These included Wartime Housing Ltd., War Supplies Ltd., Wartime Oils Ltd., and Allied War Supplies Corp. They co-ordinated policy with private sector activities; they regulated and directed. C. D. Howe preferred the corporate form of organization to the departmental form because of lower costs and greater autonomy. These agencies were managed by successful business executives such as E. P. Taylor, who volunteered as "dollar-a-year-men." Administrative Crown corporations were lean and mean.

After the war, many Crown corporations were terminated; most administrative corporations were terminated, and many production corporations were privatized or re-privatized. Others were retained in key sectors (weapons, housing, and uranium refining) or in areas where C. D. Howe perceived a promise of commercial viability. If a production Crown corporation could survive after the war without protection from market forces, then it was retained. Howe was not ideologically opposed to public enterprise *per se.*

Some of Howe's personal decisions have helped shape Canada's economy as we know it today. He kept Polymer, which has grown into Polysar, one of the world's largest petrochemical companies. He sold Canada's merchant marine; in a matter of months, Canada went from one of the world's great naval powers to a dependent one. Howe privatized Canadair and A. V. Roe, but still used them as instruments of the government's policy goal of self-sufficiency in airframe production. He dismantled and sold Research Enterprises Ltd. (REL), an optics research and production firm, because it was of no strategic interest to the government. This last decision heralded a major turning point in Canadian research and development and accelerated the "brain drain" of researchers to the United States.

TYPES OF PUBLIC ENTERPRISE

By 1951, there were only 56 federal Crown corporations left in Canada. Thirty years later, that figure had climbed to 464 (see Figure 7-1), with 23 wholly-owned by the Government of Canada; 25 were *mixed enterprises* (or joint ventures with the private sector); 213 were subsidiaries, and the remaining 126 were administrative agencies.[20] The Department of Finance reported in 1984 that since 1968, the federal government had created a new corporation at the rate of one every three months.

Technically, according to the Financial Administration Act, federal Crown corporations are "ultimately accountable, through a Minister to Parliament." In practice, however, where a share structure exists, the federal government's shares of a Crown corporation are held by a cabinet minister in trust. Shareholder rights and prerogatives are exercised by that minister on behalf of the government. Budgets and annual reports are tabled in Parliament for information only.

Today, Crown corporations can be classified within one of five categories of public enterprise listed in ascending order of managerial autonomy: *departmental, agency, proprietary, mixed enterprise,* or *investment management.*

Departmental Crown corporations are strictly administrative and do not produce any goods or services. The Atomic Energy Control Board, Economic Council of Canada, and National Research Council are examples of departmental corporations. They can regulate or advise, but are less autonomous than a special purpose body *per se.*

Agency corporations are more autonomous than departmental corporations, but are still only quasi-commercial. Although they operate as corporations, they are not considered profit centres. Examples of agency corporations are the Canadian Commercial Corporation (which exports Canadian public enterprise expertise), and the Canadian Film Development Corporation.

Proprietary Crown corporations are relatively few, but are the most common in the public's mind. They produce goods and/or services, operate at arm's length from the government, and are completely

---

[20] In 1980, the Comptroller-General of Canada prepared a comprehensive listing of federal enterprises. This had never been done before, and has not been duplicated since.

Figure 7-1

Government of Canada Corporations – 1980

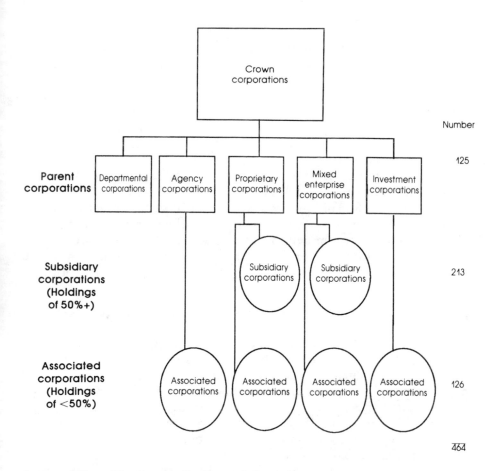

Source: Office of the Comptroller General, Government of Canada, 1980.

commercial. Air Canada, Petro-Canada, and Eldorado Nuclear Ltd. are well-known examples of this type of public enterprise.

Mixed enterprise simply refers to the increasingly popular joint ventures between state and business. Here, on the plus side, risk is shared by government and private investors; the corporation benefits from management expertise and technology from both sectors, and it has access to a larger, more diversified source of risk capital. However, mixed enterprise tends to strongly resist following non-commercial policy activities without appropriate compensation from government for losses incurred. Even then, it is less effective as an instrument of social policy than as a "window on the industry," or source of revenue. The now-defunct Canada Development Corporation was probably the highest-profile example of this genre. A very successful example of mixed enterprise is Telesat Canada, a world leader in satellite communications. In 1988, Air Canada began offering public shares, and was transformed from a wholly government-owned Crown corporation to a mixed-ownership enterprise.

Finally, the most recent type of public enterprise to evolve is the *investment management corporation*. These companies have been established by both federal and provincial governments to manage public pension and insurance funds. Quite often, they possess vast and varied holdings in numerous private-sector corporations. This enables them to reap an above- average rate of return on their funds and generate investment income for other government programs.

State investment management corporations are completely autonomous. Some, like the Caisse de dépôt et placement du Québec (Canada's largest, with over \$23 billion invested), have made it clear that they are not passive investors, but have every intention of influencing the management of their companies for the betterment of Quebec. The Caisse owns 10% or more of the voting rights, or has invested at least \$5 million, in about 130 companies. It is legally classified as an "insider" in about thirty of these.

PRAGMATIC INSTRUMENT OF PUBLIC POLICY

Public enterprise has a distinct political advantage over regulation in government's point of view. Whereas only a small number receive the benefits under regulation, with costs widely dispersed across the general population there is a wide dispersal of both the benefits and the costs of public enterprise. This was a major reason for the proliferation of Crown corporations during the 1960s and 1970s, as opposed to new economic regulatory regimes or revenue-enhancing tax reform. Public enterprise thus maintains the basic political principle of equity.

There have been other reasons for, and benefits from, public enterprise in Canada. One has been technological innovation. Private-sector research and development has been limited in this country for several reasons:

1. its conservative, mercantilist government policies;
2. its limited, branch plant economy, wherein research and development is performed in parent companies' home countries;
3. a lack of domestic risk capital from a conservative, mercantilist banking community; and
4. a small, unprofitable domestic market.

When expenditures have been made, they have been in research, not commercial development.

Crown corporations therefore became a means by which to infuse risk capital into the economy and perform research and development. As a result, Canada has been a leader at one time or another in the development of railroad, hydro-electric, pulp and paper, nuclear, and petrochemical technologies. This has stimulated Canadian enterprise where there was none previously, has safeguarded key sectors of the economy, and has earned foreign exchange by exporting these technologies.

Public enterprise has also secured supply and continued service where the private sector could not profitably do so. For example, several years ago both the CNR's and CPR's tracks were covered by a snowslide in British Columbia's Fraser Canyon. CPR responded by following standard operating procedures — all very bureaucratic and cost-conscious. Government-owned CNR was much more flexible and quicker to respond. CNR's identification with the nation gave it the incentive to serve. When the emergency had passed, CNR had restored service more quickly than CPR, was operating just as efficiently, and had spent no more money than CPR to clear its tracks.

As mentioned earlier, public enterprise has also provided local industrial entrepreneurs with an opportunity to flex their muscles, create wealth, and command industrial companies which would never have been supported by the private sector. More than one disillusioned entrepreneur has moved from the risk-averse business community into the public sector. In fact, a major export of Crown corporations today is Canadian Commercial Corporation's sale of industrial/entrepreneurial management technology to foreign governments.

American competitors of Polymer/Polysar predicted its demise once the war was over. What they did not appreciate was its passive vertical integration and the strength it possessed in its ambitious, entrepreneurial managers. Polysar followed the American rules of business, grew, and became a self-sustaining success. *It may have been bureaucratic—any large organization by definition is going to be bureaucratic—but it was not bureaupathetic.*

Finally, public enterprise has safeguarded the public's interest. In a small, domestic market, monopolies are often more efficient than competition. The greater use of assets by monopolies makes a country more competitive internationally in global industries. Canada's general lack of ideological conflict has encouraged government monopolies in those areas requiring high levels of fixed capital investment, such as utilities, transportation, and communications.

However, some problems do exist with this instrument of government policy. The most difficult of these to address is the mixture of objectives under which many Crown corporations are forced to operate. These involve the pursuit of commercial success while also pursuing public policies to create employment, provide public transportation, or protect the incomes of agricultural producers. Those Crown corporations charged only with being commercially viable, such as Canadian Cellulose Company Ltd., have few problems in this regard. However, the vast majority remain inefficient by private-sector standards because of their mandate to meet government's social priorities.

Given these mixed objectives, evaluating public enterprise's performance becomes difficult. Business' benchmark of profit has little meaning when measuring a Crown corporation's effectiveness. Profitability is but one of many objectives of public enterprise.

Managerial control is another gray area. Government maintains nominal control of most Crown corporations as sole or major shareholder, with the power to appoint the board of directors and chief executive officer. In some cases, Crown corporations also operate under legally binding government directives. However, business experience in general (let alone specific to an industry) is not always a prerequisite for appointment. Today, board appointments in particular are more often forms of patronage or regional representation than good business sense.

What happens, then, when the autonomous management of a Crown corporation with no overseeing body disobeys government? When a Petro-Canada becomes obsessed with becoming a retail giant with little exploration to its credit, despite a mandate to be much less ambitious and far more development-oriented? When a Canada Development Corporation has 80% of its portfolio in resource-related industries because that is where profits will be made? Yet its mandate was to stimulate investment in less attractive secondary industries. How does government control its creations when profit takes precedence over social policy? The answer is, not very well.

Finally, financial control is an equally perplexing problem. Parliament grants Crown corporations global budgets. Their capital budgets are dealt with by Parliament separately from their operating budgets. Public enterprise is not required to operate under the same rules of disclosure as are private-sector counterparts. Of the 464 Crown corporations identified in Figure 7-1, only 56 are clearly designated as such. These fall under the financial management and general accountability provisions of the Financial Administration Act, which attempts to control government finances. In short, there is no real financial control or accountability by Crown corporations to the Government of Canada.

Crown corporations have also begun to serve another purpose—most likely unwittingly. Like statutory regulatory agencies, they have become a target of public outcry against poorly conceived or carried-out public policies. They, not the politicians, take the heat for failed government policy.

However, one must be careful in criticizing the management of Crown corporations. For instance, Petro-Canada was sharply criticized by the business community for its grossly overpriced purchase of Petrofina in 1981. It is true that Petrofina was overpriced, but so was everything else.

In early 1981, the Toronto Stock Exchange Industrial Index traded around 4400. Later that year, it rose to 5200. By mid-1982, it had dropped by almost 50%. Petro-Canada paid too much for Petrofina; the Bay paid too much for Simpsons; Dome Petroleum paid too much for Hudson Bay Oil and Gas and Cyprus Anvil Mine; Noranda paid too much for Macmillan Bloedel, and so on. In fact, of the $35 billion worth of takeovers in 1981, half was lost within a year of acquisition. Private industry should note that "those in glass houses . . . ."

PRIVATIZATION OF PUBLIC ASSETS[21]

One of the additions to the vocabulary of public management during the 1980s was the term, *privatization*. This refers to the transfer of activities and/or assets from the public to the private sector. Such transfers can take several forms. In Canada, privatization can now refer to:

(a) *Liquidation*: government sale of a state-owned enterprise to the private sector, as was done with the Canada Development Corporation, de Havilland Aircraft of Canada Limited, Canadair Limited, and Teleglobe Canada.

(b) *Subsidization*: government provision of grants to non-profit organizations for public services, such as day care and home care;

(c) *Nation-building*: government franchising of a private company to exclusively provide a geographical area with a certain service, as was done with the provision of transportation services to the North;

(d) *Contracting-out*: government retention of responsibility for providing a service, but hiring a private contractor to deliver it, as with waste collection and snow removal.

One answer to the problems inherent in public enterprise is to get rid of it—that is, to privatize Crown corporations. Three strong arguments can be made for privatizing a state-owned business, although some may not apply in all cases.

The first is under-capitalization of the public sector. As in the private sector, Crown corporations and government services require capital to modernize and expand. However, within government these enterprises must compete with other public services, as well as with government support of private business, for a limited amount of public funds.

Second, the public sector is often less efficient in business because it is frequently protected by a monopoly position—whether natural or artificial—and thus lacks the incentive to operate efficiently.

---

[21] Some of the material in this section was contained in an earlier paper written by Mackenzie Kyle and adapted by the author.

Finally, public enterprise is often unresponsive to the market because its customers are a captured entity.

Although many Crown corporations *are* profitable and meet their social obligations, collectively, federally owned Crown corporations have not been profitable since 1981. The larger, best-known corporations have, in fact, been major money-losers: Canada Post, VIA Rail, Eldorado Nuclear, St. Lawrence Seaway, Canadian Wheat Board, and the Canadian Broadcasting Corporation. There are as many reasons for this as there are Crown corporations. Ironically, in the last few years, the three darlings of Canadian public enterprise, which account for 35% of all federal Crown corporation assets, have been quite profitable: Air Canada, CNR, and Petro-Canada.

In 1985, eight Crown corporations were terminated.[22] During 1985-1988, fourteen more were privatized for a total of $1.4 billion (see Figure 7-2).

Any effort to successfully privatize a government service will depend upon:

1. establishing strong, central political leadership;
2. assuring comprehensive advance planning, with clear criteria to weigh public benefits against public costs of choosing suitable candidates for privatization;
3. involving business and organized labour in the process of privatization initiatives;
4. encouraging employee ownership;
5. including a method of objectively measuring the level and cost of service before and after privatization; and
6. beginning with companies or services that will make the easiest transition to the private sector, so that the process will be constructive, rather than disillusioning.

The federal government has not scored well on these points. A 1988 study by the Office of Privatization and Regulatory Affairs (OPRA) criticized the government for a "perceived lack of direction, control and political will," with no one clearly in charge. The privatization process of 1985 to 1988 was plagued with long negotiating delays, poor communication between the government and employees of the companies sold, and a failure to sell the public on its ambitious and controversial scheme. The report also criticized several cabinet ministers for "spreading misinformation" and fumbling their public-relations role.

Yet, despite these weaknesses, the same report claimed that "all companies report improved commercial potential, increased access to capital

---

[22] These were: Canadian Sports Pool, Lotto Canada, Canagrex, Uranium Canada, Mingan Assn., Societa San Sebastine, St. Anthony Fisheries Ltd., and CN (West Indies) Steamships.

Figure 7-2

Federal Crown Corporation Privatizations, 1985–1988

CROWN CORPORATION/DATE	BUYER	NET PROCEEDS (*in millions*)
Northern Transport Co. Ltd. July 1985	Inuvialuit Development Corporation and Nunasi Corp.	$27
deHavilland January 1986	Boeing Commercial Corp. (U.S.)	90
CN Route April 1986	Route Canada Holdings (Mgmt.)	29
Pêcheries Canada Inc. April 1986	La co-operative agroalimentair Purdel	5
Canadian Arsenals May 1986	SNC Group	92
Canada Development Corp. September 1986	Publicly-held shares up from 75% to 90%	258
Nanisivik Mines October 1986	MRI International	6
Canadair December 1986	Bombardier	123
Northern Canada Power Commision March 1987	Yukon Territory	76
Teleglobe Canada April 1987	Memotec Data	608
Fishery Products Intl. April 1987	Public share offering	104
Canada Development Corp. (Polysar) June-October 1987	100% public	102
Eldorado Nuclear Ltd. February 1988	Saskatchewan Mining Development Corp. (Provincial Crown Corporation)	merger of assets
Air Canada	45% public (raised $300 m in new equity for Air Canada and cost the federal government $100 m in the dilution of its equity position)	(100)
		$ 1.4 billion

markets and product markets, and increased opportunity to compete aggressively." Quite revealing, given our earlier assumptions about the role and advantages of government ownership.

When the federal Cabinet met in Alberta in early 1988, its attitude towards privatization had changed. At that meeting, the Cabinet realized that the remaining 400 or so Crown corporations either:

1. were not at all profitable and therefore not saleable;
2. had no commercial future and therefore were not saleable;
3. provided government with much-needed revenue and therefore were too profitable to sell; or
4. were well-liked by the public, which opposed their privatization.

Cabinet was advised by the Deputy Minister of Privatization and Regulatory Affairs that divestment in the economy's present bearish market would not be practical. The federal government also realized that the 315 or so commercial Crown corporations employed 263 000 workers—more than the federal government's total departmental staff. As jobs would be lost with privatization, it would not occur if guaranteed, continued employment was a term of sale. And jobs mean votes.

Since 1988, the federal privatization initiative has been on hold. Political pragmatism has prevailed once again. Meanwhile, present Crown corporations have extended their reach into the national economy and acquired even more subsidiaries. *As a result, the net equity base of federal state enterprise under Prime Minister Mulroney has actually increased!*

Before the decision to privatize is made, it is vital to define *success*, in order to measure the impact of privatization. A successful privatization strategy should result in at least the following:

1. a level of service at least as good, if not better than, that provided by government; and
2. a lower cost of service than when the service was provided by government, with a discernible trend towards even lower costs.

If privatization is not a workable solution, an alternative could be *sunset laws*. Any legislation incorporating a Crown corporation would require Parliament to review the *need* for such a corporation every five years or so. In such a review, a no longer useful Crown corporation could be terminated. Money-losers not serving a social need could be closed. Money-makers could be sold, returning at least some of the public's investment. The rest? Well, that still requires a weighing of the public interest against the public cost.

IMPLICATIONS FOR MANAGEMENT

The growth of government, by whatever means, restricts individual and collective freedoms. Yet, true to their heritage, Canadians seem little concerned.

Private-sector business in direct competition with a Crown corporation, however, does have reason for concern. Public enterprise is not held accountable for its performance by its shareholders, usually pays no taxes, and enjoys easier access to risk capital than do many segments of the business community. Regulations are often skewed to favour Crown corporations or are waived altogether.

Yet, to date federal politicians have not favoured increasing the accountability of public enterprise to Parliament. This may be due to the implicit design of Crown corporations to distance elected officials from the implementation of public policy by public enterprise. In some cases, government-owned enterprise may actually enhance competitive market situations.

On the other hand, economists see private corporations, operating in a highly regulated environment, as less concerned with competition, their customers, productivity, efficiency, and managing technological change than their less-regulated peers. *Compared to regulated companies in regulated industries, some Crown corporations often appear downright aggressive and entrepreneurial.* While 80% of business success is based upon "doing the right things," such as meeting and beating the competition, most Crown corporations are preoccupied with "doing things right." They are sensitive to public scrutiny and criticism. They take their social policy mandates seriously. And given their efforts to achieve these social policy ends, they are efficient and productive.

As a result, public enterprise incorporates right-wing and left-wing political ideology into a pragmatic ethos which wins over public opinion time and time again. Canada's public enterprise culture reflects a collective, organic heritage and a passive desire for nominal, economic, and political independence.

Americans had a genius for modern private enterprise; Canadians had a genius for modern public enterprise. Canada *is* different, and it is futile to compare it to an American model to determine what works best.[23] *Canadian nationalism is concurrently the cause and the result of its public enterprise culture.*

If John Kenneth Galbraith is correct, ownership no longer matters. It is professional management that charts the course of enterprise today. And it is the behaviour of corporations, not its ownership, that has an impact upon Canadians' daily lives and national best interest. In that respect, government ownership is in the same category as foreign ownership.

---

[23] It is only natural, though, for a colony to try to imitate the culture of its metropole.

Public enterprise, like foreign-owned enterprise, is no more environmentally conscious than its Canadian-owned private-sector counterparts. Its research and development expenditures are no higher; prices are no lower, and so on. On the other hand, public enterprise, like foreign enterprise, fills market gaps with goods and services which local private capital is not interested in providing or cannot do so profitably.

The only problem with all this is the cost. Billions of dollars are spent each year by the government of Canada to subsidize most Crown corporations, commercial or not. If this expense were somehow eliminated, the federal government's so-called "deficit" would be considerably reduced.

Can privatization be a successful public management strategy? Certainly, it was successful in the postwar years and during 1985 to 1988. Once privatized, Crown corporations can still remain closely tied instruments of government policy, such as the aircraft industry, both after the war and today.

It remains to be seen if there are any more Crown corporations of interest to the private sector. If so, privatization offers business a unique three-way opportunity. It will serve the nation, help government emerge from its crippling financial burden, and make a profit. Anything business can do to help government meet its economic and social policy goals will surely improve business-government relations in this country.

SUGGESTED FURTHER READINGS

Baumol, W. J., ed. *Public and Private Enterprise in a Mixed Economy*. New York: St. Martin's Press, 1980.

Boardman, A., R. Freedman and C. Edsel. "The Price of Government Ownership: A Study of the Domtar Takeover." *Journal of Public Economics*, 31, 269-285.

Borins, Sanford F. "World War II Crown Corporations: Their Wartime Role and Peacetime Privatization." *Canadian Public Administration*, 25:3 (Fall 1982), 380-404.

————. *Investments in Failure*. Toronto: Methuen, 1986.

Brooks, Stephen. *Who's in Charge? The Mixed Ownership of Corporations in Canada*. Halifax: Institute for Research on Public Policy, 1987.

Butt, H. A. and D. R. Palmer. *Value for Money in the Public Sector*. New York: Basil Blackwell Inc., 1985.

Economic Council of Canada. *Minding the Public's Business*. Ottawa: Supply and Services Canada, 1986.

Gordon, M. *Government in Business*. Montreal: C. D. Howe Institute, 1981.

Grafftey, Heward. "Government and Business: The Caisse de dépôt et placement du Québec." *Business Quarterly*, 48:2 (Summer 1983), 107-110.

Hardin, H. *The Privatization Putsch*. Halifax: The Institute for Research on Public Policy, 1989.

Kirby, Michael J. L. "Restructuring the Atlantic Fishery: A Case Study in Business-Government Relations." *Business Quarterly*, 50:2 (Summer 1985), 115-118.

Mazzolini, Renato. *Government Controlled Enterprises*. New York: John Wiley and Sons, 1979.

Prichard, J. R. S., ed. *Crown Corporations in Canada: The Calculus of Instrument Choice*. Toronto: Butterworths, 1983.

Savas, E. S. *Privatization: The Key to Better Government*. Chatham, N. J.: Chatham House Publishers Inc., 1985.

Sexty, R. W. "Autonomy Strategies of Government-owned Business Corporations in Canada." *Strategic Management Journal*, 1 (1980), 371-384.

Strong, Maurice. "The Necessary Private-Public Mix." *Policy Options*, 5:6 (November 1984), 6-12.

Tupper, A. "The State in Business." *Canadian Public Administration*, 27 (1979) 124-150.

Tupper, A. and G. B. Doern, eds. *Privatization, Public Policy and Public Corporations in Canada*. Halifax: The Institute for Research on Public Policy, 1988.

INTERPRETING BUSINESS–GOVERNMENT RELATIONS

In analysing business-government relations, it is not sufficient to understand only the past and the role of the key players in the relationship, but to be able to critically evaluate, or interpret, the present state of these relations. The next two empirically based chapters not only clarify the state of business-government relations in Canada, but also address business' ambivalence towards the state. This section of the book completes the task of placing Canadian business and government in their proper contexts.

CHAPTER 8

THE CURRENT STATE OF BUSINESS-GOVERN-MENT RELATIONS

CHAPTER 9

THE RIGHT KIND OF GOVERNMENT INTERVENTION

CHAPTER

8

THE CURRENT STATE OF BUSINESS-GOVERNMENT RELATIONS

Since the general or prevailing opinion on any subject is rarely or never the whole truth, it is only for the collision of adverse opinions that the remainder of the truth has any chance of being supplied.

John Stuart Mill, 1806-1873

Nothing appears more surprising to those who consider human affairs with a philosophical eye, than the ease with which the many are governed by the few.

David Hume, 1711-1776

Business-government relations in Canada today are often said to be in poor shape. Some observers claim they are even worse than those in the United States. To date, however, little empirical research has been conducted to confirm or deny this.

Are some business-government relations better than others? If so, then why—and in what areas? If not, why has this general assumption been so uncritically accepted? How has this perception evolved and why?

Much of the research on current business-government relations in Canada has assumed a problem exists: that government intervention is emasculating the private sector; that business interests are no longer synonymous with the "public interest"; *that what was once the workplace of a national socio-economic partnership is now the battleground for two disparate solitudes.*

Most investigations have been largely issue-oriented case studies, such as those found at the end of this book. Case studies generally provide specific information helpful in understanding a more generalized theory. They offer little else, however. Other publications on the topic have been commentaries, criticisms, and/or advocacies with little empirical research as a foundation.

---

[24] Some of the material in this chapter originally appeared in *Canadian Public Administration* and *the Canadian Journal of Administrative Sciences*.

In fact, most literature, both descriptive and prescriptive, available to Canadian scholars and practitioners, is American. Given the significant differences between Canada and the United States, as identified in Part I of this book, American material has little relevance to Canadian business-government relations.

THE INTERPRETIVE APPROACH

Prior to the 1984 federal election in Canada, one heard cries from all sides for "improving" the relationship between business and government. Most critics sought to improve the means by which government made decisions on major economic policy issues. These reforms would have resulted in a stronger voice for certain preferred interest groups. It was hoped that, if the "right" people could be brought together at the "right" time with the "right" information, they might agree, or at least compromise, on crucial economic issues.

The possible reasons why behavioural and structural reforms in the business-government dynamic have not been made are many. The "macro socio-political" school of thought blames deeply rooted economic, political, and social conditions prevalent throughout the Western world over the past thirty years.[25] Such conditions do not lend themselves to being changed easily.

The "failure of business" school tends to emphasize more specific problems in the way business is organized to deal with government, while the "failure of government" school—a somewhat larger camp—concentrates on a variety of equally specific organizational problems within government.

Yet another school offers an "interpretive approach"; this emphasizes the underlying values and beliefs that the parties hold about each other, their relationship, and the specific policy issue(s) under discussion. These subjective interpretations are believed to colour the actions of the parties, making accurate communication and collaboration virtually impossible.

This interpretive approach to understanding business-government relations is predicated on several assumptions:

(a) in the case of large, complex economic, social, and political problems, it is not possible to *prove* what causes them or what will *cure* them by any of the usual tests of scientific rationality;

(b) in spite of (a), people interested in these problems form *beliefs* about their causes and cures;

---

[25] For a comprehensive survey of thought see V.V. Murray and C.J. McMillan, "Business-Government Relations in Canada: A Conceptual Map." *Canadian Public Administration*, 26, Winter 1983, 591-609.

(c) these *subjective interpretations of reality* influence and, along with situational variables, shape the actions of parties in dealing with one another; and

(d) changes in *behaviour* can only be achieved in conjunction with changes in related beliefs, attitudes, and values.

Figure 8-1 provides a sequential schematic interpretation of the relationship among values, attitudes, beliefs, perceptions, and actions with regard to business-government relations. First, any actor in a business-government relationship is bombarded with a complexity of incoming stimuli. These stimuli are filtered by his or her values, attitudes, beliefs, and sociological and hereditary learning factors into a manageable form. This, in turn, produces a *psychological predisposition* as illustrated in Stage 1 of Figure 8-1. Behaviour at this stage is highly predictable.

However, the influence of intervening *situational variables,* such as *social constraint,* can distort perception and reduce the predictability of behaviour. They can influence the individual to *selectively perceive* a given situation such as a business-government relationship. This selective perception (Stage 2 in Figure 8-1) provides the basis for one's choice of behaviour. The combination of all actors' responses results in a particular strategic choice or policy output (Stage 3 in Figure 8-1). Outcomes then join incoming stimuli as feedback and the process may be reiterated.

Figure 8-1

Selective Perception and Business-Government Relations

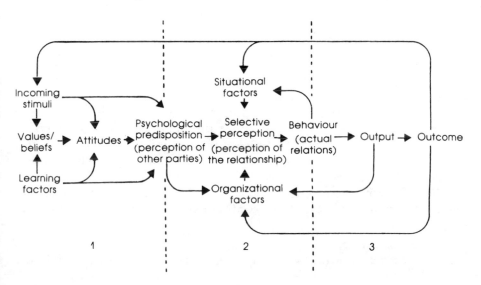

Historically, there has been hardly any consideration given to sociological variables such as values, attitudes, beliefs, and perceptions to help define problems, interpret data, or formulate theories and/or recommendations about Canadian business-government relations. This is startling, given that perceptions are significant factors in understanding social relationships and organization.

Often, what people perceive to be real, is real in its consequences for them; perception determines reality for the individual.

It is important to understand this process of "selective perception," because while values may not change, attitudes can, given changes in situational variables. For example, a change in government leadership may alter a person's attitude towards government without affecting other values. As a result, one's perception of the business-government relationship may change even if the substance of the relationship does not.[26]

When striving to improve business-government relations, it is extremely valuable to understand the subjective, interpretive elements that exist in the minds of business and government leaders. It is also important to explore what factors may shape the way these feelings are created and changed. Unfortunately, few studies have attempted to measure empirically some of these beliefs and values among the interested parties.

This section of the book will summarize the results of perhaps the most extensive study ever conducted to determine these beliefs. It empirically measured how Canadian business and government elites perceived their overall relationship during the spring of 1984, prior to the federal general election. It also tested the hypothesis that there is a similarity between the beliefs held by business and government elites about their relationship, and the perceptions they hold about themselves, and each other.

Before examining these findings, however, let's take a closer look at Canadian elites, and the role they play in Canada's socio-economic drama.

THE ROLE OF ELITES

Every society has its elites. Tribal societies had their hereditary warrior chiefs; feudal societies had their noble and religious elites; today's industrial societies have their economic and political elites. Canada is no exception: the existence, structure, and processes of Canada's elites have been extensively documented. In fact, since the publication of *The Vertical Mosaic*, John Porter's pathfinding study of ethnic and socio-economic elites, most Canadian social science research and commentary has concentrated on "elites," rather than on "class."

For Canadian researchers, elites are a much more meaningful sociological grouping because less conflict exists between those who have

---

[26] A study to test this hypothesis was being conducted by the author while this book was being published.

power and those who do not, rather than between those who *already* have power. This country's powerful minority is composed of the leaders and primary decision-makers within its numerous hierarchies. This is Canada's elite.

The great Italian economist, Vilfredo Pareto, was one of the first modern scholars to study the differences between elites and non-elites, or "the masses." Within an elite, he differentiated between the *governing elite* (the faction possessing real power) and the *non-governing elite* (which possessed wealth, learning, and position, but no power). Pareto also noted that each elite group, whether industrial, religious, political, or military, held consistent values, attitudes, and ideologies.

Twentieth-century studies have shown that a society's governing elite can contain its political elite as well as other elites; these groups could also affect political decisions. Specifically, industry's owners, managers, and the highest government officials have inherited roles once performed by the ruling class of feudal society. John Kenneth Galbraith, in his ongoing analysis of the modern industrial state, has frequently referred to this group as a *technostructure*.

In this technostructure, elites not only compete for, but co-operate in, the exercise of power and influence to keep society running smoothly. Of course, co-operation and competition suggest periodic alterations to the status quo. These changes may be of an evolutionary or revolutionary nature. As change occurs, the relationship among elites is also altered. New elites may arise and assume the positions of power vacated by graying elites. Political science refers to this whole process as *elite accommodation*. This process has much to offer in improving both the understanding and the conduct of Canadian business-government relations. Robert Presthus, Canada's dean of elite theorists, has actually proposed that elite accommodation is inherent in the process of democratic government today.[27] Business and government would do well to acknowledge this.

Elites are leaders of all bureaucracies in which power is concentrated at the top. Over time, these elites develop the means to maintain their position, and to keep in check the power of other elites. Elites are less concerned with further subjugating those within their hierarchies and under their control. Certainly, this is true of business and government in Canada today.

In the 1960s and 1970s, Presthus identified a considerable degree of cohesion and frequent interaction between Canadian business elites and government elites. There were high levels of mutual interdependence between the private and public sectors, and an omnipresence of departmental-clientele relationships. To neo-corporatists, of course, this sort of

---

[27] R. Presthus. *Elite Accommodation in Canadian Politics.* Toronto: Macmillan, 1973, page 4.

convergence and even interpenetration was a symptom of the tech-nocratic, corporatist state which they believe Canada to be.

In 1986, T.K. Das wrote a monograph about how strategic choices, corporate performance, and process outcomes were partly shaped by the backgrounds of an organization's senior managers. Found to be relevant were values, attitudes, beliefs, learning stimuli, demographics, and a host of situational variables. All these characteristics of business and govern-ment leaders help form their perceptions. A manager's understanding of a situation, along with his or her values, attitudes, and beliefs, provides the basis for choices and behaviour. Therefore, it is vital to these elites in order to improve strategic management in both the private and public sectors. *It is incumbent upon the key actors in both camps to be as familiar as possible with each other's qualities. Only then can they effectively influence and manage their business-government relationships.*

Lacking this type of knowledge, business people often make two common errors when dealing with politicians or public servants. First, they believe that government is, or ought to be, run like business. There-fore, they expect that government behaviour can be predicted using business management processes as models. The second error is the belief that public officials, both elected and appointed, are completely different from their business counterparts, and operate in a world the latter can never comprehend. In reality, most senior bureaucrats plan and implement strategies in a way strikingly similar to senior managers in the private sector. They set goals, gather information, develop options from which they choose one, allocate resources, and set into motion an action plan.

However, theorists claim that *business elites*—the leaders of the major firms of a country—are not as hostile towards, and ignorant of, govern-ment as is business in general. Thanks to their companies' longer-term, broader perspectives, business elites recognize the benefits, as well as the costs, of government intervention. In fact, this inner group is likely to differ sharply from other members of the private sector when it comes to determining government's role in the economy. The elite recognizes the stability government offers society through its social and economic inter-ventions, thus lessening the economic turbulence which plagues corporate managers. This suggests that chief executive officers in more frequent contact with government would espouse a political ideology more favourable to state intervention than might others.

It is a dangerous error on anyone's part to assume that business and government elites are internally homogeneous.

Canada's business elites have lacked unity; in fact, a significant gulf has developed between the financial and industrial elites over the years. The adversity to risk demonstrated by Canadian chartered banks has often discouraged industrial entrepreneurs in this country.

It is equally absurd to assume that all politicians and career public servants think and act the same way. Usually, a spectrum—no matter how small—of differing political, economic, and management thought will exist among the ranks of a government elite. To the untrained eye, such a spectrum is hidden from view due to party discipline, Cabinet solidarity, and a silent (silenced) public service.

CHALLENGES TO THE CONVENTIONAL WISDOM

A recurring theme of modern business-government relations has been the changing dynamics between business and government. This has been the result of the growth of Canada's government in both scope and in size during the 1970s, and the resultant increasing complexity of its decision-making processes. From this awareness have come many of the proposed solutions to improve an apparently volatile, if not deteriorating, relationship. Contributing to the overall discord is business' failure to have a sufficient impact on the determination of the public interest, and government's failure to operate effectively.

Solutions proposed to improve the situation range from "mutual accommodation," issue management, and direct political involvement, to the more effective use of trade associations, public affairs consultants, and in-house government affairs staff. Many perceive a need for business to prove to society the value of an efficient and unencumbered private sector. As well, it is said, business must better understand factors behind government growth, as well as politicians' responses to the electorate's ever-increasing expectations and demands.

Business must also appreciate more fully changing social values and their impact on government's agenda, as well as the legitimate right for government to intervene in business' affairs. Most studies have agreed that problems exist on both sides of the Canadian business-government relationship, and that cultural, sociological, educational, and vocational gaps exist between them.

Such has been the conventional wisdom about business-government relations in Canada, but such is no longer the whole truth.

Results of a survey conducted by the author and Vic Murray of York University in 1984 showed that 61% of the business elite perceived Canadian business-government relations to be fair.[28] Yet 70% of the government elite assessed them as good.[29] Fifty-three percent of the business elite believed the relationship had deteriorated over the past ten years, while 69% of the government elite saw no change, unless perhaps for the better. A majority—62% and 59% respectively of Canada's business and government elites—considered relations worse here than in the United States.

---

[28] These were the 635 CEOs whose companies appeared in the 1984 Financial Post 500.
[29] This refers to the 185 ministers, deputy ministers, associate deputy ministers, and assistant deputy ministers in the federal government in 1984.

It was not surprising that both business and government regarded business-government relations as better in the United States—the home of free enterprise and a neo-conservative Republican president. Nor is it odd that business-government relations in Canada were considered worse than they were ten years before. What *was* surprising was to discover that neither business nor government considered business-government relations in general all that bad. Given the rhetoric, the business-bashing by government, and the government-bashing by business, this was indeed refreshing to see.

Also not surprising was the finding that both elites' perceptions of the status of business-government relations reflected their political values and beliefs. If the business elite perceived government policies as ideologically "too far left," they went on to perceive business-government relations as "poor." If government policies were "just about right," the business elite tended to regard business-government relations as "good."

Most business respondents assessed their own company's specific relations with government as "good." On the government side, too, almost all judged their relations with specific businesses to be either "good" or "very good."

The study also showed that certain interest groups in Canada have had more influence than others in the formulation of public policy; some have benefited more than others from public policy, and the distribution of influence among groups in Canada has changed over time.

The biggest gains in influence were considered to have been made by the media and the Prime Minister's Office. Differences in opinion, however, clearly were influenced by elite membership. For example, the business respondents believed senior federal civil servants had gained in influence, whereas government respondents had not. The government respondents thought that the influence of large corporations had increased, while business respondents thought that it had generally remained about the same. The business respondents saw an *increase* in the influence of federal Cabinet ministers, while government respondents perceived it to have *decreased.* The business elite felt that the ministers' *gain* of influence had worsened business-government relations. Government respondents, who thought that the influence of ministers had diminished, believed that this *loss* of influence had made relations worse.

When a factor analysis was conducted for a 26-part question which asked the respondents whether they agreed or disagreed with various explanations for the state of business-government relations in Canada, four significant, underlying dimensions to the responses were discerned.

The first two dimensions, which together summarized 29% of a variation, supported the "failure of government school." This implied that the main reasons for ineffective business-government relations were due to various faults *within* government: faults of the politicians, the civil servants, or the structure and process for the making of policy decisions.

The next two dimensions supported the "failure of business school." They suggested that the fault was primarily with business in the roles played by business leaders, and with ineffective organization for bringing the business point of view to government. When government responses were factored separately, the most significant dimension (16%) supported the "mechanisms of interaction" school. This group attributed the main cause of problems not to what goes on within the ranks of the two parties so much as to the mechanisms of interaction between the two: the details of who gets to see whom about what, plus when and how the interaction is conducted.

In essence, the business elite believed that both business and government were to blame for any problems between them, but that government shared a larger portion of that blame. Government, on the other hand, perceived the major problem to be the mechanisms of interaction between the two sectors, and then placed the blame on business and government respectively. These findings, of course, are in strict keeping with the first two principles of attribution theory: failure is externally blamed; success is internally credited.

Two external factors were also agreed upon as having influence on business-government relations: the extent to which the electorate had succumbed to the social value of entitlement (the feeling that the government must protect them against all misfortune), and the role of the media as biased reporter and editorializer shaping public opinion. In both instances, each set of respondents agreed substantially that these were important factors.

The frequencies of personal interaction that members of one elite had with members of the other elite are displayed in Figure 8-2. Overall, nearly 70% of the business respondents interacted with government once or more per month; 25% interacted with a government official at least once per week. Of those interactions, almost two-thirds were with the federal government as contrasted with provincial or municipal levels of government.

Members of the government elite reported that they interacted with members of the business community even more frequently. In fact, almost 84% of the government respondents interacted with business once or more per month; 45% interacted with business at least once per week.

Interestingly enough, though, there was no significant consistency in the pairing of businessperson and government official with respect to the frequency of their interaction. *This would clearly suggest that the days are gone in which a chief executive officer had a personal contact within government and in which government officials saw themselves as serving a specific business interest.*

The business elite was asked what level of personal experience they had in government and/or politics while the government elite was asked what level of business experience they had. Of the business elite, 64% had some

Figure 8-2

Elite Interaction

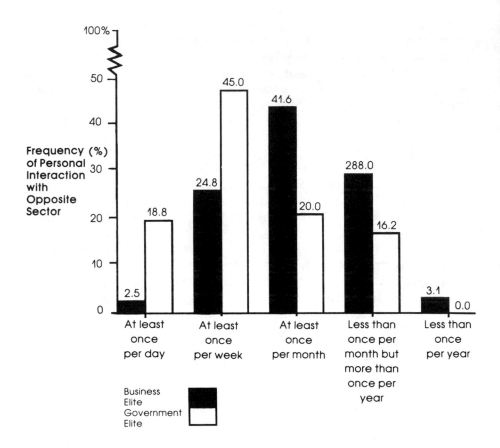

sort of experience in either government or politics. A little over a third belonged to a political party, but only about one-half of that number was active in a riding association or in political fund-raising. Nine respondents had actually run for public office, with seven having won. Ten percent actually had been senior civil servants, while 35% had acted in some sort of formal advisory capacity to government (see Figure 8-3).

On the other hand, 61% of the government elite had some sort of experience in business but only 44% had had full-time experience. Thirty-six percent had some or all of their experience in "big business" while 29% actually had been senior managers in the private sector (see Figure 8-4). These findings, for both the business and government elites, were surprising given the conventional wisdom of one side not understanding the

Figure 8-3

Business Elite's Experience in Government or Politics

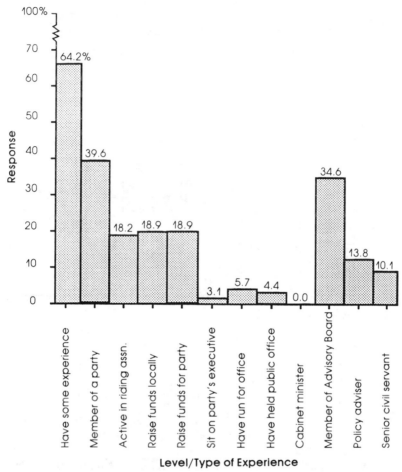

other, and of either side never having had experience in the management of the affairs of the other.[30]

Finally, Figure 8-5 reveals that more than two-thirds of the time it was the chief executive officer who was a firm's most active person in formulating business-government policy. In the public sector, 92% of the time it was the Minister, the Deputy Minister, or an Assistant Deputy Minister, with the frequency fairly evenly distributed across the three.

---

[30] I.A. Litvak. "The Ottawa Syndrome: Improving Business-Government Relations." *Business Quarterly* 44, Summer 1979, 22-39; N. Islam and S.A. Ahmed. "Business' Influence on Government: A Comparison of Public and Private Sector Perceptions." *Canadian Public Administration*, 27, Spring 1984, 87-101.

Figure 8-4

Government Elite's Experience in Business

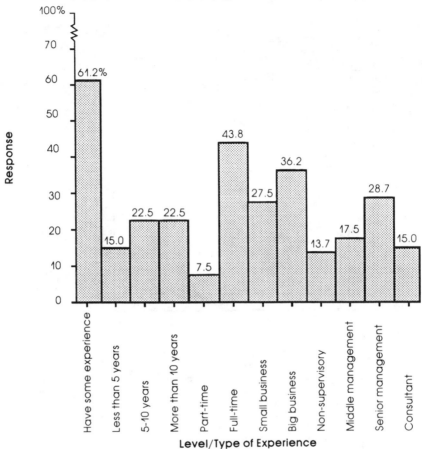

Within the business elite, individual CEOs and their companies had differing perceptions about a number of things. For example, the more senior was the person responsible for government relations in a company, the better that company perceived business' relationship to be with government. For the firms which reported that their CEO was responsible for government relations, 29% reported that relations were good and 56% reported that they were fair. Of those companies, 60% thought that relations in Canada were worse than those in the United States. However, when the responsibility for government relations was delegated downwards within a firm to a vice-president, director, or manager of public affairs or government relations, only 13% reported that their relations with government were good and 81% reported that they were fair. Of this number, 74% thought that relations were worse than those in the United States.

Similar results were depicted when the business elite was asked their perception of the state of their organizations' specific relations with government. Of those firms whose CEOs were responsible for business-government relations, 57% reported that relations were good for the firm. Of those firms who had a vice-president, director, or manager responsible for business-government relations, 39% reported that relations were good and 35% reported that they were only fair. Firms with CEOs responsible for business-government relations were happier with their firms' relations with government than were those firms who delegated the responsibility for this function to a vice-president, director, or manager. *It was quite clear that only the CEO could, in most cases, effectively manage the company's corporate relations with government.*

The relationship between industry concentration and perception was highly significant (see Figure 8-6). The CEOs of firms in industries where four or fewer firms accounted for 100% of the industry's production, reported the most favourable perceptions of the state of business-government relations in Canada: 38% perceived relations to be either very good or good, and 50% perceived them to be fair. *As industry concentration decreased, so did the respondents' perception of the state of business-government relations.* For industries where the top four firms produced 40-59% of industry output, 23% perceived relations to be good and 62% perceived them to be fair. When the top four firms of an industry accounted for less than 20% of industry output, 100% of the respondents answered that relations were fair.

Figure 8-5

Management Responsibility for Business-Government Relations

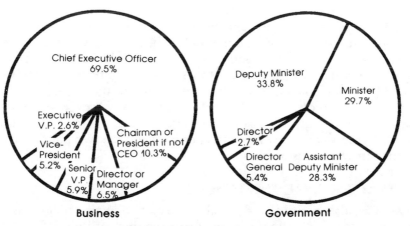

Business **Government**

Question: The one person most active in formulating business-government policy in your organization is:

Figure 8-6

Economic Concentration and Business-Government Relations

PERCENTAGE OF MARKET ACCOUNTED FOR BY TOP FOUR FIRMS	STATE OF BUSINESS-GOVERNMENT RELATIONS IN CANADA				
	Very Good	Good	Fair	Poor	Total
100%	12.5%	25.0%	50.0%	12.5%	5.4%
80-99%	6.7	26.7	63.3	3.3	20.3
60-79%	3.6	25.0	60.7	10.7	37.8
40-59%	–	23.1	61.5	15.4	17.6
20-39%	–	31.6	57.9	10.5	12.8
20%	–	–	100.0	–	6.1
TOTAL	3.4%	24.3%	62.8%	9.5%	100.0%

However, there were exceptions when vested interests were involved. For example, the manufacturers of metal products approved of tariffs and quotas that protected labour-intensive industries, whereas the rest of the business elite did not. Similarly, the secondary manufacturing businesses disapproved of government regulation of industries in which there was little competition due to concentration of ownership, but then again the secondary manufacturing sector is the least concentrated of the three sectors of Canada's economy. The lower technology primary sector disapproved of, and thought that there was too much government subsidization of potential "high-tech winners."

There was also disagreement about whether it made a lot of difference to business-government relations which political party was in power at the federal level. Respondents from the following industries believed that it did make a difference because the Liberals and Progressive Conservatives had different ideologies and attitudes about business: manufacturing-nonmetal products, petroleum/chemicals, food/beverages/tobacco, transportation/communications/utilities, and real estate. The remainder did not agree — they saw no difference between the two political parties' attitudes towards business.

TOWARDS A NEW WISDOM

Given Canada's political and social history of collective pragmatism and consensus-seeking, it should not be surprising that conflict and confrontation are unpopular with both sides when seeking a middle ground.

Collectivism in Canada has developed a popular value that society as a whole comes before the individual, and that government should be responsible for guaranteeing that it does. Here, collectivism does not translate into participative democracy beyond the ballot box. The state remains a very paternalistic force.

Canadian politics, as a result, tend to be *brokerage-style,* whereby compromises among various elite interests are negotiated. Along with the traditional English, French, federal, and provincial elites, there are now business and government elites — definable, recognizable, and effective.[31]

The basic aim of the foregoing was to highlight a number of general concepts, beliefs, perceptions, and values held by leaders in business and government. These focused on attitudes towards each other and their relationships, since these subjective interpretations could have a significant impact on policy-making as well as on the outcome of any interactions between them. Differences were apparent between the two parties in their interpretation of their situation.

Results of the 1984 survey of business and government elites in Canada showed that the business elite considered business-government relations to be mediocre, to have deteriorated over the past ten years, and to be worse than those in the United States. The government elite, on the other hand, assessed relations with business to be good, to have remained about the same, or to have improved, but also to be worse than those in the United States.

More strikingly, the survey produced evidence that personal values, attitudes, beliefs, and perceptions correlated positively with elite perceptions of business-government relations. This supported the hypothesis that ideas about what is real can significantly affect the outcome of business-government interactive/consultative processes.

Specifically, statistical analysis of the above results showed that attitudes often arose from previous experiences by members of the business elite in government or politics. For example, those in the business elite with previous governmental or political experience often approved of maintaining tariffs and quotas that protected labour-intensive industries. They also looked favourably upon government regulation of non-competitive industries. Those with no such experience tended to disapprove.

Furthermore, business leaders with political experience approved of federal participation in resource megaprojects, and of Petro-Canada's purchase of the marketing operations of Petrofina and BP Canada. Those who had not been politically active did not approve.

---

[31] Business and government elites have always existed in Canada; researchers and managers have just never considered them as such. This paradigm excludes organized labour. Unions represent less than one-third of the work force, are highly fragmented, job-conscious, and not class-conscious. Although each union bureaucracy and hierarchical labour congress has its leaders or elites, Canadian labour is not an elite by the Canadian definition-in-practice.

Similarly, certain attitudes of government respondents reflected their levels of prior experience in the private sector. For example, those with prior business experience strongly disapproved of the government's participation in the Syncrude megaproject; those who had no such experience approved of Syncrude.

Further analysis showed that as members of the business and government elites interacted more often, their responses to government interventions became more similar. For example, those in the business elite who communicated with the government elite at least once daily (as opposed to the median frequency of once a month) completely approved of Petro-Canada's growth through acquisition, while others disapproved and called for fewer such government takeovers.

In another example, government leaders who had daily business with the private sector generally approved of existing competition legislation; those with less contact called for tougher, more exhaustive competition legislation.

Situational variables also play a significant role in the shaping of perceptions. In a situation of high social constraint, both elites' leaders are strongly pressured from many sources to respond according to what they perceive their peers wish them to do (see Figure 8-7). For instance, business leaders must not be seen as having been compromised by government. They must maintain their "legitimacy" in the eyes of their shareholders and potential investors, regardless of how beneficial government policy may actually be for their firms. Thus, *business may take a public posture of not liking government, regardless of the reality of the situation.*

Eventually, some participants may begin to believe their posturing and adjust their perceptions accordingly. This is when business-government relations really do start to deteriorate—all because of misperception and public posturing.

Further, it is not unusual for survey respondents to report a high level of satisfaction with more general relationships from which they are somewhat removed. In response to a mail questionnaire, both elites reported a slightly higher level of satisfaction with their personal business-government relations than that for business-government relations in general. This response was consistent, whether the respondents chose not to admit that their own business-government relations were poor, or because they thought it was socially desirable to be seen to be dissatisfied with overall business-government relations.

In his seminal work on strategic crisis management, Graham Allison coined the phrase, "where you stand depends on where you sit."[32] According to Allison, a player's stance can be quite reliably predicted by observing his or her seat, or position, vis-a-vis the others.

---

[32] Graham T. Allison. *Essence of Decision: Explaining the Cuban Missile Crisis.* Boston: Little, Brown & Co., 1971.

Figure 8-7

Contingent Consistency Among Attitudes, Situational Variables, and Actions

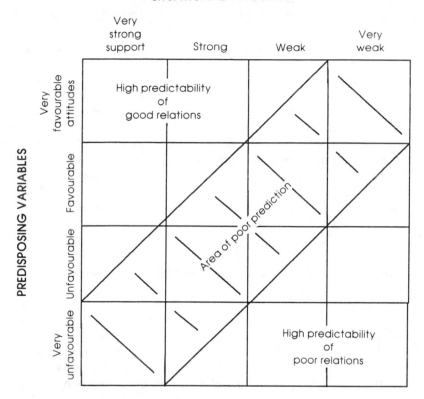

SITUATIONAL VARIABLES

Source: Adapted from Warner and Defleur. "Attitude as an Interactional Concept: Social Constraint and Social Distinction as Intervening Variables Between Attitudes and Action." American Sociological Review, 34:2, 1969, 168.

Consistent with this theory was the finding that elite perceptions had been influenced by elite membership. Simply stated, chi-square tests showed that a respondent's perception of business-government relations was influenced by having been a member of a particular elite. Government respondents were more satisfied overall with business-government relations *because* they belonged to the government elite. Business respondents were less satisfied *because* they belonged to the business elite. The business elite was not expected to be happy with government, and of course, government would think everything was just fine. Where they stood *did* depend upon where they sat.

However, as mentioned above, the business elite's response was not internally consistent. As Pareto would have expected, there were a number of attitudinal differences within the group. For example, there was a correlation between a CEO's industry and a positive or negative perception of the state of business-government relations.

Also, the more senior the position of the person responsible for a firm's government relations, the better that company perceived its relationship to be with government. When a firm's CEO personally dealt with government, the firm was satisfied with government policy; when someone else did, the firm felt dissatisfied.

Business' ambivalence towards government intervention indicates "an elite within elites." The business elite resented government intervention when taxes eroded profits, regulation curtailed freedom of economic behaviour, and Crown corporations stimulated competition. Such competition, by an economist's definition, lowers industry profitability. On the other hand, the business elite liked government intervention when tax expenditures, grants, and subsidies lowered their start-up and/or operating costs, when direct economic regulation closed entry, raised profit levels and decreased competition, and when government provided markets for business' goods and services.

Not surprisingly, firms in the industries with the *highest* levels of concentration were the *most satisfied* with business-government relations. The CEOs in industries where four or fewer firms accounted for 100% of industry production reported the most favourable perceptions of the state of business-government relations in Canada. As industry concentration lessened, so did the respondents' enthusiasm for the status of the relationship.

The CEOs, boards of directors, and management teams of satisfied firms had worked closely with government to secure preferential policy treatment from which they were benefiting. *Where business was satisfied with government policies, there was an identifiable "inner circle" of CEOs and state officials that worked together much more frequently than was the norm. There was also a high level of career crossover and inter-recruitment.*

As a result, the attitudes of these CEOs towards state intervention and business-government relations were closer to the government elite's attitudes than were those of their business peers. They seemed to understand, appreciate, and respect the other side's point of view, the constraints the other side might have to endure, and the other side's public posturing which might not reflect the reality of the situation.

IMPLICATIONS FOR MANAGEMENT

Based upon this analysis, a tentative conclusion can be reached. *Canadian business-government relations are not in an era of mutual mistrust and* misunderstanding, *as the popular press would have us believe, but an era of selective elite accommodation.* If profits are considered a measure of satisfactory business-government relations, then Figure 8-8 would support this conclusion.[33]

Figure 8-8

Canadian Business After-Tax Profits, 1970-1988

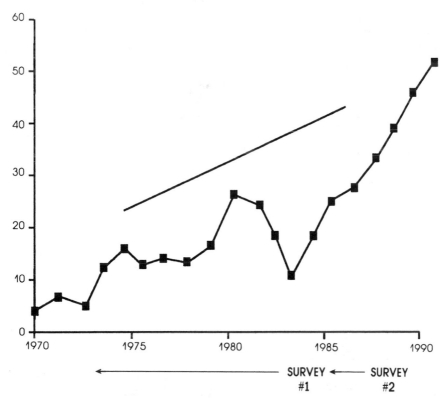

Source: "Corporation Financial Statistics, 1984," Statistics Canada. Reproduced with the permission of the Minister of Supply and Services Canada, 1990.

There is a significantly higher degree of career exchange between business and government elites than previously suspected. Members of the business elite who had once belonged to the government elite, and members of the government elite who had been part of the business elite, collectively formed a subset of the two elites. Business attitudes here were more sympathetic towards government policy, and government attitudes were more sympathetic towards business' needs.

---

[33] Research presently underway will generate evidence to either support this conclusion or not.

A similar meeting of minds was evident where CEOs and their government counterparts communicated much more frequently than did their respective elites as a whole. Where firms and industries had secured favourable legislation and regulation, CEOs were much more supportive of government intervention than was the business elite at large. The business elite supported government intervention when an "inner group" of CEOs and government elite members interacted more frequently than normal, with numerous career crossovers and inter-recruitment.

Business and government are not two disparate solitudes in Canada; nor are they united as a ruling class. An inner circle of business and government elites exists in Canada: a small fragment of the business elite is closely aligned—for practical, if not ideological, purposes—to sympathetic members of the government elite. Leading segments of Canada's business and government elites have embraced a set of relationships in order to accommodate the interests of both the private sector and the state.

SUGGESTED FURTHER READINGS

Bottomore, T. B. *Elites and Society.* Harmondsworth, Middlesex: Penguin Books Limited, 1973.

Carroll, William *et al.* "A Network Analysis of Interlocking Directorates Among the 100 Largest Canadian Corporations." *Canadian Review of Sociology and Anthropology*, 21, 1981.

Clarke, S. D. *The Developing Canadian Community.* 2nd ed., Toronto: University of Toronto Press, 1968.

Clement, Wallace. *The Canadian Corporate Elite: An Analysis of Economic Power.* Toronto: McClelland and Stewart, 1975.

Das, T.K. *The Subjective Side of Strategy-Making.* New York: Praeger Publishers, 1986.

Heap, J. L., ed. *Everybody's Canada: The Vertical Mosaic Reviewed and Re-examined.* Toronto: Burns and MacEachern Ltd., 1974.

Islam, Nasir and Sadrudin A. Ahmed. "Business' Influence on Government: A Comparison of Public and Private Sector Perceptions." *Canadian Public Administration*, 27, Spring 1984, 87-101.

Murray, V. V., ed. *Theories of Business-Government Relations.* Toronto: Trans-Canada Press, 1985.

Murray, V. V. and C. J. McMillan. "Business-Government Relations in Canada: A Conceptual Map." *Canadian Public Administration*, 26, Winter 1983, 591-609.

Murray, V. V. and D. Wayne Taylor. "Towards Understanding Business-Government Relations at the Federal Level in Canada" as in V. V. Murray, ed. *The Consultative Process in Business-Government Relations.* North York: York University, 1986.

Olson, D. *The State Elite.* Toronto: McClelland and Stewart, 1980.

Panitch, Leo. *The Canadian State: Political Economy and Political Power.* Toronto: University of Toronto Press, 1977.

Pareto, V. *The Mind and Society.* Vol. III, London: Jonathan Cape, 1935.

Porter, John. *The Vertical Mosaic.* Toronto: University of Toronto Press, 1965.

Presthus, Robert. *Elite Accommodation in Canadian Politics.* Toronto: Macmillan, 1973.

————. *Elites in the Policy Process.* Cambridge: Cambridge University Press, 1974.

Pross, A. P., ed. *Pressure Group Behaviour in Canadian Politics.* Toronto: McGraw-Hill Ryerson, 1975.

Taylor, D. Wayne. "An Interpretive Approach to Understanding Business-Government Relations." *Canadian Journal of Administrative Sciences*, 4:4, December 1987, 353-366.

Taylor, D. Wayne and V. V. Murray. "An Interpretive Understanding of the Non-Fulfillment of Business-Government Relations." *Canadian Public Administration*, 30:3, Fall 1987, 421-431.

Thomas, W. I. *On Social Organizations and Social Responsibility.* Chicago: University of Chicago Press, 1966.

Useem, Michael. "The Inner Group of the American Capitalist Class." *Social Problems*, 25, 1978, 225-240.

Warner, L. G. and M. L. DeFleur. "Attitude as an Interactional Concept: Social Constraint and Social Distinction as Intervening Variables Between Attitudes and Action." *American Sociological Review*, 34:2, April 1969, 153-169.

9 THE RIGHT KIND OF GOVERNMENT INTERVENTION

However much the Canadian taxpayer may favour a policy of strict economy in government in the abstract, he likes nothing so little as its application.

Sir Joseph Pope, 1854–1926

In previous chapters, business' ambivalence towards government policy has been frequently referenced. Business likes government policies that help keep its bottom line healthy; business dislikes government policies that do not. In theoretical terms, different types of government policies were categorized and business was seen to favour those whose benefits accrued to business, but whose costs were indirectly borne by the masses. But, specifically, what kinds of government intervention are these, and at what cost to those non-beneficiaries are they implemented?

While researching this book, the author discovered that 82% of the business elite believed government economic policy to be "too far left," while the government elite was evenly divided between "too far left" and "just about right." More than twice as many business as government respondents thought there was *too much* government intervention overall. However, when pushed, both government and business leaders overwhelmingly agreed it was not a question of *degree* of government intervention, but of *too much of the wrong kind of government intervention.*

WHAT *IS* THE WRONG KIND?

A question with twenty elements was included in a mail questionnaire to determine elite attitudes about certain actual and proposed government policies and actions. This question provided the opportunity to examine what the "wrong kind of government intervention" actually meant.

Business respondents generally disapproved of government equity investment, such as that manifested by Petro-Canada and the (now privatized) Canada Development Corporation. An overwhelming 82% of the business elite opposed Petro-Canada's purchase of the Canadian marketing operations of Petrofina and BP Canada. On the other hand, 57% of the government elite approved of these actions. Their attitude towards the establishment of the Canada Development Corporation was similar. The government elite generally approved of the public sector being an equity investor. *Public enterprise was clearly the wrong kind of government economic intervention for the business elite.*

At the opposite end of the spectrum of interventionist activities, an impressive 80% of the business elite and 84% of the government elite opposed the government "bailout" of major corporations in financial difficulty. *Bailouts were another wrong kind of government intervention.*

Business and government elites both generally approved of direct government assistance to business for developing and adopting new technologies, creating new jobs, enhancing export capabilities, and financing megaprojects, such as Syncrude. The only exception was the government elite's attitude towards potential "high-tech winners." Government leaders were almost evenly divided between approving the existing policy and/or calling for more such assistance, and disapproving of it and calling for less such assistance.

Business and government leaders were united in approving of regulations for four purposes:

1. to allow foreign banks to compete with chartered banks in Canada;
2. to regulate industries in which there was little or no competition;
3. to deregulate the airlines; and
4. to institute the government's "6 and 5" voluntary restraint program.

Both elites disapproved, however, of mandatory wage and price controls. Interestingly, 84% of the government officials favoured government restraint, as opposed to only 70% of Canadian business executives. (Sir Joseph Pope was right!) *Generally, economic regulation was considered the "right" kind of intervention.*

The two elites also disapproved of the government maintaining tariffs and quotas that protected labour-intensive industries: 76% of government officials were disapproving—nearly 15% more than business elite respondents. *One could speculate that free trade with the United States was inevitable, regardless of the political party in power at the time.*

With respect to foreign investment, 62% of the government elite approved of the mandate of the Foreign Investment Review Agency (FIRA)—now Investment Canada — to screen foreign investments. In comparison, 68% of business leaders disapproved of FIRA and thought that there should be much less of this kind of economic intervention.

Finally, both business and government elites *approved* of existing consumer protection legislation and occupational health and safety legislation. However, 45% of the business elite disapproved of existing labour relations laws and preferred less government intervention; 46% of the government elite approved of the existing legislation.

Overall, both business and government elites *approved* of government financial assistance to business. They also endorsed existing economic and social regulation of business, with the exceptions of foreign investment review and labour relations laws.

Both sectors generally *disapproved* of, and wanted less, government "bailing-out" of major firms in financial difficulty, and tariff protection of labour-intensive industries. These policies were clearly the wrong kind of government economic intervention for *both* elites.

In essence, competition was preferred over government regulation if it meant that the strong would get stronger and the big could get bigger; if not, then government intervention was acceptable, if not downright desired.

Ironically, when public enterprise had the effect, whether deliberate or not, of stimulating competition, it was generally disliked by business and supported by government officials.

DETERMINANTS OF ELITE ATTITUDES: CAREER EXPERIENCE

Why do elites think and feel the way they do about various forms of government intervention? Survey and interview results showed that, once again, many of the above attitudes are rooted in the level of personal experience that members of the business elite had previously had in government or politics, or the level of prior experience that members of the government elite had had in the private sector.

For example, those members of the business elite who had some form of experience in government or politics tended to approve of the maintenance of tariffs and quotas that protected labour-intensive industries. Those with no or little such experience tended to disapprove of them and thought that the country needed less. Furthermore, business leaders who had held public office most definitely approved of tariffs, as opposed to those who had not been elected. Members of the business elite who had been involved in government or politics approved of government regulation of industries where there was little or no competition. The others, who had no government or political experience, generally disapproved of such regulation.

More specifically, business leaders who were members of a political party approved of the federal government's participation in megaprojects such as the Syncrude project. Those who did not belong to a political party did not approve of it. CEOs who were active in their respective riding associations tended to approve of Petro-Canada's purchase of the Canadian marketing operations of Petrofina and BP Canada, and other government equity investments. Those who were not active in this manner did not approve of such actions.

Ironically, those business leaders who sat on the executive of their political parties disapproved of government regulations which permitted foreign banks to compete with Canadian chartered banks; those who did not hold such a post approved of the government's policy. Finally, business executives who had not been policy advisers or consultants to elected officials or senior civil servants strongly approved of current occupational health and safety regulations. Those who had been such advisers or consultants thought that there was not enough regulation in this area and called for even more.

Some of the attitudes held by government leaders were similarly dependent upon members of the government elite having or not having experience in the private sector. Those government officials who had previous business experience in the private sector strongly favoured mandatory wage and price controls, whereas those members of the government elite who had no such experience did not favour them. Of particular interest was the finding that government leaders who had only non-supervisory business experience favoured the increased usage of mandatory wage and price controls on a more widespread basis. Public servants who had senior management experience in a large corporation did not favour mandatory controls. Government respondents who had business experience strongly disapproved of the government's participation in megaprojects such as the Syncrude project, whereas those who had no such experience approved of the government's actions.

Finally, members of the government elite who had no experience in the private sector favoured current consumer protection legislation; those who had been business executives actually called for more consumer protection legislation.

DETERMINANTS OF ELITE ATTITUDES: FREQUENCY OF INTERACTION

The only other independent variable which had a significant influence on business' and government's attitudes towards government initiatives was *the individual's frequency of personal interaction with politicians and/or civil servants, or business executives respectively.* For example, those members of the business elite who interacted with members of the government elite the most frequently (at least once per day) completely approved of Petro-Canada's expansionism, while the others disapproved and called for less such government intervention in the marketplace.

In a similar manner, the attitude of the government elite towards current competition policy was influenced by the frequency of the government respondents' personal interaction with those in the business sector. Those government leaders who interacted with business on a daily basis generally approved of the existing competition legislation. As the individual's frequency of interaction with business decreased, his or her level of disapproval of current competition policy increased, as did the call for even tougher competition legislation than presently existed.[34]

IMPLICATIONS FOR MANAGEMENT

As one followed the development and growth of the federal government's involvement in the private sector in Part I, it was clear that business often solicited and economically benefited from government intervention. After all, who asked the federal government to set up agricultural marketing boards to bail out Maislin, Chrysler, and Massey-Ferguson, and to negotiate the Auto Pact?

However, business' rhetorical preference for free enterprise and its opposition to government involvement in the economy is not merely a form of role-playing. It also indicates that business has clear preferences with respect to government policy and actions.

Both business and government approved of government financial assistance to business, existing government direct economic regulation of business, and government social regulation of business. Both sectors, however, disapproved of government assistance in the form of "bailouts." Nor did they want tariff protection for labour-intensive industries.

Major disagreement existed, however, with respect to government equity investment. Although this was clearly the wrong kind of government economic intervention for business elites, government elites generally approved of the public sector being an equity investor in the economy.

In short, the state of specific business-government relationships depended upon the type of government policy involved.

Results also indicated that these attitudes often depended on the *level of personal experience* that members of the business elite had had in government or politics. Similarly, the *frequency of interaction* by an executive with a counterpart in the opposite sector influenced his or her attitudes.

As interest in the business-government *problematique* has heightened, normative works either have addressed the subject with a *macro*, policy-making model of elite accommodation, or a *micro*, firm-level model of issues management. The macro approach assumes that business-government relations are singular in substance: that one political model can easily fulfil the needs of all organizations experiencing difficulty with "the other side." Common sense, of course, tells us that in reality there is a myriad of different, simultaneous business-government relationships: firm-specific, sector-specific, cross-sector, national, provincial, local, issue-oriented, administrative, ideological, and so on. Business-government relations,

---

[34] One other variable interceded as well, but to a much lesser extent. CEOs who managed companies which were 100% Canadian-owned tended to approve of Petro-Canada's growth and the government's growth within the economy. The rest did not approve of it, and wanted state enterprise growth through acquisition halted.

therefore, with the exception of learning how national economic strategies are developed (of which there are few cases in Canadian history), cannot be studied meaningfully using such a reductionist approach.

On the other hand, the micro approach assumes that managing business-government relations is simply a task for a skilled, competent public-affairs department. If that were true, then the growing importance of the public-affairs function in business should have contributed to an improved relationship, rather than its deterioration, as reported by Canada's business and government elites.

To overcome this conceptual gap in business-government theory, the findings reported in this and the preceding chapter would suggest that a middle-ground approach would be more useful in helping managers to better handle their business-government relationships.[35] In fact, this interaction can best be studied at the level of the public policy-type. Thus, if public policies are grouped by type, each with its own identifiable policy network and set of dynamics, at least an equal number of generic types of business-government relationships would exist, each with its own set of characteristics. "Reinventing the wheel" thus would be avoided each time a fracture occurred in a firm's relationship with government, or vice-versa.

By definition, business-government relations are political relations; a specific business-government relationship is a political relationship. Each such relationship is determined by the type of policy at stake, as every type of policy is likely to call for a distinctive type of political relationship. Since each of the four types of public policy: *distributive, regulatory, redistributive,* and *constituent* has a distinct nature, so, too, will the relationships involved in each type.[36]

There will also be a direct correlation between policy type and business' satisfaction with business-government relations. For example, a firm whose largest percentage of time spent interacting with government is within a policy network which yields benefits concentrated on its particular industry, and whose costs are widely dispersed, predictably will have satisfactory relations with government. Such a firm will also perceive the overall state of business-government relations to be good.

Conversely, a firm whose industry does not benefit from a specific distributive policy will not be as satisfied with business-government relations, and will perceive them to be "fair" or "poor." Further, a firm that spends most of its time relating within a policy network from which it does not directly benefit, and for which it perceives itself paying a progressive share of the costs, will be less satisfied with government. In fact, it will assess the relationship as "poor." Between these two extremes there will be a close correlation between policy-type and the perceived state of a business-government relationship (see Figure 9-1).

---

[35] Of course, a multiple approach would be best, but is not always practical.

[36] See also Chapter 4 in W.D. Coleman, *Business and Politics.* Montreal: McGill-Queens University Press, 1988.

Figure 9-1

Perceived State of Business-Government Relationship

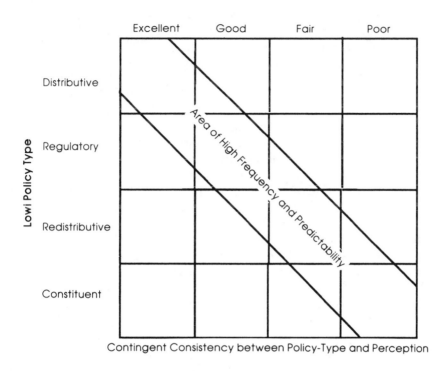

Contingent Consistency between Policy-Type and Perception

Based upon the research findings contained in this book, both business and government elites generally approved of distributive-type government policies, except for tariffs and quotas. In fact, business respondents overwhelmingly approved of them when they directly benefited the respondents' industries. *Those sectors which benefited most from various distributive policies were the most satisfied with their relations with government and perceived overall business-government relations to be quite good.*

Next, when questioned about direct, economic regulatory policies, the government elite consistently approved existing and proposed regulatory policies, while business was ambivalent. Respondents from highly market-competitive industries disapproved of regulation much more than those from the least market-competitive (and most heavily-concentrated) industries. *The majority of those in highly regulated (highly concentrated) industries were generally satisfied with business-government relations.* After all, regulatory regimes generally inhibited entry to newcomers, which awarded earlier entrants into these sectors with economic profit.[37]

Referring back to Figure 9-1, the next order of public policy examined was redistributive policy. Again, a strong 79% of business leaders disapproved of the government's attempt to redistribute wealth through progressive income taxation and various forms of social insurance. However, 70% of the government elite approved of such redistributive policies.

Finally, when the question turned to constituent-type policies (macroeconomic, "rules of the game") an overwhelming 83% of the business respondents were dissatisfied. The business elite generally did not approve of the federal government's monetary or fiscal policies. Instead, they called for less government equity investment in the economy and fewer Crown corporations. The business elite strongly disapproved of mandatory wage and price controls and other such policy instruments.

On the other hand, government respondents were ambivalent. They approved of the government's constituent policies by a narrow margin. They also approved of most public enterprise, fiscal, and monetary policies, but disapproved of mandatory wage and price controls.

There is a distinct consistency and predictability that exists between policy-types and business' perceptions of business-government relations. It also affects the respondents' sense of satisfaction with their organization's specific relations with government. Various public policies can affect the perceptions held by different industries. This depends, of course, upon which types of policies are important to a firm, and how a firm is primarily affected by them. Based on this, business' satisfaction with government will range from being poor to very good.

CEOs will usually approve of distributive policies if they benefit the respondent's firm. If a CEO were immersed in a distributive policy network, feelings about the state of business-government relations would be good. Most regulatory policies also meet with business' approval—especially when directly affected by them; such approval, however, is slightly lower than for distributive policies.

In short, businesses most affected by either a distributive policy network or a regulatory policy regime are satisfied with business-government relations. They approve of said policies which tax the general public to give business an economic advantage. However, businesses most affected by either redistributive or constituent policies, or which are not beneficiaries of distributive or regulatory policies, are displeased with the state of business-government relations in Canada.

Therefore, to understand and improve upon this relationship, a much more interpretive, middle-ground approach is needed than has been previously used. This does not imply that other methods have no merit. To the

---

[37] *Economic profits* on goods sold are the difference between revenues received from the sale and the opportunity cost of the resources used to make them. The opportunity cost includes charges required to use the firm's capital, and to take risk.

contrary, these pioneering works have gained for business-government relations a lot of attention in management research studies lately.

Now, business-government studies can be meaningfully broken down or combined into policy fields, each with its own set of characteristics and dynamics. Some business-government relations have been found to be healthy; others are not. Some need work; others do not. Common threads run through heretofore isolated instances, and there are boundaries between discrete sets of interactions. This approach to business-government relations provides the opportunity to generalize more than through case studies, yet is more pragmatic than universal systems theory.

Business and government are not two isolated, disparate solitudes as Trudeau proclaimed in 1981; nor are they fragmented beyond redemption. They simply need to be identified as they actually exist—as an array of differentiated clusters and networks, each centred around a generic type of public policy, and each with its own set of variables.

Business-government relations in Canada are no longer an illustration of mutual political accommodation. Nor have they disintegrated to a state of mutual misunderstanding and distrust, as often suggested in the popular press. Rather, they exhibit characteristics of mutual dependency.

However, business management in Canada does not seem to see it that way, or at least is not willing to admit it.

SUGGESTED FURTHER READINGS

Atkinson, M.M. & W.D. Coleman. "Is There a Crisis in Business-Government Relations?" *Canadian Journal of Administrative Sciences*, Vol. 4, no. 4 (December 1987), 321-340.

Bartha, Peter F. "Organizational Competence in Business-Government Relations: A Managerial Perspective." *Canadian Public Administration*, Vol. 28, no. 2, (Summer 1985), 202-220.

Gillies, James. *Facing Reality: Consultation, Consensus and Making Economic Policy for the 21st Century.* Montreal: Institute for Research on Public Policy, 1986.

Gollner, A. *Social Change and Corporate Strategy: The Expanding Role of Public Affairs.* Stamford, CT: Issue Action Publications, 1983.

Lindblom, C.E. *Politics and Markets: The World's Political-Economic Systems.* New York: Basic Books, 1977: especially Chapter 13.

Stanbury, W.T. & G. Lermer. "Regulation and Redistribution of Income and Wealth," *Canadian Public Administration*, Vol. 26, no. 3 (Fall 1983), 378-401.

IV MANAGING BUSINESS-GOVERNMENT RELATIONS

With a fuller understanding of past and present business-government relations, and the variables which have shaped them, managers can now address the question of how best to manage them in the future. As with strategic planning, there is no one best choice, but an array of techniques and mechanisms of interaction, the choice from which will be contingent upon business' and/or government's objectives, needs, and circumstances.

CHAPTER 10

BUSINESS DEALING WITH GOVERNMENT

CHAPTER 11

GOVERNMENT DEALING WITH BUSINESS

CHAPTER
10 BUSINESS DEALING WITH GOVERNMENT

Government and co-operation are in all things the laws of life;
anarchy and competition, the laws of death.

John Ruskin, 1819–1900

Government in Canada (and the federal government, in particular) has been called a *monolith* and a *leviathan.*[38] These words imply not only that government is big and totalitarian, but that everyone in government thinks identically, behaves identically, and seeks to achieve identical goals. Yet, nothing could be further from the truth! *The biggest mistake that those outside government make is believing in a "single player" theory of government.*

In fact, there are as many "government" points of view on any subject as there are outside of it. Nowhere else do we expect two people to be exactly the same, so why should government be an exception? In fact, there are myriad opportunities to win support over a policy issue; one must simply find the right person at the right time.

Who is the right person? That depends on the issue. When is the right time? It's usually before the issue becomes an issue!

To illustrate this principle, one needs only look at business' greatest triumphs in its dealings with Ottawa recently. For decades, Boeing Aircraft of Seattle and McDonnell Douglas of St. Louis supplied Air Canada with its fleet of commercial aircraft. However, Canada's national airline will be acquiring its 1990 shipment of aircraft from Airbus Industrie of Europe. Why? Because Airbus hired a consulting firm headed by Frank Moores, former Progressive Conservative Premier of Newfoundland, to represent it in the corridors of Parliament Hill. The other two manufacturers worked through the trade service of the United States' State Department. Did Moores open doors and push buttons? Probably not; he simply showed Airbus which doors to open and which buttons to push.

Another victory was the Canadian Brewers' Association's success in excluding the beer industry from the terms of the Canada-United States Free Trade Agreement. The federal government saved the beer industry from its own diseconomies of scale, its price maintenance ritual, and the

---

[38] W.T. Stanbury. *Business-Government Relations in Canada.* Toronto: Methuen, 1986.

149

provinces' outdated barriers to inter-provincial trade. The ante: thousands of jobs. The price: the probable loss of the much smaller, mass-production segment of the Canadian wine industry. After all, Hockey Night in Canada without a Molson's would be inconceivable.

Not to be overlooked is how effective Canada's lawyers and accountants can be in getting their own way. Remember Finance Minister Wilson's proposed Value-Added Tax? It was the legal and accounting professions which, fearing client revolt at higher prices for the same level of service, convinced the Minister that a national sales tax would be a better idea—at least for them.

Finally, even neighbourhood grocers have Ottawa's ear these days. This has been largely due to the Grocery Products Manufacturers of Canada, who developed an information system that impresses upon local MPs the number of jobs and other economic benefits the grocery trade provides in every riding. The association's success in doing this almost rivals that of the consistently recognized dairy farmers and their provincial marketing boards.

There are also several CEOs who devote so much of their time to dealing with government, it eventually pays off. Jean de Grandpré, Chairman of Bell Canada Enterprises, received the nod to expand his monopoly from both Liberal and Progressive Conservative governments several times during the 1980s. He then was invited to chair Prime Minister Mulroney's task force on implementing free trade. Robert Blair of Nova and Paul Desmarais of Power Corporation have also deftly transcended political dynasties, the latter having once been Prime Minister Mulroney's employer.

However, the list is short. There are far more failures than successes when talking about business dealings with government.

BLUNDERS, BLUNDERS, BLUNDERS

When dealing with political and governmental issues, business managers continue to perform poorly more often than not. They cry out against government intervention (except when it benefits them), unaware that Canadians are highly tolerant of state involvement in most aspects of their lives. In all, there are seven fundamental errors that business makes when dealing with government.

First, politicians come and they go, but the bureaucracy and the acolytes who dwell therein change far more slowly.[39] Still, *upper managers, especially CEOs, continue to disdain the public service and demand to deal with the Minister.* Yet, it is often the middle-manager of a department or central agency who can best assist an outsider. A political quick-fix is rare. Beware anyone selling the promise of a quick-fix. Furthermore, it is the

---

[39] . . . although deputy ministers now change jobs almost as frequently as their political masters do.

politician's job and nature to be open, friendly, and sympathetic; such appearances, though, are often calculated to be deceiving.

Second, *business loves to prepare comprehensive "briefs" at great expense to its organization and shareholders.* These are presented to the appropriate public forum—a committee of the House of Commons, a committee of the Senate, or a government task force.[40] By then, however, it is too late. When a government goes public with a policy, it is committed to adopting it. The best a company can hope for is to dilute, slow down, or change the policy's packaging. Briefs are devoured by the information-hungry bureaucracy, but are largely ignored by the information-over-loaded politician. Too little, too late.

Third, *some businesses still believe that economic power emanates totally from their boardrooms.* Yet, in the past quarter century, a shift has taken place. Equal if not greater economic clout now emanates from the Prime Minister's Office, the Privy Council Office, and the shadowy bowels of line departments. CEOs ignore at their peril the fact that they are only additional players in a pluralist, political system, wherein government must appease numerous competing interests. Business' concerns are not necessarily the public's—at least, not so far as the public (a government's shareholders) is concerned.

Fourth, *business fails to deal with government in a businesslike manner.* The basic tasks for business managers are gathering and analysing data, identifying and solving problems, formulating and implementing strategies, making decisions, organizing, and motivating. All these require reasoning. Yet, when business deals with government, passion—not reason—comes to the fore. Business leaders plead cases of self-interest, rather than offer to help government analyse, organize, decide, and solve problems. Demands are often unsupported by evidence, options may not be suggested, and the competition is often ignored.

Fifth, *when business' intentions are good, its approach to government is all wrong.* Often, businesses approach the wrong people with the wrong information at the wrong time; they have failed to analyse and understand government's organizational dynamics, as well as the institutional setting of political problems. They may ignore potential allies and miss potential antagonists. Worse still, they fail to see that the machinery of government evolves over time, as do appropriate pressure points within it.

Sixth, *business goes to government in a state of disarray.* Often, there is no agreement within an industry, let alone a sector of the economy or the business community as a whole. Government then faces the same dilemma as when facing the electorate. Its only two options are to provide for the majority as reflected in public opinion, or to do what it thinks is best, regardless of public opinion. Unless a company pleads an exceptional case,

---

[40] Royal Commissions are not listed because they are more often used to diffuse an issue rather than to develop a policy or make a decision.

going solo is unlikely to bring positive changes in government policy. Nor is business adroit in identifying a political constituency it could mobilize for support. Strange, considering that government is politics and politics is government.

Seventh, *business generally lacks a commitment to successful ongoing business-government relations.* There are relatively few cases of significant resources being allocated for this purpose within organizations. Whether these resources be financial, human, attitudinal, or specific expertise, the key is commitment from the top. And that takes the rarest resource of all—a CEO's time.

The two key ingredients for any successful business-government relationship are: (1) identifying the most influential *target(s)* within government, and (2) choosing the most effective *tactic(s)* by which to approach and influence them.

GOVERNMENT TARGETS—PLURALISM AND CONSTITUENCIES

Although Part 1 of this book revealed that Canada is hardly a true pluralist democracy, it does possess three of its characteristics: political parties, an unfettered media, and numerous interest or pressure groups vying for public attention and government largesse. Each of these factors can either impede or expedite business' dealings with government.

Political Parties. These play a minimal role in Canadian public policy; they simply select and get elected members of Parliament or legislative assemblies. Political parties in Canada fail to aggregate and articulate particular viewpoints along the political spectrum, as do those in Europe. With the advent of executive federalism in the mid-1960s, parties have become even more irrelevant to the governing of the nation and to business' interests. Therefore, they are not likely targets for business' lobbying efforts.

The Media. Since the 1960s, media's intensified coverage of current events has increased the pressure for short-term "quick-fixes" to social and economic problems. These ready solutions often result in new budgets, new spending initiatives, or more regulation. In the extreme, an election will be called to cloud the issue with euphoria and promises, later found to be too expensive. Acting as intermediary between government and its public is the media, which channels public opinion to government decision-makers and sells (whether wittingly or unwittingly) government programs to the electorate.

This has a profound effect on public policy. Theoretically, the media is neutral. However, this assumption has been repeatedly challenged as the concentration of ownership in the media increases.[41] Not only can the media report public opinion—it also has the potential to filter, shape, and distort both public opinion and government policy. As a result, the Prime Minister is a "media junkie," reading every major newspaper and watching the network newscasts before breakfast and before retiring.

News-clipping and monitoring services are a major growth item in most federal government departments. Two new sections have even been added to the form for a Memorandum to Cabinet (reviewed by Cabinet before making a policy decision) entitled, "Possible Best Headline" and "Possible Worst Headline."

Canadian journalism has lost its strong investigative past; its present strength lies in the editorial boardrooms. Therefore, a public servant's main task today is to keep his or her minister out of trouble with the media. Business can learn from the media what government is thinking, or at least is considering, when making policy. Also, business has a powerful potential weapon in the media, but one which could turn and attack it just as quickly. Public opinion and the media are *exogenous* variables in a business-government relationship: they can strongly influence government, but are very difficult to influence.

Interest or Pressure Groups.   Almost every organization in Canadian society has been an interest or pressure group at one time or another: it has tried to influence in its favour the output of the political system. Unlike Europe and the United States however, formal, full-time interest groups in Canada have not aligned themselves with political parties. As a result, business must first compete for government's attention; then, for its favour. This makes the government relations function all the more crucial to business' long-term survival.

Although Canada is a pluralist democracy, it is not a highly developed participatory democracy. Party politics are split between federal and provincial levels, and are not significant at either level outside of the legislature. The media, on the other hand, is concentrated but not terribly aggressive. Interest groups are numerous, but not politically active in a partisan sense. Nor are there signs of any of this changing. If anything, parties will become increasingly irrelevant in the technocratic age, the media more concentrated, and interest groups more numerous.

Business must, therefore, develop an effective relationship with government, or be swept aside. Political parties will not help; the media is as much a threat as an opportunity, and business is not alone in courting government's favour.

What, then, are business' targets? Whom in government should business approach? When? And for what?

---

[41] Canada has a duopoly in national television: the six largest newspaper conglomerates account for more than 80% of the market.

GOVERNMENT TARGETS—TECHNOCRATS, CENTRAL AGENTS, AND POLITICAL ADMINISTRATORS

It should now be clear that if business' concerns are truly of national importance (however defined by the politicians or media of the day), the key player—or target—should be the Prime Minister. Even though the vast majority of Prime Minister Mulroney's Cabinet reportedly had grave reservations about the Meech Lake Accord and the Canada-U.S. Free Trade Agreement, both have been primary agenda items for this government. The Prime Minister's opinion counts. When it comes to national or international issues of great urgency, sometimes *only* his opinion counts. Given the centralized nature of decision-making in Ottawa today, this would be true regardless of who held the office.

However, today's Prime Minister of Canada is not accessible to most. He represents the nation; at best there will be time to meet with large, national organizations. But the PM's key advisers and *their* advisers *are* accessible. These include staff of the Prime Minister's Office, Privy Council Office (the *central agents*), assistant deputy ministers, directors-general and directors (the *technocrats*).

Other interest groups who always seem to get their way with government have known this for years. As ministers and their deputies get shuffled around every eighteen months or so, only the second-rank bureaucrats—the assistant deputy ministers, directors-general, and directors—have a real grip on the reins of power and the information base by which to use them. That is why assistant deputy ministers in current business-government research are considered the equivalent of CEOs in the private sector. *If chief executive officers like talking to their counterparts, they had best forget about ministers and get used to talking with assistant deputy ministers and their immediate subordinates.*

Nowhere is the contingency theory of management more applicable than here. *Whom you target depends on what you want.* Generally, the more detailed and routine a matter, the lower down the hierarchy business should go; the more abstract and singularly unique an issue, the higher.[42] Correspondingly, the higher the government official, the more imperative that the CEO be involved; the lower the government official, the more practical it is to involve someone closer to the technicality of the issue. Either way, business has to take the initiative.

In addition to these central agents and technocrats is one often overlooked target: the growing class of *political administrators*. These include the chief of staff who controls a minister's agenda; the chief of staff who controls a deputy minister's agenda; executive assistants, special assistants, speechwriters, and policy advisers. No longer are all these players young

---

[42] Another way of looking at this is, the larger the number of jobs potentially affected, the higher up one should go within government.

men and women hot off a campaign trail, embarking on new careers. Instead, they will likely be professional people, often in mid-career, sometimes co-opted from the public or private sectors, and capable of influencing their political masters. However, even in the Prime Minister's Office, there are only about three key staff who really have the Prime Minister's ear. There are many political administrators, but only a few who count.

Ministers and deputy ministers have been omitted from this list of targets. They have little more time than the Prime Minister does (except for those rare business concerns of national importance), and prefer to meet with coalitions or sectoral representatives to conserve their time. In essence, a policy must be well-developed by outside interests, with due consideration given to its political ramifications, before a minister or deputy minister will take it seriously. Ministers and deputy ministers will most often be courteous if accessed, but that is all. After all, both owe their positions to the Prime Minister, and therefore will likely defer to "the government." There will be exceptions, but they will be few and far between.

Despite the case for approaching central agents, technocrats, and political administrators, there is still one to be made for approaching ministers, MPs and the Opposition. These approaches should not be aimed at achieving one's ends, but should rather be of a courteous nature. One day, one of those ministers may become Prime Minister; some of those backbenchers will become ministers; and the Opposition could become the government. Consider this contact an investment in the future. And when you approach these individuals, provide them with information; whatever is available to other policy-making contacts that is not confidential, of national importance, or relating to corporate security.

This approach has brought de Grandpré, Blair, Desmarais, and even Jack Gallagher of Dome Petroleum success in Ottawa. By working with government full-time, they are able to create a sense that their causes take priority.

Even here, however, things are changing. Under the new procedures of the House of Commons, committees of the House now have increased investigative and policy review powers. So far, only the Finance Committee has flexed its muscles, convincing the government to urge five of Canada's "big six" banks to review their customer service fee structures and policies.

All of this: working with people in the Prime Minister's Office, Privy Council Office, and line departments, and educating members of the Cabinet, backbenchers, and Opposition may appear to require considerable time and resources. It certainly does not seem a logical continuation of the concept of *targeting*, or focusing one's efforts. But in fact, it is. This is not a shotgun approach which dissipates business' efforts to no avail. It is not a "minister only" approach, which is also likely doomed to futility. *It is a concentrated, all-out effort to influence those key players who do, or perhaps will, influence the making of policy.*

The first thing to be done by any CEO not yet plugged into Ottawa's pulse is to purchase the latest edition of the Government of Canada Telephone Directory for the National Capital Region. Here, one will find the key players. A good consultant can help, and more will be said on this later.

As Chapter 6 explained, decision-making power has become increasingly centralized, even within the central agencies. In essence, the Prime Minister, the Prime Minister's Office, the Privy Council Office, and a very small number of ministers and deputy ministers run the show, making accessibility to the top even more difficult than it was under the Liberals. This increased centralization of decision-making and the politicization of deputy ministers has pushed the real nuts-and-bolts of policy-making down into the middle levels of line departments and central agencies. The same group is also responsible for implementing policy. Of course, budget time is where the gamble will always lie; another unknown is what priority the Prime Minister, the Deputy Prime Minister, the Minister of Finance, and the President of the Treasury Board will place on a request.

Here is where *tactics* become important. *The key remains, though, to reach one's targeted policy-makers before a policy is made—or needed.*

REACTIVE BUSINESS TACTICS: THE ADVERSARIAL MODEL

Business has two classes of tactics by which to consult with, influence, or otherwise interact with government: *reactive and proactive.* As the names imply, business can either react to government's initiatives after the fact, or can develop a relationship giving it input into government's policy-making process before decisions are made or program changes are announced.

As any student of management will readily see, proactive interaction offers business more significant, longer-term benefits. It also allows business to present its case within a public interest framework—something very difficult to do later, when it must take a defensive mode.

The reactive method will provide only short-term solutions to immediate problems, and presents business as acting only in self-interest. It is usually issue-oriented and intended to prevent a change in policy after government has made its decision to do so. *Surprisingly, the majority of today's business-government dealings are still of a reactive nature.*

Reactive-type tactics cover a wide spectrum, but can be grouped best as follows, from shortest-term to longest-term; from most reactive to least reactive;[43] from simplest to most complex:

---

[43] In fact, the potential proactive capacity of these tactics increases for each one as you go down the list.

- Issues Management
- Government Relations Function
- Consultants (Lobbyists)
- Trade Associations
- Sector Associations (Coalitions)
- Advocacy Advertising
- Political Mobilization

Each of these will be explored briefly below.

1. Issues Management

The past and current practice of most businesses has been to fight government's increasing involvement in economic affairs on an issue-by-issue basis. This should not be surprising, given business' pragmatism and conservative ideology. In fact, this method of dealing with government was prescribed by texts for years — *texts written in the United States for an American audience.*

Thus being of American origin, issues management assumes that policy development in the federal government moves from the bottom up (which is, generally speaking, incorrect in Canada), and is based upon the art of persuasion rather than a position of strength. Issues management also erroneously assumes the private sector's unchallenged legitimacy in the eyes of both government and the public. Managing business-government relations on an issue-related basis is difficult at best, given the ever-evolving nature, decision-making process, and priorities of government and its key players. However, to manage these relations with no full-time staff dedicated to the task is not to manage them at all.

For some companies, this may be an optimal strategy; there may be little else they can afford or need to do. However, this is not true for all Canadian businesses. With the passing of C.D. Howe and the halcyon days of the 1950s, so went the use of issues management as the primary means by which to deal with government.

2. Government Relations Function

During the OPEC crisis of the early 1970s, both business and government were completely taken off guard by the premeditated actions of the Arab oil-producers and several of the world's largest oil conglomerates. Since then, strategic management theorists have urged the addition of environmental scanning, strategic planning, and government-relations functions to corporate organizational processes at the highest level. These were expected to help corporations survive by easing their adaptation to externally driven change. The intent was to monitor and anticipate both public opinion and government actions, plans, legislation, and regulations, and prepare a company for possible government change.

Ideally, the head of a government relations department would know exactly how government operates and what government needs. This individual would play an integral role in corporate strategy-making and senior management decision-making. Reporting would be done directly to the CEO, with high levels of respect from within the organization as well as in the halls of Ottawa. In essence, improving government relations could be a new form of intelligence function.

This option was widely prescribed by well-meaning but naive Canadian academics, consultants, and practitioners during the early 1980s. However, for the most part, companies with a government-relations department do not benefit from it. Most companies view government relations as a staff function to be tolerated, not a line function of importance. For all the resources Imperial Oil has spent on government affairs, it was still humiliated in the late 1970s in the Bertrand Report, which alleged that Imperial and the other oil companies had "ripped off" the public by $12.1 billion.

Less than ten percent of Canada's major corporations have chosen to adopt a full-time government-relations function that reported to the CEO.[44] Such a procedure costs money, and most Canadian businesses were too parsimonious to oblige. Those who did represented the most concentrated and regulated industries.

Today, the trend is actually away from the institutionalized government-relations function. The government-relations function itself is doomed to failure until CEOs assume responsibility for the political impact of their corporations' actions, and rise to the challenge of defending Canada's private sector.

3. Consultants (Lobbyists)

Consultants in business-government relations may be paid consultants per se, or paid third-party lobbyists. *Lobbying*, which simply means influencing the powers-that-be to change legislation or policy, involves a series of learnable skills. These include: defining one's goals; identifying who has the power to shape a policy to fulfil those goals; doing one's research; finding allies, if possible; packaging one's message; and communicating it in a positive manner.

Some consultants provide the early warning advice; others help companies develop policy position papers and briefs. Still others will help companies identify key players on government's side, and educate business managers about the intricacies of government policy-making. Of course, some will do all three.

Unfortunately, a large number will actually plead business' cases, rather

---

[44] Only one-third of the *Financial Post 500* corporations had such a function. (M.C. Baetz, "The Organizational Status of the Government Relations Function Among Canada's Largest Firms." Unpublished working paper, Waterloo: Wilfrid Laurier University, no date.)

than help them do it themselves. Hiring such firms often proves a waste of a company's money. A busy assistant deputy minister or director-general would much rather meet with a CEO in a candid conversation, rather than speak to a go-between.

CEOs and companies successful in dealing with government may hire consultants to help them research and prepare for the task, but they always deal with government personally. Consultants who promote their own "influence" with Ottawa and their ability to "get things done" tend to be the snake-oil salesmen of today.

The legitimate consulting firm, though, has a valuable role to play. Most of these are staffed by knowledgeable former cabinet ministers, government technocrats, mandarins, or political administrators. When hiring a consultant, note what is promised and compare this with the firm's track record. Generally, the "one-man shops" have currency valuable for two to three years after they leave government. The larger companies tend to have a *revolving door*, which keeps their personnel fresh and in touch with current issues, key players, and processes. But reputation alone does not assume success. Good government-relations consultants should have solid experience in the business world, as well.

Lobbying Canadian-style is big business. Canada's largest firm in the field, British-owned Public Affairs Research Group Ltd. (PARG), grossed only $1 million ten years ago, but grosses over $25 million today. The federal Lobby Registry, first issued in 1989, listed over 20 000 practitioners. The business is also rapidly becoming more professional. Increasingly, lobbyists and consultants in Ottawa hold graduate degrees in economics or political science. Large multinational communications and advertising firms have also entered the industry by acquiring smaller Canadian firms.

Smart companies will use consultants to complement, rather than replace, in-house expertise. *The best government consultants will not only help resolve a current problem, but will also help devise a strategy to avoid future ones. (Unfortunately, there are too few such firms around.)* As one 1988 advertisement for a major government affairs consulting firm said, "There's a lot more to government relations than opening doors."

4. Trade Associations

The term, *trade associations*, refers to industry associations, product associations, professional associations, vertical trade associations, horizontal trade associations, and so on. All of these represent a group of companies with similar interests.

Theoretically, trade associations are designed to exchange information within an industry, trade, or group, and to promote their members' views to outsiders, particularly to government. They tend to (with varying success and in varying proportions) monitor government actions and plans, develop consensus within their specific business communities, and promote their members' needs. Over three hundred trade associations are at work in Ottawa, employing over 2 000 people and spending millions of dollars annually.

Government officials like these associations for two reasons. First, they save the harried minister or bureaucrat a lot of meeting time. Second, they provide a forum in which to reach a consensus, rather than leaving it to government. However, different associations have varying success in influencing government. Either they cannot develop that elusive consensus among their members or, if they do, they may be unable to offer government practical, detailed proposals.[45] National, broad-based associations such as the Canadian Manufacturers Association (CMA) and the Canadian Chamber of Commerce (CCC) now have little effect in Ottawa. Reading one of their position papers is like listening to a politician's speech; there's plenty of hyperbole but little substance.

The two most significant exceptions today are the Business Council on National Issues (BCNI) and the Canadian Federation of Independent Business (CFIB). Both arose when ministers were no longer seen to cater to specific business constituencies on a one-to-one basis. The BCNI has succeeded in influencing government policy because it represents 125 to 150 of the largest corporations (private-sector employers) in Canada. It also develops timely, well-balanced research papers providing new information on issues of importance to both government and business. The BCNI is led by Tom D'Aquino, a former staffer of Prime Minister Trudeau's and university roommate of Prime Minister Clark's.

The CFIB has been extremely successful on behalf of small business in Canada. It directly represents 80 000 independent businesses, which account for nearly one million voters, and has been relentless in its pursuit of its mission. It is headed by John Bullock, a successful second-generation Toronto small businessman.

Even though these two trade associations appear opposite in all of their characteristics, they are both successful for the same reasons: hard work, knowledge of the government system and actors, consistency, openness, good information, and forthrightness. They do not always win, but they do well in a city not known for succumbing to lobbyists. Both have won the confidence of decision-makers in Ottawa.

5. Sector Associations (Coalitions)

A special subset of trade associations worth separate mention is *sector associations.* These represent the manufacturers/processors/producers, buyers, suppliers, labour, investors, and creditors of sectors of the econ-

---

[45] A 1981 study by the Economic Council of Canada reported that business and professional associations spent more than $122 million promoting their interests. Only $2 million was spent by public-interest groups.

omy. They are not national, all-embracing associations like the CMA or CCC, nor are they as specific in their membership as an industry association such as the Canadian Carpet Institute. They are cross-sectoral, not unlike the BCNI and CFIB, representing varying interests within the same economic grouping.

Successful sector associations exchange and promote information like any other trade association. They also develop a consensus which includes labour, thus representing a true political constituency. Smart associations never call for increased government spending unless they can identify where government can save elsewhere in the same sector. Unlike many of their industry counterparts, they promote job creation, and court the Opposition and backbenchers for the long haul. Their approach is to accommodate, not to confront.

The best example of a sector association at work is not a formal association at all, but rather a coalition of interests representing the auto industry. This is comprised of vehicle manufacturers, auto parts manufacturers, and the Canadian Auto Workers' Union (CAW). These three mutually interdependent groups who often find themselves in fundamental disagreement have put aside their differences more than once. Their objective: to work with government to agree on a policy direction in which everyone—big business, small business, labour, government, and the public—wins. A win-win proposal to government will seldom be turned aside.

Good business groups, whether formal associations or ad-hoc coalitions, also recognize that not everyone in Ottawa wants to see them. The Prime Minister's Office likes associations if they truly represent a consensus. Middle-level managers of line departments like them because they can offer at least information and often solutions for their policy dilemmas. *Sector associations succeed because they are partnerships bonded together for one common purpose—survival!*

6. Advocacy Advertising

Simply defined, *advocacy advertising* is designed to promote opinion, not sell goods or services, through paid media advertising. It is aimed at influencing the public's political, economic, or social behaviour, not its purchasing behaviour. The most successful type of advocacy advertising (for its paid sponsors) is directed at influencing public policy choice, rather than improving one's image or appeal.

Regardless of the type employed, advocacy advertising is aimed at a company's employees as much as at external publics. It is hoped to boost management and labour morale, where, in fact, it is often more successful than in shaping public opinion. Advocacy advertising stops being propaganda when the audience agrees with the opinions being expressed. However, this is difficult to measure. The public's understanding of information and how well it receives it are two different phenomena.

However, business is no longer a spectator sport, and advocacy advertising has a deserved place in the private sector's arsenal. Like any other weapon, it should be treated with respect. It is expensive, and often a gamble. It can also backfire as easily as it can succeed.

Although advocacy advertising is not new to the United States, it has only become actively employed in this country within the last decade. Most advocacy advertising has not worked because companies or trade associations started too late to fight off the perceived enemy. As a result, the actual advertisements were defensive. In the early 1980s, The Petroleum Resources Communication Foundation spent millions informing the public that 67 cents out of every dollar spent on gasoline went to government. The Canadian Petroleum Association spent millions touting its role in frontier exploration. Its message was, "Solutions begin with understanding." Viewers confused the two and ignored both.

Regardless of this disappointing start, business is slowly beginning to recognize that winning over the public means winning over the government. If business can shape public opinion to its favour, then government will be hard-pressed to ignore business' case. Political parties and governments engage in various forms of advocacy advertising all the time. They call it "campaigning" and "informing the public."

Successful advocacy advertising avoids posturing and belligerence, but focuses on a short-term issue with long-term consequences, presented in its audience's best interests. It will present an ongoing case for its argument spanning several months.

The highest quality advocacy advertising (see Figures 10-1a and 10-1b) really came of age in Canada only recently. During the 1988 federal general election, voters saw an overwhelmingly successful $5.2 million, pro-free trade campaign by the Canadian Alliance for Trade and Job Opportunities. This was actually a coalition of the CFIB, BCNI, CMA, CCC, Canadian Exporters' Association, Consumers' Association of Canada, and nineteen other trade associations and interest groups.

7. Political Mobilization

The least attractive option to business is that of political mobilization and direct involvement in the political process.[46] This option assumes that business minds think ideologically, that business deserves special status within the political bargaining forum, and that there is an open, public policy arena in which economic power is distributed and benefits are conferred. All three of these assumptions, as we have seen earlier, can be easily challenged. Political mobilization is, again, an American concept. It does, of course, have some merit for business in Canada.

---

[46] This, of course, excludes financial contributions to political parties, since these are now limited by the Election Expenses Act.

Many researchers still urge CEOs to run for public office and represent business' interests in Ottawa. Someone must carry business' message to Ottawa, and Ottawa claims it would benefit from proven management skills, whether in caucus, Cabinet, or the public service. As we know, a successfully elected former CEO would have to represent many diverse interests, not just personal ones. As an MP, one would have no choice but to follow party discipline and government policy, if a member of the government party. These would be good lessons for a CEO to learn, as well as the fact that power no longer resides in the House of Commons or even in the Cabinet as a whole; that government is too busy to just accommodate business. Listening, the new MP would learn, does not necessarily mean agreement, and action does not necessarily follow consultation.

Of course, the CEO wants to be in Cabinet, but the odds of becoming a Cabinet Minister are not high. This would depend on the region represented, sex, religion, ethnicity, and age — not just merit.

Worse still, if one does make minister, an authoritarian business executive used to a formal, rational, directive decision-making structure will not feel at all comfortable—let alone excel in —Ottawa's much more fluid, intellectual, social decision-making process. Dynamic, achievement-oriented business leaders are often quite frustrated in government's cumbersome management environment.

Finally, the $75 000 salary of an MP or $100 000+ for a minister will be a far cry from the salary, stock options, and bonuses received as a CEO or senior executive. Preoccupation with income may lead one into that ill-defined territory of conflict-of-interest. This has happened before.

However, political mobilization means more than just CEOs seeking public office. *It means business developing consistent positions, identifying allied constituencies, and mobilizing votes as labour unions do.* Speeches to one's peers will change nothing. Bashing government from time to time plays right into someone else's hands.

Delivering or denying votes, though, gets results directly in proportion to the number of votes at stake. Witness Quebec's success at the federal-provincial bargaining table over the last twenty years, regardless of the political colour of the governments in Ottawa or in Quebec City.

Unfortunately, there is no natural political constituency for business in Canada today. There is much work to be done in this regard, and it will take time. Business must also be prepared to play to win: anything goes in the political arena. Politicians and bureaucrats seldom get angry in public, but they can and do get even!

PROACTIVE BUSINESS TACTICS: THE ACCOMMODATION MODEL

There should remain little doubt that, in business' present environment, modern business management must learn to monitor environmental

Figure 10-1a

Canada/U.S. Free Trade A Majority View

Question: Will free trade diminish our sovereignty?

I t was the great Canadian Marshall McLuhan who coined the term "Global Village" to describe the interdependence of our modern world. Nations, albeit sovereign politically, need each other economically. Trade is a prerequisite of prosperity.

Freer trade between Canada and the United States is a way to ensure our prosperity in the years to come. It will not diminish our independence. Indeed, it will strengthen it.

Throughout our history, we have signed a number of tariff reduction agreements with the United States. Largely as a result, our economy and our standard of living have grown tremendously. And we're more "Canadian" now than ever before.

Other industrialized countries have had similar experiences. The New Zealanders and Australians enjoy a free trade association; they have not sacrificed their sovereignties. Many other nations have similar agreements; their political sovereignties remain intact.

We believe that the vast majority of Canadians will be well served by a properly constructed free trade agreement. It will mean more prosperity. It will mean more jobs. It will make us stronger as a people. That's what sovereignty and independence are all about.

Figure 10-1b

Canada/U.S. Free Trade: A Majority View

C A N A D A / U . S . F R E E T R A D E : A M A J O R I T Y V I E W •

TRADE IS OUR BREAD AND BUTTER

TRADE is vital to us in Canada. It always has been. Our advanced standard of living is built on centuries of success in exporting our goods to the markets of the world.

Today, we Canadians export more per man, woman and child than most major industrialized nations in the world. Our exports amount to some 30 percent of all the goods and services we produce. Over 3 million jobs in all parts of Canada depend upon our trade.

ALL CANADIANS BENEFIT FROM TRADE

Who benefits from our trade in the markets of the world? We all do. We are all consumers – and access to goods and services of quality at competitive prices is important, in particular to those with lower incomes. Jobs – we need them – and with close to one and a half million unemployed, we need them more than ever. Our industries, small and large, which are the engines of our economic growth and prosperity, need to export to survive. This they cannot do without a well-trained workforce, advanced technology, and an expanded capacity. Without exports, this will not happen.

EXPANDED GLOBAL TRADE MUST BE OUR GOAL

Today, our export trade is under threat. In the world at large, fierce competition is driving countries and trading blocs ominously close to global trade war. We in Canada have fought these trends in the past and we are doing so today by being one of the most vigorous supporters of trade liberalization on a world-wide basis.

But while we try our hardest to improve the rules for world trade, this will take patience and time – years, in fact. We must at the same time secure access to our most important markets in Europe, the Pacific, in North America, and elsewhere. Let's not forget that we are the only country among leading industrial powers that does not have unimpeded access to a market of 120 million people or more.

Peter Lougheed
Co-chairman for Canadian
Alliance for Trade & Job
Opportunities

Donald Macdonald
Co-chairman for Canadian
Alliance for Trade & Job
Opportunities

WITHOUT RULES, THE LAW OF THE JUNGLE PREVAILS

A free trade agreement offers both Canada and the United States a badly needed set of rules to guide the relationship. The current negotiations must find ways in which the two nations can trade more securely, ways to avoid costly trade disputes before they arise, and ways to solve them more quickly when they do. Without such a set of rules, the law of the jungle will prevail and the biggest players will almost certainly always win.

CANADA'S SOVEREIGNTY IS NOT AT STAKE

A small but vocal minority of Canadians is suggesting that a free trade agreement with the Americans will lead to the disappearance of Canada as an independent country. This is nonsense.

A great deal of the trade that passes between Canada and the United States is already free – indeed considerably more so today than a decade ago. And yet are we a less independent, less confident, or for that matter less prosperous nation today? The reverse is true. And the free trade arrangement we are exploring with the Americans is not unique. Free trade arrangements are in place around the globe – in Europe, in Asia, in Africa, in South America, and in Australasia. In no instance, under these arrangements, has a smaller country lost its independence to its larger partner.

A GOOD DEAL OR NO DEAL

No informed Canadian would support a free trade deal with the Americans at any cost. The deal must be in the national interest. Our negotiators are currently working hard to secure such an agreement. They are supported by the federal government, a majority of Parliamentarians, every province and territory of Canada, and a majority of Canadians. Until we see what such an agreement looks like, we must keep an open mind and an eye on opportunity. To do anything less, would be to ignore our best interests.

WE MUST SECURE ACCESS TO OUR LEADING MARKETS

By far the most important market that we must secure is the United States. Close to 80 percent of our total exports go to the United States. Over 2 million jobs in Canada depend on our trade with the Americans. And the two-way trading relationship is the world's largest. This year, some $190 billion of goods and services will pass between our two countries. We are by far the United States' most important trading partner.

This enormous two-way relationship, which has brought so much prosperity to Canadians and Americans alike, is in need of greater certainty. Protectionist forces are at work in the United States that threaten our access to the American market. In recent years, over $8 billion worth of Canadian exports have been threatened by American quotas, surcharges, anti-dumping and countervailing duties. The industries in Canada that have been threatened provide over 200,000 jobs. Shakes and shingles, softwood lumber, steel, hogs and pork, are recent examples of our exports that have been hurt. But many more have been affected: steel, copper and sugar products from Ontario; rail passenger cars from Quebec; potash from Saskatchewan; salmon; herring, raspberries and cut flowers from British Columbia; rock salt, ground fish and salted cod from the Atlantic provinces, to name only a few.

Currently, American legislators are considering trade bills that potentially could severely restrict imports into the United States. We in Canada must vigorously oppose this dangerous trend because we have more at stake in the outcome than any other nation. A free trade agreement would help shield our workers and our industries from the impact of these protectionist actions.

Do we have the potential as a people to reach an accommodation with the Americans that will enhance our prospects for an even stronger and more secure Canada – able to expand our political and economic influence throughout the world? Of course we do! Millions of Canadians share our confidence. We trust you will too.

THE CANADIAN ALLIANCE

This message is from the Canadian Alliance for Trade and Job Opportunities. Formed in March of this year, the Alliance is a non-partisan, broadly based body composed of citizens from all parts of Canada, and economic organizations representing some one-half million Canadians. The Co-chairmen of the Alliance are the Honourable Peter Lougheed and the Honourable Donald Macdonald. Founding organizations of the Alliance are the Business Council on National Issues, the Canadian Chamber of Commerce, the Canadian Exporters' Association, the Canadian Federation of Independent Business, the Canadian Manufacturers' Association, and the Consumers' Association of Canada. These are being joined by a growing number of organizations and individuals every day.

Membership in the Canadian Alliance is welcomed. No fee is required, but voluntary contributions would be appreciated. Upon receipt of your completed coupon, you will be sent a membership card and Alliance lapel pin. Complete this form and send it to The CANADIAN ALLIANCE FOR TRADE AND JOB OPPORTUNITIES, P.O. Box 6077, Montreal, Quebec H3C 3A7.

CANADIAN ALLIANCE FOR TRADE AND JOB OPPORTUNITIES

Canadian Federation of Independent Business
Consumers' Association of Canada
Business Council on National Issues
Canadian Manufacturers' Association
Canadian Chamber of Commerce
Canadian Exporters' Association

*National surveys show a majority of Canadians in favour of a Free Trade Agreement with the United States.

change, interpret these changes, adapt where practical, be flexible, and anticipate future change. However, most important, business management must understand the need, and develop the capability, to influence public policy, rather than managing its effects once passed. This will require hiring personnel with significant understanding of government, giving them adequate resources to do their jobs, and having them directly accountable to the CEO who must take charge of dealing with government. After all, this is a question of survival — and the CEO is charged with the survival of the firm.

Business, not government, must take the initiative to restore the old government department-clientele relationships, once the cornerstone of early Canadian business-government relations. Of course, many such linkages still exist at the routine, technical, administrative level. It is at the general policy-making, senior management levels that they must be re-established.

In other words, business must be *proactive*. It must objectively, professionally, and discretely demonstrate to the *real* powers that form government policy how vital business enterprise is in Canada's economy. Business must provide policy-makers with accurate, complete information before policy options are eliminated, decisions taken, and a government department drafts its Memorandum to Cabinet. Above all, business must actually do the above *in the public interest.*

In effect, business must interact more often with government to enhance mutual understanding. This requires a strategy, whether at the firm or sector level, to identify the right people and the right time in government, and the CEO must take the lead in all of this. After all, *decision-makers want to deal with decision-makers* in any bargaining arena. By doing so, business will be able to prevent as well as initiate change.

Such a proactive stance would return business and government to an era of mutual accommodation and co-operative planning. It would narrow the perceptual gap between business and government, and develop once again shared beliefs in how national goals could best be achieved; perhaps even what those goals ought to be. Above all, it would restore trust between these two solitudes and forge a national partnership. Business-government relations are not in such desperate disrepair; it is just that the challenges facing business and government today are so awesome.

This is not to be construed as lobbying. This is having *input* before decisions are made. It is an exchange of information and co-operation for favourable legislation and regulation. It is business offering to implement government policy through the mechanisms of the marketplace, as well as showing government why business needs it to redress the imbalances in that marketplace from time to time.

The answers to business-government misunderstanding do not lie in Parliamentary reform or improved reactive tactics, but in business showing government and the public that a healthy private sector is in the best interests of the nation. Going to government with a ready-made consensus within part or all of the business community, of course, would be Utopia for both business and government.

What are the rules for proactive government relations?

1. Business' policy recommendations must be sound, legal, and specific. It should not ask for the impossible, or succumb to hyperbole—that is the politicians' job in selling policy.

2. Business should avoid the discussion of specific benefits and the need to disperse costs. Government will assume as much. Business must go to government with a plan, not more problems for government.

3. Business must be able to lose gracefully. After all, it will not always win. It should be prepared to play a long game for that all-important big win someday.

4. It must deal with the *real* decision-makers, and deal with their very real problems. Business must understand the needs of government and its policy engineers.

5. Business must support its brief oral submissions with completely documented written verification and research.

6. Business must be patient. The wheels of government move cautiously—and that is good for everyone. There is no single channel of authority for any one matter.

7. Being bilingual will certainly help.

8. Business must be aware of the political ramifications of its proposals or information, and be able to offer intelligent, informed advice about them. This does not mean that its advice will be taken, but it will show that business is sympathetic to the constraints upon government policy-makers. For example, business should understand that in "bad times" government must be seen to be doing something.

Of course, the CEO of a firm (or one who chairs a sector association) should do all of this.[47] Here are some characteristics of a successful CEO dealing with government. The individual should be:

1. Articulate, well-informed, and consistent in presenting one's case.

2. Frank, candid, positive, and sensitive.

3. Competent and popular in the business community.

4. Not overly extroverted, aggressive, or strident.

5. An "organization person," self-confident and socially adept.

---

[47] Chief executive officers of large Japanese firms spend almost all of their time dealing with government, at home and abroad.

Efforts must be conducted on an ongoing basis, but should not appear to be overtly persistent. (This raises government's suspicions — and rightly so — and wastes its time.) Although these efforts have little impact upon quarterly profits and market share, they have great bearing on a company's, industry's, or sector's long-term prospects for survival. The overall process is more important than the immediate outcome.

Canadian business may not be able to shape world economic trends, but it does have the potential to again influence domestic economic policy. Information is the key.

Reactive confrontation produces a lose/lose situation at worst; compromise is still a lose/lose situation, but of less consequence all around (that is why most erroneously view compromise as a win/win situation). Only proactive co-operation and consultation can produce a true win/win situation.

IMPLICATIONS FOR MANAGEMENT

Business no longer has (if it ever did) a monopoly on relations with government. Government now meets with, and sometimes even listens to, a large number of very diversified interest groups. Yet business has not clearly recognized or understood this fact and has not learned to adapt.

To compound this situation, the private sector lacks effective leadership. The Canadian business community has not been united in its efforts to influence the public policy-making and implementation. Different business interests often talk at cross-purposes, which allows government to play one segment against the other. This diminishes any impact business might have had on public policy. In this respect, business' rivals may actually be their best friends. Banded together, there would be a cohesiveness and strength in numbers never experienced by business when dealing with government.

Even though individual interest groups, including segments of the business community, have sometimes succeeded with short-term, reactive issue management, they have as often failed to promote their own interests in the longer term and over a broader spectrum of public policy issues. Cross-business compromise and co-operation would probably lessen much of the short-term individual gain, but would achieve a greater collective gain overall.

In Japan, business makes the tough economic decisions and government implements them. This works in a homogeneous society, but Canada is very much a pluralist society. To expect the CEOs of the *Financial Post 500* to unanimously agree on all government policies would be unrealistic. However, CEOs must accept business-government relations as an important addition to their mandate. If they are, in fact, responsible for strategically managing their enterprises, they should realize that *there is nothing more vital to the survival of their firms than government and its collective impact upon them.*

Chief executive officers must also adopt a much broader perspective when approaching or dealing with government. At the very least, they should envelop their parochial interests in a greater national interest, fine-tuning them to more closely match the national interest — however defined by the government of the day. Working with and through sector associations which include buyers, suppliers, and labour, and taking a more personal role in the leadership of these associations, would expose CEOs to the consensus-building mode of decision-making so vital for effective public policy.

Business leaders often are dismayed to discover that government operates by the principles of political science. Business should therefore strive to understand government's convoluted agenda and processes. Hiring senior line managers or lobbyists from senior government ranks is one way to do this. Maintaining an office in Ottawa with staff directly responsible for improving contact with appropriate government staff is a second option.

Improving the quality of trade associations, working through them more often, and developing them as training schools for executives is a third option. The Business Council on National Issues type of association would be an ideal candidate for the latter. It has the support of many key players within the business elite, has been fairly effective in lobbying and working with government, has demonstrated that it knows how and why government works as it does, and is respected by many in government circles. Such organizations would contribute substantially to improving business' understanding of government if it assumed the role of an academy. This would be designated to train senior business executives in the art and principles of political science. *Business leaders would then learn that in the short-term, it is the process that counts; in the longer term, it is the results that count.*

In short, business should move away from firm-specific, individual efforts to more collective, representative, cross-sectoral approaches to government. Business should concentrate more on the *real* decision-makers in government and less on the public figureheads. Business must concentrate less on *ad hoc* responses to announced government policy, and become more proactive in influencing government policy. It needs to stop automatically opposing every government program it does not like, and address economic issues before they become political issues.

All of these recommendations require an increased allocation of resources to the business-government function, not necessarily in the form of a department, but in recognition of the fact that a CEO needs advice, research, contacts, support, and time to do the job. Although this practice may erode short-term profits slightly, it will improve substantially business' longer-term position within the economy. Canada needs business to get more involved in the public policy process.

SUGGESTED FURTHER READINGS

Bartha, Peter F. "Organizational Competence in Business-Government Relations: A Managerial Perspective." *Canadian Public Administration.* 28: 2 (Summer 1985), 202-220.

Bregha, F. *Bob Blair's Pipeline: The Business and Politics of National Energy Development Projects,* 2nd edition. Toronto: James Lorimer Publishers, 1981.

Calvert, John. *Government, Limited: The Corporate Takeover of the Public Sector in Canada.* Ottawa: The Canadian Centre for Policy Alternatives, 1984.

Coleman, W.D. *Business and Politics: A Study of Collective Action.* Montreal: McGill-Queen's University Press, 1988.

Fleck, J.D. and I.A. Litvak, eds. *Business Can Succeed: Understanding the Political Environment.* Toronto: Gage Publishing Limited, 1984.

Gillies, James. *Where Business Fails.* Montreal: Institute for Research on Public Policy, 1981.

Gollner, A. *Social Change and Corporate Strategy: The Expanding Role of Public Affairs.* Stamford, CT: Issue Action Publications, 1983.

Institute for Political Involvement. *A Report on the Prospects For Increased Involvement of Business People in the Canadian Political System.* Toronto: Institute for Political Involvement (April 1978).

Lyon, J. *Dome: The Rise and Fall of the House that Jack Built.* Toronto: Macmillan of Canada, 1983.

Sawatsky, John. *The Insiders: Government, Business and the Lobbyists.* Toronto: McClelland & Stewart, 1987.

Stanbury, W.T. *Business-Government Relations in Canada.* Toronto: Methuen, 1986.

Thompson, Donald N. "The Canadian Pharmaceutical Industry: A Business-Government Failure." *Business Quarterly.* 48 (Summer 1983), 120-123.

11 GOVERNMENT DEALING WITH BUSINESS

He that would govern others, first should be the master of himself.

Philip Massinger, 1583-1640

The federal government of Canada has traditionally sought public input in the policy-making process *after* it has drafted its policy intentions. More recently, however, the government has genuinely started to seek public input, and that of business in particular, before the details of a policy are finalized. The rounds of business-government consultation while the free trade agreement was being negotiated best demonstrates government's new proactive stance. Might this be the trend for the future of business-government relations, or is it an aberration in how government deals with business? What more should government be doing?

These questions and more form the substance of this chapter on how government deals with business. But first, it should be recognized that government can be just as reactive as business is. The best, most glaring case of its reactive approach to business' needs is the bailing out of firms in deep financial trouble, or *corporate welfare*, as New Democratic Party leader David Lewis called it in the 1968 general federal election.

BAILOUTS AND CORPORATE WELFARE

Government financial assistance to business (aside from regional and employment development initiatives) usually takes one of three forms: loans or loan guarantees; so-called bailouts, or the last-minute infusion of funds, either of a debt or equity nature; or grants, a more common, less reactive form of direct subsidization.

During the Great Depression of the 1930s, government loans and loan guarantees to failing businesses represented up to 14% of the GNP. By the time of the postwar economic boom of the 1950s and 1960s, that figure had dropped to an average of 4.3%. However, throughout the 1980s that figure has risen to 18.5% of the GNP!

The vast majority of this amount comes from the federal government. In fact, Ottawa is the fourth-largest lender to the business community. No fewer than 42 federal agencies loan money or guarantee loans for business, with about 60% of that money in the housing market. Another 14% supports other forms of domestic business (primarily resource upgrading); 11% encourages exports; and another 11% goes to the agricultural sector.

Nearly all export financing today is done by the Export Development Corporation (EDC), and over half of all mortgage insurance is through the Canada Mortgage and Housing Corporation (CMHC). In fact, the CMHC has become the 14th-largest financial institution in Canada, with assets of $10 billion. The farm community receives 30% of all its credit from government loans and loan guarantees.

And government does not discriminate between borrowers. Take the case of Peter Pocklington and the government of Alberta. Pocklington is the outspoken defendant of free enterprise who ran for the federal Progressive Conservative leadership. His platform was to minimize the role of government. In fact, he was totally opposed to all government support for business. In his regular Alberta newspaper column on March 6, 1988, he once again censured "government funded movements of the liberal-left." On March 10, however, he accepted a $12 million loan from Alberta's Treasury Branches for his meat-packing company, Gainers Inc., and a $55 million loan guarantee. Why the sudden shift in philosophy? Because the "free enterpriser" needed the money to compete with Fletcher's Fine Foods (a government-controlled enterprise) in central Alberta, where he planned to build a new plant and modernize his existing one. Nor was this the first time that Pocklington had fed at the government trough. In 1984, he accepted a $31 million loan from Alberta, and in July, 1987, received a $100 million line of credit for his Palm Dairies, Ltd.

Of course, this was not a bailout, and Pocklington does oppose bailouts. Over the past 15 years or so, the federal government has bailed out or rescued ten major firms: six of these subsequently went under; one turned around; and three remain in limbo. This spate of corporate welfare occurred between 1976 and 1983, when "anti-business" Trudeau had been Prime Minister for all but nine months. In 1976, 49% of the equity of Consolidated Computer was purchased by the federal government for $30 million. It was later sold for $100 000, with the government losing $119 million overall on the deal. On the other hand, one year later Ottawa poured $15 million into Electrohome, was paid back by 1980, and *made* $10 million.

In 1979, CCM received $22 million from the federal government and went bankrupt in 1982. Taxpayers lost $16 million. In 1981, $13 million was given to White Farm Equipment, which went bankrupt in 1983. Also in 1981, Massey-Ferguson received $125 million from Ottawa and another $75 million from the Ontario government to save its combine manufacturing operations. By 1988, this division of the now-renamed Varity Corporation was in receivership, with the federal government writing off previous loans totalling $226.3 million.

The following year, 1982, was a watershed year for business. Maislin received $33 million from Ottawa in 1982 and went bankrupt in 1983. The Lake Group received $13 million and lost $23 million in 1983 alone. The East Coast fish-processing industry was nationalized, and subsequently partially re-privatized at untold costs to the taxpayers. Co-op Implements received $13 million.

So-called bailouts ceased by 1983, with Petromont of Quebec receiving $25 million that year. Chrysler Canada and Dome Petroleum both negotiated with the federal government, but both refused the government's terms. Chrysler succeeded; Dome failed.

Bailouts are a total waste of time and money. They are usually "too little, too late." Most of the companies bailed out had exhausted every other form of government largesse. Corporate welfare fosters inefficiency, dependency, and misallocation of resources, but it does save jobs.

The only difference between a *subsidy* and a *bailout* (both are essentially free money) is that bailouts are for losers, and subsidies are for winners. The rich get richer at the public's expense in order to increase capacity, relocate, open a new plant, or create jobs. For example, the auto industry is continually being subsidized by the federal, Ontario, and Quebec governments for one reason or another.

The forest products industry—Canada's number one industry with 1987 profits of over $1 billion—is continually being subsidized for machinery, jobs, reforestation, infrastructure, exports, and so on. Normick, Perron and Forex's new $400 million newsprint mill in Quebec was heavily subsidized by that province's government. The company is now selling out to American interests. Daishawa Paper of Japan, when building its $500 million pulp mill in Alberta, received $65 million from the province and $10 million from Ottawa. Why? Not because it needed it (as they admitted) but because they tried "to follow the Canadian way of doing things."

Is government subsidization of business dangerous? It can be. Over-capacity already exists in both the auto and forest products industries, and in most industries or firms subsidized. Government subsidization drives industry profits down further, creating a vicious circle. Over-capacity reduces profitability, which means layoffs, so government subsidizes new capacity to create jobs. This new capacity reduces profits, and so on.

Why do governments loan money to business as a lender of last resort, bail out losers, and subsidize excess capacity? There are nine generally accepted reasons:

1. *Jobs, Jobs, Jobs* - (votes, votes, votes)

2. *Market Failure* - The private sector cannot profitably or does not want to provide a public good or service.

3. *As an Instrument of Public Policy* - This is rare, and was accounted for only in the East Coast fish-processing industry as seen above.

4. *"Favoured Son"* - This is for purely political reasons, as some critics claim Maislin and Petromont were because they were in Quebec; the fishing case; Massey, White and Co-op for the farmers' sake; and Electrohome in that bastion of Liberalism, Kitchener-Waterloo.

5. *Regional Development* - Pressure is felt from provincial governments, especially Quebec, the East Coast, and the Prairies.

6. *Key Sectors* - Forestry, oil and gas, agriculture, mining, and fishing are heavily capitalized and have huge unemployment, and have a major share of the GNP. Six out of the ten bailouts above were in key sectors.

7. *To Promote/Retain Canadian Ownership*

8. *To Save Sources of Future Corporate Tax Revenues*

9. *To Promote/Retain Reasonable Levels of Competition within an Industry*

But what is the cost when government deals with business in this way? To begin with, there is greater industrial inefficiency, higher prices, and higher taxes. Unfortunately, these actions neither address nor cure the root problems. Worse still, government simply raises others' expectations that they, too, are entitled to funds. *Business has now joined the age of entitlement.*

How does government decide whether business failure is due to outside variables or to mismanagement? Will the United States government challenge Canada's right to support business, considering it an unfair trade practice under the terms of the Canada-United States Free Trade Agreement? Although it says it will, only time will tell. (But then, the U.S. is equally guilty of this practice.)

Surely there must be a more sensible approach for government to deal with business than to transfer 25% or more of the nation's wealth from the consumer/taxpayer to the producer. One alternative is for business to get involved in government policy-making. This would enable it to develop an economic climate that would avoid failure. But to what extent should government get business involved?

NORMATIVE LEVELS OF BUSINESS INFLUENCE

In the same survey discussed in Chapters 8 and 9, business and government elites were asked whether they believed that business should have more, less, or the same amount of influence as they had in forming the following government policies:

- monetary policy
- fiscal/taxation policy
- competition policy
- wage/price regulation

- foreign investment
- tariffs and trade regulation
- development/location incentives
- bailouts of financially troubled companies
- government investment in or ownership of business
- labour legislation
- social/environmental regulation

The majority of business leaders thought that business should have more influence in shaping all the above policies listed. Specifically, respondents felt strongest about having more influence in creating the following policies. They are listed in descending order of importance to them:

- fiscal/taxation policy
- government investment/ownership of business
- foreign investment
- labour legislation

Interestingly, a strong inverse relationship existed between a business leader's level of satisfaction with business-government relations and the wish for greater influence in the making of public policy. In other words, *the more satisfied one was with business-government relations, the less interest there was in having more influence.* In fact, those who perceived business-government relations to be in very good shape actually thought that business should have less influence. On the other hand, *those who were less satisfied thought business should have more influence.*

The government elite was ambivalent. It was satisfied overall with current levels of business input, but was open to greater input. There were only two exceptions: most leaders thought that the business community should have *more* influence on the granting of development/location incentives. They also thought business should have *less* influence on the bailing out of financially troubled firms.

In an earlier survey, Campbell and Szablowski[48] revealed that fully half of central agents—those powerful, if shadowy decision-makers in the Prime Minister's Office, Privy Council Office, Treasury Board Secretariat, and Ministry of Finance—actually consulted with business leaders for policy advice. In the United States the response was 75% and in the United Kingdom, 81%. More striking, though, was the fact that out of the 16 groups most often consulted, business was considered the most reliable—tied with provincial government officials.

In short, both business and government see the benefit of greater business involvement in the public policy-making process. How, then, can government facilitate this most effectively?

---

[48] Colin Campbell and George Szablowski. *The Superbureaucrats: Structure and Behaviour in Central Agencies* (Toronto: Macmillan, 1979) 208, 292-3.

COLOURED PAPERS AND TRADITIONAL CONSULTATION

The most time-honoured mechanism by which business and the general public can have policy-making input in a parliamentary monarchy is through Green and White Papers.

A *Green Paper* is usually a collection of propositions about a subject released by government for public debate and discussion; it is not actual government policy. These papers are released at the very earliest stages of the policy process, usually when government is genuinely unclear about a new area of public concern. There are generally few precedents to follow, or the subject may be a very difficult one involving many irreconcilable differences and vested interests. A Green Paper usually precedes a Royal Commission, Task Force of Inquiry, or White Paper. Only once has the federal government deliberately released a Green Paper after it had already drafted legislation. This was in 1975, regarding the changing of Canada's immigration laws.

A *White Paper* is a government document outlining intended government policy about a specific issue or policy. It usually describes planned legislation and the scope of any necessary accompanying regulation. Its contents are more refined and directed than are those found in a Green Paper which may have preceded it. If a Green Paper debated options, a White Paper will expand upon the chosen option. White Papers are usually only issued after government has decided what to do, but is still interested in business' (and/or public) reaction to its proposals. Often White Papers will follow the deliberations of a Royal Commission or Task Force of Inquiry. The advantage of a White Paper for government is that if its proposals are unpopular, they can be withdrawn more easily than if they had been tabled in Parliament.

The Liberal governments of Prime Minister Trudeau discovered from their frequent use of Green and White papers that, although it did open up the policy-making process somewhat, only elites actually took advantage of it. Business elites unfortunately rarely did. The one exception was Trudeau's White Paper on Tax Reform. The business community took it seriously and responded most vociferously.

Today, the Progressive Conservative Government in Ottawa sometimes refers to its papers as *blue papers* in recognition of the dominant colour of the party's logo. The Liberal government in Ontario has started to refer to *red papers*. Regardless of this change in terminology, the types of papers remain two: general discussion or proposed policy. Their purpose is to gain feedback from outside the government before policy decisions and public commitments, either in Parliament or in the media, are made.

Like most things in life, Green and White Papers are not fully appreciated until they are absent from the scene. For example, the Liberals' National Energy Program of the early 1980s offered no warnings—not even the customary phone calls by the Deputy Minister or Assistant Deputy Minister to the industry the night before the announcements were made. Nor had there been a Green or White Paper on repatriation, socialization, nationalization, or self-reliance in energy supplies and capitalization capacity within the oil and gas industry.

Business has a responsibility to respond to Green or White Papers. The private sector should take every opportunity to know its government counterparts better, and to have its opinions heard. However, even if business does not accept government's offer to get involved in this way, these coloured papers offer business an early warning of things to come. If a firm or industry is conscientiously monitoring its environment for threats and opportunities, the messages contained in these papers can often prepare it for one or the other.

TRIPARTISM

Many of the economic and social problems facing this country over the past quarter century have arisen from high inflation, low productivity, commodity shortages or surpluses, and high unemployment. All these are set against a backdrop of rising expectations. To fully address these national problems, government must view them in both a global context, and one in which business and labour can assist in resolving them.

This level of consultation, co-operation, and consensus-building among government, business, and labour has become known as *tripartism.* This concept has actually become an institution in Austria, Denmark, Norway, Sweden, Holland, and Belgium; alas, such has not been the case in Canada. However, the process holds great promise for the future.

Given the environmental changes identified in Part I of this book, neither the classical, political model of interest brokerage nor the traditional, management-labour model of problem-solving works. *Tripartism is an admission that the process of decision-making is more important in achieving desired economic or social outcomes today than is rigid adherence to outdated economic formulas or political ideologies.*

Tripartism is *not* a panacea. Consensus is difficult to reach at the best of times. It has not always been reached in the six countries mentioned above, and the few tripartite experiments in Canada have had mixed results. It also excludes environmental and consumer interests.

Tripartism will only work if government is actually willing to bargain with business and labour, and then follow through on its agreements. Traditionally, government has balked at this, claiming that the supremacy of Parliament must never be eroded. However, the new Constitution and the Charter of Rights and Freedoms allows for individuals to challenge this supremacy in the courts.

The real opposition has come from the federal bureaucracy. The public service enjoys a very privileged position, serving elected officials both as policy advisers and policy administrators. Tripartism threatens that privileged position. Over the past twenty years, central agencies have usurped much of the policy-making role of line departments. Now, business and labour are regarded as potential incumbents to this role, as well as to the overall prestige and power of the line departments.

The very logistics of tripartism are staggering. Who represents business? The CMA? CCC? BCNI? CFIB? Who represents labour? The CLC? CFL?

However, a more realistic drawback to tripartism is the belief that neither self-interested business nor labour can approach or deal with the range of socio-economic policies which government must address every time a major issue arises. Nothing can be handled by government without compounding some other situation; otherwise, it would not be in government's lap in the first place. Business and labour think uni-directionally; government by necessity thinks circuitously.

The greatest drawback to tripartism is government's preference for selling pre-arranged policy initiatives, rather than working towards a three-way consensus. In the two most familiar cases of tripartism described below, the Canadian government took the initiative both times. One case met with mixed reviews; the other was a resounding success. Neither would have occurred if government had not taken the lead.

The first genuine attempt at tripartism has come to be known as *Tier I/ Tier II*. Jean Chretien was appointed Minister of Industry, Trade and Commerce (ITC) in 1976 by Prime Minister Trudeau. His mandate was to improve relations with business by listening to it, and to develop an industrial strategy. Chretien's Deputy Minister proposed an interdepartmental committee to prepare sectoral profiles based upon business, federal, and provincial input.

When Jack Horner was appointed Minister of ITC in 1977, he included labour in what was to become a tripartite (with continued provincial involvement) study of these 23 sectoral profiles. Meetings would be chaired by business, with committees staffed by public servants. All 23 studies would be published as Tier I.

Each sector then set up a Tier II committee with six representatives from business (including the chairman), five from labour, and one academic. These would determine the optimal government policy for that sector. The whole exercise took one and a half years and cost $25 million.

Labour cried foul throughout the process, claiming its participation was an afterthought and that it lacked the staff resources to compete with business and government. (In fact, the CLC refused to participate until after the task forces had actually begun to meet.) Eight sector reports were unanimous, with labour dissenting in another eleven. Over 600 recommendations were made in the energy, transportation, and research and development fields alone; government responded to every one. (Coincidentally, there were slightly over 600 participants in all.) Not surprisingly, there was neither agreement nor government action on taxes or tariffs. For six years afterwards, the federal government continued to consult with sectoral task forces, but on a smaller scale.

The outcomes of Tier I/Tier II were important. The differences among segments of the private sector were clearly seen to be greater than was the traditionally assumed gulf between business and government, or business and labour. The levels of appreciation, understanding, and rapport with the "other side" markedly improved. Government wanted information, and got lots of it. Fifty-eight percent of participants said they learned something substantive and 53% made new, lasting contacts.

Tier I/Tier II failed primarily for two reasons. First, business thought this tripartite body would forge an industrial strategy; meanwhile, government simply sought information with which to develop an industrial strategy. Second, sectoral task forces were asked to address problems which were not sector-specific. Thus, little real consensus was ever formed, or even possible.

The second example of tripartism in Canada was a true success. In the early 1980s, the Canada-United States Auto Pact became more favourable on a net basis to Canada than it was to the United States. Successful renewal of the pact meant tough negotiations from a position of strength for the Canadian government. This led Minister of ITC Ed Lumley to create a sector task force which included the presidents of the three major auto manufacturers, representatives of the auto parts manufacturers, and representatives of the auto workers' union. The President of the Automotive Parts Manufacturing Association of Canada, Pat Lavelle, and the President of the Canadian Autoworkers, Bob White, were co-chairmen. It worked.

The final, unanimous conclusion of this task force was that producers of imported vehicles should have to invest in the countries in which they sold their cars. This meant that foreign cars produced in Canada would be exempted from Canadian import duties, provided 60% of the vehicle content was Canadian. The same applied to the United States. This kept domestic producers price-competitive and meant more business for the parts manufacturers. New plants also meant new jobs. Although ITC's Lumley did not accept the task force's recommendations as government policy, it gave the government much-needed ammunition to negotiate hard with the Japanese and save the Auto Pact with the Americans. They could invest in Canada, or face higher barriers to trade. The rest is history.[49]

The conclusion is that, although untried to any degree in this country, tripartism could work. However, it must be initiated by government in good faith and should follow these rules:

1. concentrate on longer-term issues (5 years);

---

[49] Seven years later, however, the industry has a whole new set of problems as a result of investment by Japanese auto manufacturers in Canada and the United States.

2.   concentrate on sector-specific issues;

3.   include business, government, and labour from the start;

4.   set ground rules at the beginning, which are agreed upon and understood, with clear objectives;

5.   keep expectations realistic (given #4)

6.   limit it to those sectors that want to do it (when one or two are successful, the others will follow.) Start with those predisposed to success, and

7.   have business and labour share the cost with government. (After all, it will share the benefit).

There is no doubt that government is sheltered from and immune to the realities of the business world. Consultation—tripartism—is therefore a necessary educational process. However, business is even more ignorant of the realities and constraints of government. Business also needs to work on developing a consensus within the segment of its community invited to participate—*before* participating. Labour will definitely show up united.

Finally, government must realize that effective consultation and consensus-building among business, labour, and government cannot be done in public, where posturing overtakes substance. Tripartite meetings must be held behind closed doors, so that when one party concedes and changes its position it need not lose face. After all, that is why most federal-provincial conferences fail today.

FREE TRADE AND THE NEW CONSULTATION

The Progressive Conservative Government of Prime Minister Mulroney learned well from the Tier I/Tier II exercise of 1977-1979 and the Auto Task Force exercise of 1982-1983. The lesson: *it pays for government to consult with—not just to listen to—business.*

For the first time since World War II, business and government have begun to collaborate on current issues. The most prominent example of this closeness was in negotiating the Canada-United States Free Trade Agreement.

The government developed a relatively elaborate system to consult with business and develop an agreement to benefit Canada on a long-term, net basis. In August, 1986, an advisory group of business leaders was appointed for each of the fifteen major sectors of the economy.[50] These were collectively called the Sectoral Advisory Groups on International Trade (SAGIT). The chairs of these groups reported through the International Trade Advisory Committee (ITAC) to the Minister of International Trade.[51] Both levels were staffed with government officials and supported

---

[50] Nine groups have token representation from labour.
[51] ITAC was formed in January, 1988, to advise the Minister and the government on bilateral and multilateral (GATT) trade negotiations.

by academics and consultants. While very little has been made public about the dynamics and impact SAGIT and ITAC had on the free trade agreement, both the business community and the federal government have glowed over the success of the process. Business communicated its concerns to government; government priorities were influenced by those concerns.

This is a vast change in government technique since the days of the National Energy Program. Time will tell whether or not SAGIT and ITAC signal the beginning of an era of more co-operative, effective government consultation with business. If so, business had best be prepared to accept every opportunity government offers it to become more involved in the making of public policy.

The success of SAGIT and ITAC rests on two inherent characteristics of the bilateral free trade talks. First, there was a clear deadline for both Prime Minister Mulroney and U.S. President Reagan to establish a free trade treaty, which had to be met by both negotiating teams. Working a time line backwards placed the consultation process in a very compressed and urgent time frame. Second, the issue at hand was one of survival for Canadian business, and for Canada as an economically prosperous polity, given the alternative of increased U.S. protectionism. Trade is a strategic priority for Canada.

Thus, *the key to successful consultation between business and government is that the process address a strategic priority for both parties; something that is both urgent and important, that threatens their very existence.* Only then will a true consensus emerge, and public policy in the best interests of the nation be created.

But SAGIT and ITAC worked for another reason, as well. The process was created by and supported by the Prime Minister of Canada. He set goals; consultation developed the policies. Prime Minister Mulroney dismissed Parliament, Parliamentary reform, and executive federalism as a totally ineffective means by which to accomplish those goals. Given the CLC's vocal, rigid opposition to free trade before the consultation process began, he also eliminated the option of any tripartite approach to the issue.

The accomplishment of the free trade agreement by Brian Mulroney is in many ways a modern parallel to the creation of the National Policy by Sir John A. Macdonald. As back then, and as in Japan today, it was business that chose which industries were winners and which were losers, not government. This had been a tough but important lesson for government to learn: that sometimes business *does* have a better idea.

IMPLICATIONS FOR MANAGEMENT

Government must act if business-government relations in Canada are to improve. In Chapter 10, it was recommended that business attempt to better understand government's agenda. To help business accomplish this, government must set clear ground rules and terms of reference for any consultative or interactive process. It must also clearly communicate its objectives to business for specific consultations or interactions. Government should thus tell business whether it is only in search of information, or that it wishes to make a deal. This would prevent business from becoming unduly disappointed and wasting resources.

As a show of good faith, and in its own fact-finding interest, government should consult with business on a continuing basis, not just in crisis situations or before elections. Government could clearly identify whether it was offering a proactive, maintenance type of consultation, or a reactive, crisis-management one. The first would be designed to reach an agreement with business on certain facts, and to diminish the differences between their viewpoints. The latter would respond to a perceived problem.

Second, government should provide more opportunities and incentives for business-government executive interchange. (On business' part, of course, it must be willing, and be seen by government to be willing, to capitalize upon such opportunities). The area of most agreement by both elites was a desire for more crossover in careers between business leaders, senior civil servants, and political officeholders. A career in either sector in Canada was expected to be more of a lifelong commitment than it was in the United States, where mid-career crossovers—and even re-crossovers—were much more prevalent.

If one's beliefs about society are tied into one's position in society, then senior managers in both private and public sectors must learn to cross-pollinate with the opposite sector. Only thus will they understand the values, attitudes, beliefs, and ideas of the other side. As a result, they can begin to forge common links, goals, and avenues to achieve mutual understanding—an objective obviously in the best interests of the nation.

Executive exchanges promise to help weld together the two elites. Here, senior executives from one sector visit the opposite sector to take up a similar position for a year or two. This has already begun to close the "personal and personnel gap" between the two sectors, but more is needed.[52] Senior civil servants should be trained and more fully experienced in the intricacies and imperatives of competitive strategic management in the private sector. Not only will they better understand their private sector counterparts, but they will learn to formulate more effective economic and industrial policies. Similarly, chief executive officers in the private sector should be trained in the complexities of both political process and political economy. Only thus will they fully appreciate the temporal and political constraints which political leaders must face.[53]

---

[52] I.A. Litvak. "The Ottawa Syndrome." *Business Quarterly* 44, 22-39.
[53] For evidence of the success of this approach, see O.L. Bon and K.D. Hart. *Linking Canada's New Solitudes*. Ottawa: Conference Board of Canada, 1983.

The objective would not be to compromise one side or the other, but to promote a better understanding of the other side. Having said that, one-year or two-year executive changes are not really adequate. Strong incentives must be developed to encourage and support senior executives from both sides to switch careers, preferably along sectoral lines, in order to close that perceptual gap which exists between them. The evidence in this book clearly suggests that this interchange would be successful. *It is government's place to facilitate such an endeavour.*

Finally, government must realize that for consensus to exist among industries, and between business and government on major economic issues, there must be some form of compensation for the "losers." In any major change of the Canadian economic system, some industries will gain, while others will lose. Government itself should not pick winners and losers, but let technological and economic trends identified by business determine them. This was done in 1989 in the free trade agreement with the United States. As in Japan, and to a lesser extent in other countries, government should assist those "losing" businesses in changing their products, financing, or even their industries. The funds used for this assistance should appropriately come from marginal taxation of the winners.

Of course, *political will* remains an absolute necessity for any recipe of consultation or interaction to be successful. Sometimes, though, the political will to *not* get involved is greater than that required to *get* involved.

SUGGESTED FURTHER READINGS

Atkinson, M.M. and Wm. D. Coleman. "Is There a Crisis in Business-Government Relations?" *Canadian Journal of Administrative Sciences*, Vol. 4, no. 4 (December 1987), 321-340.

Blair, Cassandra. *Forging Links of Co-operation: The Task Force Approach to Consultation.* Ottawa: Conference Board in Canada, 1984.

Bon, D.L. and K.D. Hart. *Linking Canada's New Solitudes: The Executive Interchange Programme and Business-Government Relations.* Ottawa: Conference Board in Canada, 1983.

Doern, G. Bruce and Glen Toner. *The Politics of Energy: The Development and Implementation of the NEP.* Toronto: Methuen, 1985.

Eglington, P. and M. Uffelmann. *An Economic Analysis of Oilsands Policy in Canada— the Case of Alsands and Wolf Lake.* Ottawa: Economic Council of Canada, 1984.

Gibson, J.D. "The Flow of Policy Ideas Between Business and Government" as in D.C. Smith, ed. *Economic Policy Advising in Canada.* Montreal: C.D. Howe Institute, 1981, 105-120.

Gillies, J. *Facing Reality: Consultation, Consensus and Making Economic Policy for the 21st Century.* Montreal: Institute for Research on Public Policy, 1986.

McLaren, Roy. *How To Improve Business-Government Relations in Canada: Report of the Task Force on Business-Government Interface.* Ottawa: Queen's Printer, 1976.

Murray, V.V., ed. *The Consultative Process in Business-Government Relations.* Toronto: The Max Bell Business-Government Studies Program, York University, 1987.

Pratt, Larry. *The Tar Sands: Syncrude and the Politics of Oil.* Edmonton: Hurtig, 1976.

Rugman, A.M. and A. Anderson. "Business and Trade Policy: The Structure of Canada's New Private Sector Advising System." *Canadian Journal of Administrative Sciences*, Vol. 4, no. 4 (December 1987), 367-380.

V CHALLENGES FOR BUSINESS AND GOVERNMENT IN THE 1990s

If the Meech Lake Accord is about the political future of Canada, then industrial strategy is about the economic future of Canada. To meet the challenge of developing a national economic strategy that will secure a place of leadership for this country in the new evolving world order, while safeguarding the integrity of Canada's natural environment, business and government need to work together as partners. Effectively managing business-government relations in the 1990s is a national strategic imperative. To do this requires understanding, awareness, honesty, trust, and above all, political will.

THE QUEST FOR AN INDUSTRIAL STRATEGY

Come, my friends, 'Tis not too late to seek a newer world

Lord Alfred Tennyson, 1809–1892

As the Japanese realized over twenty years ago, the key to a successful economic future is productivity. Canada can improve its productivity by effectively combining and integrating technology, capital, labour, management skills, and education. It must increase its expenditures on research and development, loosen the reins on its ultra-conservative, risk-averse banking community, include labour in the national policy agenda, improve its management expertise, and instill in the educational system a new sense of pride, a commitment to quality, and a heightened degree of competitiveness.

In short, *Canada needs an industrial strategy—a coherent and consistent set of policies implemented by government and designed to increase the performance of the economy.* This will be the greatest career challenge to the managers of the 1990s. To be effective, however, such a group of policies should be developed by all the major stakeholders as partners.

Industrial strategies are used to correct imbalances in an economy's performance. They implicitly offer government an interventionist role, but not necessarily in a planning capacity. Nor do such strategies focus on the secondary manufacturing sector alone, but on primary resource and tertiary service sectors, as well. An industrial strategy allows the nation to capitalize on opportunities and strengths. It is designed to achieve effective competitiveness, success in the global marketplace, and long-term survival.

An international trade policy would be only one policy in an overall industrial strategy. As seen earlier, trade is an important part of the Canadian economy. About half of all economic activity in this country depends upon trade. For the past decade, exports and imports have each averaged 30% of the GNP.

Such a trade policy would also capitalize on the country's competitive advantage(s)—those goods and services that can be produced at less cost than in other countries. Thus, economies of scale and related gains would be introduced into production.

Of course, this Ricardian model of trade is over-simplistic. The costs associated with coaxing and re-training workers from one industry to another to increase competitive advantages may be substantial. However, these costs and the policies needed to make re-training practical are also part of a comprehensive industrial strategy.

An emphasis on product-specific, plant-level economies of scale will ultimately lead to a rationalization of assets within an industry. This will increase economic concentration and decrease internal competition. The costs and unemployment associated with this idea also must be considered. Given Canada's pluralist, democratic institutions, employment and its opposite will be both a reason for and a consequence of an industrial strategy.

Creating and implementing an industrial strategy for Canada is the greatest challenge to business and government. Nothing demands greater co-operation than forging a competitive economic strategy for the entire nation. The Canadian economy, although more buoyant than that of most other G-7 nations, has performed far below its potential for almost two decades. Part of the problem is cyclical; certainly, the 1980s have been more favourable than the 1970s. As described in Chapter 1, however, significant structural shifts have occurred in the world economy which make past tactics outdated. Today, Britain is one of the poorer nations in the European Economic Community; Korea is no longer a sleepy agricultural and fishing nation. How can Canada escape being tossed upon the scrap heap of economic history?

THE NATIONAL POLICY—110 YEARS

Although debate about an industrial strategy is recent, economic planning and industrial policies are hardly new to the Canadian political economy. Sir John A. Macdonald's 1879 National Policy was an industrial strategy; it was a collection of measures to stimulate economic growth. The building of a transcontinental railroad, encouraging immigrant settlement of the west, and protecting Canadian industry with a tariff barrier were all designed to boost the economy's performance. It was hoped that a secondary manufacturing sector would develop in Ontario, the markets for which would be the Maritimes, the rest of central Canada, and the growing agriculturally based prairie economy. Canada could be an economically self-sufficient, sovereign entity—or so it was planned by both business and government. Of course, the consequences of being an economic island are clear 110 years later—Canada has a tertiary sector-based economy, with a foreign-owned secondary sector and habitual reliance upon natural resources.

Ironically, tariff and non-tariff barriers did not create high levels of economic concentration across the board, as was predicted. Some industries show a direct correlation between protection and concentration; others have demonstrated the opposite effect (see Figure 12-1).

One unarguable benefit that emerged from the National Policy was the

Figure 12-1 Trade Barriers and Concentration Ratios Selected Industries, 1970

Industry	Nominal Tariffs	Non-Tariff Barriers (expressed as Tariff Equivalents)			Total Protection	Concentration Ratio (CR$_4$)
		Quota Restrictions	Subsidies	Tax Concessions		
Tobacco products	24.04				24.04	97
Motor vehicles	2.95		6.13		9.08	93
Cotton textiles	15.48	25.81			41.29	93
Petroleum and coal products	7.63				7.63	79
Iron mining	0.01		1.28	8.15	9.44	77
Primary metal manufacturing	4.13				4.13	75
Aircraft and parts	0.02				0.02	72
Ship building	9.44		17.00		26.44	62
Electrical equipment	13.71				13.71	60
Nonmetallic mineral products	7.44				7.44	60
Rubber products	14.88				14.88	53
Chemical products	9.21				9.21	50
Food and beverages	10.00	2.53	1.66		14.19	47
Vehicle parts manufacturing	0.88				0.88	46
Paper products	9.12				9.12	38
Leather products	19.59				19.59	35
Machinery	6.08				6.08	32
Metal fabricating	12.17				12.17	31
Dairy products	16.92	14.84	9.75		41.51	29
Wood products	3.80				3.80	28
Knitting mills	24.14	1.07			25.21	27
Printing and publishing	5.65				5.65	26
Gravel and aggregates	0.48			3.18	3.66	22
Furniture	17.20				17.20	18
Clothing	27.01	4.08			26.09	14

stimulation of east-west economic, political, and social activity. The National Policy accomplished its main goal—it built a nation!

The National Policy, in "protecting" Canadian industry, also led to the easy formation of cartels, oligopolies, and even monopolies. By the late 1880s, the exploitation of monopoly power had become a political issue. In response, the Canadian Parliament passed its first anti-combines or competition policy in 1889 as part of the Criminal Code.

This policy sought to codify existing English common law on the subject, which had thus far been fairly ineffective. The Act was strewn with adjectives such as "unlawfully," "unduly," and "unreasonably," which meant that there was to be a *lawful* degree of collusion, that there was an *acceptable* level of aggregation, and that there was a *reasonable* level for price-fixing. (Services were excluded.)

As a result, Canadian law became a matter for judicial interpretation, not administrative practice. Although penalties under the Criminal Code are generally greater than under the Civil Code, the costs of prosecution and the burden of proof under the Criminal Code are far greater. This makes it very difficult to enforce an act as vague as the Anti-Combines Act. Canada's policy was actually a non-policy—a toothless paper tiger.

It was not until 1986 that some parts of the Anti-Combines Act were removed from the Criminal Code and placed under the Civil Code. A Competition Tribunal was also established to handle such matters. The Director of the Bureau of Competition Policy of Consumer and Corporate Affairs Canada can now investigate conspiracies to lessen competition, mergers and acquisitions, predatory pricing, price discrimination, price-fixing, and misleading advertising and marketing practices. Banks, services, and Crown corporations are also included. The actual strength of the Act remains to be tested.

The obvious purposes of a competition policy are to reduce the inefficiencies of economic concentration and monopoly power, and to guarantee fair play in the marketplace. *Historically, Canada's National Policy has never contained an effective competitive policy.* Aggregate and industrial concentration were considered necessary evils by government, and a desirable state of affairs by business.

However, just when further rationalization of assets appears to be inherent in an effective industrial strategy, Canada is embarking upon a more serious attempt to stimulate competition within the economy. Should guaranteeing internal competition take precedence over being globally competitive? Should individual equity come before national economic survival? What is in the public interest here?

After the Great Depression of 1930, the National Policy was complemented by interventionist government monetary and fiscal policies. Keynesian economics took hold in Canada like nowhere else in the world!

Policies designed to stabilize or even control interest rates, inflation rates, liquidity levels, and unemployment rates have a major impact upon business' working environment. In effect, Keynesian macroeconomic policies are an attempt to stabilize the aggregate level of business activity. Monetary policies are used by the Bank of Canada to control the supply of dollars, market liquidity, investment and savings levels, and credit. Fiscal policies are represented by the annual and accumulated government budget surplus and/or deficit. If government chooses to have a "deficit budget," it must make ends meet by either borrowing or by printing money. If the latter, fiscal policies may influence monetary policies.

Stabilization policy is an adjunct to other government policies which address market failures, market inefficiencies, and market equity or fairness. Macroeconomic policy is really designed to address the net effect of cumulative microeconomic market problems. Keynesian policies have been used with varying degrees of success for fifty years to simultaneously create jobs, control inflation, and stimulate economic growth. But will they address the considerable structural problems which business and government must overcome, in order for Canada to compete in tomorrow's world markets?

Keynes' policies were originally a response to cyclical economic problems. When unemployment was high, government increased its spending. When inflation was high, government increased taxes. Keynesian economics affected demand. Industrial strategists recognize that Canada's problems today are centred more on the costs of production and supply, rather than on demand. The governments of Prime Minister Thatcher in the United Kingdom and President Reagan in the United States recognized this fact, and attempted to boost the supply side of the economy, again with varying degrees of success.

When Keynesian economic policies have failed, it is generally for one of three reasons. First, John Maynard Keynes was an aristocrat. He never understood that workers would demand more money than allotted them; that demand management inherently had potential for fuelling inflation. Second, Keynes believed that the United Kingdom's rising unemployment during the 1920s was the result of its stubborn allegiance to the gold standard. When Britain went off the gold standard in 1931, unemployment continued to rise. Third, Keynes urged government to increase its spending in bad times and borrow to finance part of it, and to bank its surpluses in good times for future borrowing needs. Of course, in times of surplus, governments have spent it and continued to increase spending when Keynes would have prescribed cutbacks. During a protracted period of borrowing, such as the last ten years or so, interest rates have risen, unemployment is high, and inflation has still not been "wrestled to the ground."

Therefore, Canada's industrial strategy over the past fifty years—although never intentionally conceived, developed, and implemented as such—has been a combination of tariffs, neo-laissez-faire market practices, and Keynesian-style voodoo economics. The mix has served Canada well:

it created a nation against all odds, raised it to be a middle economy and industrial power by the 1940s, and elevated it to membership in the G-7 by the 1970s. *Business and government co-operated as partners, mutually recognizing common goals.* Then things began to change.

REGIONAL ECONOMIC DEVELOPMENT[54]

Regional economic disparity has been a public policy issue in Canada since Confederation. It is most often illustrated by comparing provincial income per capita and unemployment figures with the national average. Disparities place a strain on national unity and create feelings of inequity in the less developed regions. Every federal government has, in its own way, tried to close the gap between "have-not" provinces and "have" provinces, rather than concentrating on lessening the gap between existing and potential economic development for each region.

Ontario and British Columbia have historically experienced per-capita incomes above the national average, whereas the Atlantic provinces and Quebec are generally lower. Ontario and British Columbia are thus "have" provinces, while Quebec and the Atlantic provinces are "have-nots." Throughout the 1980s, the *disparity gap* (the ratio of the highest provincial income per capita to the lowest) hovered around 1.5.

However, per-capita income statistics are somewhat misleading; they include net gains from inter-regional transfer payments. *Earned income per capita* provides a more accurate measure of a region's economic performance, since it excludes net gains from inter-regional transfer payments. This, however, only amplifies regional income disparities and raises the disparity gap to over two.

Using the second criterion for economic well-being, unemployment rates greater than the national average exist in the Atlantic provinces, Quebec, and British Columbia. Less unemployment is characteristic of Ontario and the Prairies. In 1987, for instance, unemployment in Cape Breton rose to 21%, whereas the unemployment rate in Metropolitan Toronto was only 3.2%. This is approximately the rate economists use today to represent *full employment*, taking into account those who are in transition. In both cases, disparity or well-being are measured against the national average.

What causes regional economic disparity in Canada? One explanation lies in a history of depending upon local staples for income. Regional economies have seen fluctuating demand for their respective staples: Nova Scotia with its fishing industry, and New Brunswick and its forests. The more stable regions have become those with a developed secondary manufacturing sector, such as Ontario.

Unlike Ontario, Atlantic Canada was unable to diversify and develop a

---

[54] Much of the material in this section was contained in an earlier paper written by Beth Arnold and adapted by the author.

substantial manufacturing sector, due to small regional demand and un-competitive transportation costs to larger markets. This has led to an historically low level of investment and technological change, and a high level of seasonal development in the Atlantic region. Since per-capita income directly affects gross tax revenues, provincial government per-capita expenditures on health, education, social services, transportation, and economic development have been much lower in the Maritimes.

However, staples have had the exact opposite effect in the West. The western provinces have experienced significant economic growth, due to their dependence upon resources and related products: wheat in the Pra-iries, oil in Alberta, and minerals, coal, natural gas, hydroelectric power, and timber in British Columbia. Increasing world demand for these staples and ease of exploitation with improved technology have made the West relatively prosperous. However, while British Columbia's well-diver-sified primary sector has created a high per-capita average income, this dependence upon natural resources has also resulted in seasonal fluctua-tions in employment as great as anywhere in Canada.

As mentioned earlier, Ontario has dominated the tariff-protected manufacturing sector in Canada. In particular, industrial development has centred around southwestern Ontario. As a result, Ontario has the greatest total output (40% of Canada's GDP/GNP in 1987) and income per capita of all the regions of Canada.

In fact, if Ontario were a nation instead of a province, it would have the eleventh-strongest economy on earth!

The government has, as far back as 1879, aimed at stimulating regional economic growth by providing tariffs on imported manufactured goods. This allows resources to be indirectly transferred from export industries (thus increasing costs and decreasing their output) to the protected, im-port-competing sector. This slows the growth rate of export trade and enhances that of the protected industry. Unfortunately, the traditional "have-not" provinces of Nova Scotia and New Brunswick relied most upon export industries for economic growth.

With the election of Pierre Elliott Trudeau in 1968 came radical changes in regional economic policy. Liberal Prime Minister Trudeau strongly believed that Canada was threatened by decentralization and the provinces' increasing political power, due to their enhanced roles in natural resources and social welfare programs. To centralize control over economic policies, Trudeau created the Department of Regional Eco-nomic Expansion (DREE) in 1969.

DREE's first policy was inspired by the *growth pole concept*. This argued that economic activity concentrated around certain focal points, or *growth poles*. By strengthening industry in these urban focal points in slow-growth regions, a process of self-sustaining and radiating economic growth was expected.

DREE also implemented the Regional Development Industrial

Assistance program (RDIA). This provided special industrial assistance to depressed areas which could sustain economic growth. In 1970, RDIA was expanded to include loan guarantees for manufacturing and processing facilities. Unfortunately, the program could not persuade the industries it assisted to relocate to the slow-growth regions.

In fact, between 1969 and 1975, designated growth poles within the entire Atlantic region received a smaller percentage of new manufacturing jobs than did other communities. The main factor behind this was the growing political turmoil in Quebec, which led Ottawa to intensify its efforts and resources to pre-empt the separatist movement.

A new, multi-dimensional approach to regional development appeared in 1973 under the title of General Development Agreement (GDA). The federal government, in co-operation with the provinces, would define the unique development opportunities in each province and develop a set of programs for them. These GDAs were funded up to ninety percent by the federal government, with the provinces paying the remainder. These agreements restored much of the provinces' initiative for regional economic policy. *Regional development policy had become provincial development policy.*

In the late 1970s, the federal government believed it was losing control over GDA programs. It suspected that the provincial governments were receiving most of the political credit, even though the federal government was providing most of the funds. Ottawa wanted credit for its expenditures, and the last GDAs were allowed to lapse in 1984. The role of the provinces in regional economic development was once again downplayed.

In 1979, the Ministry of State for Economic Development (MSED) was created to achieve even greater federal policy control and co-ordination. Economic development efforts were now given a sectoral focus, based on resource sector megaprojects and the resource exports of all regions. This, it was argued, would stimulate the building of both an economic infrastructure and the manufacturing sector. MSED's task was to implement this sectoral development policy. The status of DREE was diminished.

In 1981, the Industrial and Labour Adjustment Program (ILAP) was created for urban areas hardest hit by industrial change initiated by changing world economies and more liberalized trade. Communities eligible for ILAP were chosen on the basis of need. This was measured by the number of layoffs within an industry, regardless of whether they were recent or chronic, structural or cyclical. Incentive grants for relocation, higher training, and skills upgrading also were made available. Over 80% of ILAP spending went to Ontario communities, since that is where most of the industrial sector can be found.

Another initiative of the early 1980s was the Adjustment Assistance Benefit Program. Ottawa sought to revitalize the economies of those communities most vulnerable to foreign competition in the textile and clothing industry. Most of this industry was centred in Quebec and Ontario.

In 1982, DREE was disbanded. The following year, the Department of Regional Industrial Expansion (DRIE) was formed by amalgamating DREE's regional programs with the industry, small business, and tourism components of the Department of Industry, Trade and Commerce. DRIE was to focus exclusively on *national* industrial and commercial concerns, while *regional* development planning and policy became the responsibility of the Ministry of State for Economic and Regional Development (MSERD), a revised version of MSED with regional offices in each province. Regional development policy was no longer the responsibility of a line department. Regional development policy-making had now risen to the Cabinet Committee level. Regionally specific policy proposals known as Economic and Regional Development Agreements (ERDA) replaced the former GDAs in 1984.

DRIE created the Industrial and Regional Development Program (IRDP), one of whose characteristics was an index that established which census districts were eligible for assistance. Three factors were used to calculate a census district's need: its unemployment rate; its level of income per capita; and the fiscal capacity of the province in which the district was located. Financial aid would cover up to 60% of the cost of putting new plants in the census districts of greatest need.

The Economic Council of Canada has advocated for some time that regional economic development in Canada be based upon the principle of *comparative advantage*. Each region would produce what it was most able to, and trade for products and services it did not produce. This would combine both the sectoral and regional approaches to economic development. In 1987, the Progressive Conservative government created three regional agencies. Each was charged to respond to local needs and opportunities. These were the Northern Ontario Advisory Board, the Atlantic Canada Opportunities Agency, and the Western Economic Diversification Strategy (now known as the Department of Western Economic Development).

The Atlantic Canada Opportunities Agency (ACOA), the organization responsible for the economic development of Atlantic Canada, has been allocated $1.05 billion between 1987 and 1992. It is responsible for all federal programs targeted for small and medium-sized businesses in the region, and co-ordinates federal economic development activities in the region.

The purpose of the Department of Western Economic Development (DWED) is to better equip western Canada to compete in the growing global economy, since 14% and 60% respectively of its exports go to the United States and the Pacific Rim. Targeted areas for growth and diversification include agriculture, electronics, computer software, oil and gas equipment, clothing, agricultural machinery, and transportation equipment. The main requirement for eligibility for federal support is that a proposal builds upon one of the West's existing competitive advantages.

Throughout Canadian history, the federal government has financed most of the country's development. It has used numerous forms of transfer payments, such as federal-provincial shared cost agreements, income transfer payments in the form of welfare and unemployment insurance, regional economic expansion grants to needy businesses, and provincial equalization payments. On a per-capita basis, the "have-not" provinces have received up to four times the amount that "have" provinces have received.

Federal transfers to individuals, designed to improve individual living standards and thus contribute to regional development, are much higher in slow-growth regions than in the more developed areas. However, they tend to restrict worker mobility. This can alter labour supply conditions, create inefficient production and distribution of goods and services, retard indigenous regional growth, and create an increasing dependency on federal funding. This situation produces a "catch-22" for the federal government.

Without a change in the present system of individual transfer payments, regional disparity will continue to exist. Without improvement in regional disparities across Canada, the federal government to date has not and probably will not alter individual transfer payment programs.

Regional economic expansion grants, created to give business an incentive to locate or expand in certain regions, are still the cornerstone of the Canadian government's involvement in regional development. This policy's underlying aim has been to create employment and reduce the regional dependency upon transfer payments. In the past, however, the federal government distributed location incentives using a "shotgun" approach. Any manufacturer was encouraged to enter a slow-growth region if it meant creating new jobs. Little consideration was given to selecting industries with the best chance of long-term survival. Most have failed.

Equalization payments were a way of compensating for the regional variation in revenue for provincial taxation purposes. They account for approximately 25% of provincial revenue in the Atlantic region, and about 10% in Quebec and Manitoba. Every Canadian province except Ontario has at one time received equalization payments.

Yet, despite all these federally sponsored policies over the past century, regional economic disparity still exists in this country.

Along with the National Policy of tariffs and Keynesian macroeconomic policies, regional economic development policies have played a big part in government's attempt to stimulate and focus economic activity. Through various assistance programs, the federal government has sought to encourage industrial development and reduce regional disparities. *More often than not, however, regional development initiatives have contradicted the very essence of protectionist policies and stabilization policies.* In that sense, collectively they have not been an effective industrial strategy for Canada during the 1970s and 1980s.

PICKING WINNERS—A FALSE START

Much of the current interest in industrial strategy has been initiated by changing multilateral trading relations in the international trading arena. The Canadian government has been fairly active in developing international agreements and institutions, such as the General Agreement on Tariffs and Trade. GATT has sought to reduce barriers to trade (except in agriculture and textiles) and to facilitate a much more liberal, non-discriminatory trading environment. GATT, which regulates approximately 80% of world trade, has intensified the competition for domestic manufacturing industries by easing access for imports. At the same time, it offers them an opportunity to increase their output by exporting to other nations. Some Canadian companies have risen to the challenge and succeeded; some have failed; others have cowered at the prospect.

Trade liberalization implies a re-structuring of Canadian industry in order to remain competitive. Over the past thirty years, the federal government has complied with GATT requirements to reduce tariffs, and has sought to assist business through the transition. In 1963, the Department of Industry was created to help Canadian firms improve their productivity. When it merged with the Department of Trade and Commerce in 1969 to form the Department of Industry, Trade and Commerce, the government also introduced a number of industrial assistance programs. These were designed to encourage investment, improve firms' marketing capabilities, increase corporate spending on research and development, decrease foreign ownership of Canadian industries, and help industry meet foreign competition through agencies such as the Export Development Corporation. All of this came from a Prime Minister whom business leaders had publicly branded a "communist." Unfortunately, there was little coordination, little synergy among programs, and no strategy behind them.

The one exception was the Canada-United States Automotive Products Agreement, 1965: the Auto Pact. This was an industry-specific set of goals, policies, and tactics within a single agreement, with a deliberate strategic focus. In effect, the Auto Pact provided for free trade within a specific subsector of the economy and was exempted from GATT. The major U.S.-owned automobile manufacturers were allowed to import and export cars and parts duty free between Canada and the United States, provided that specified production levels were maintained in each country. As a result, Canada—and particularly Ontario and Quebec—now boasts a healthy auto-parts industry and North American production mandates for several types of automobiles.

Initially, the U.S. was the trade winner in the auto industry. But during the 1980s, the balance of trade in Auto Pact industries became more favourable to Canada. In fact, Auto Pact trade has greatly contributed to the positive balance in the Canada-U.S. goods trade account. *The auto and auto-parts industries became growth industries for Canada because a positive business-government relationship emerged while developing an industry-specific strategy.*

After his first election as Prime Minister in 1968, Pierre Trudeau demanded that Canada develop an industrial strategy. For the next five years, some of the best economic talent in the country worked in the Privy Council Office and the Prime Minister's Office trying to do just that. They failed. During the following five years, the federal government embarked upon the most extensive consultation process ever attempted, to solicit the input of both business and labour in developing a comprehensive industrial strategy. This process, known informally as *Tier I/Tier II* because of its national and sectoral focuses, also failed. The consultative process itself was a huge success, as perceived by both business and government. However, no strategy was developed. Government dropped the ball, and the various government players could not agree as to the best strategy to be used.

In 1972, the Science Council of Canada issued a report calling for an industrial strategy based upon technology. The Council subscribed to the notion that technology redefines markets; it destroys old monopolies and oligopolies, creates new market products and businesses, and is the major change agent in our economy. It recognized that firms in Canada generally lacked any technological depth and performed little innovative, applicable research and development. The Science Council's strategy was designed to support those industries that would receive a technological payoff from government assistance. Some of these included telecommunications, space, fibre optics, computer software, biomedicine, urban transportation, and energy.

In 1974, the aerospace industry was singled out as a potential winner for Canada. However, instead of sectoral free trade with the United States, the federal government stimulated this industry with investment grants, as well as grants for research and development. The government also "nationalized" two of the country's leading airplane manufacturers — Canadair of Montreal and deHavilland Aircraft of Toronto. It hoped to turn them around financially, gain for them a respectable place in the world market, and then return them to the private sector. Such hopes have not been met.

In 1980, the fourth government of Pierre Trudeau decided that the energy sector of Canada held great potential for the economy. Abandoning normal consultation with business, it promulgated almost overnight the National Energy Program (NEP). Its basic thrust was to promote Canadian ownership of the industry — both public and private — and to develop frontier resources. It was short-lived primarily because of U.S. industry and government objections and threats; it did, however, reduce

U.S. ownership of the industry. The NEP also greatly increased Canadian government ownership of the industry through its primary agent, Petro-Canada.

By 1981, the NEP had evolved into a White Paper entitled *Economic Development for Canada in the 1980s*. This was Canada's first attempt at a formalized industrial strategy. Prime Minister Trudeau sought to "ensure that the federal government is an active player in industrial development, rather than just a passive referee." The paper assumed that natural resource development in both western and eastern Canada would provide direction for future economic growth. It was also to create an impetus for increased industrial development in central Canada and diversification in the East and West. The White Paper was heavily layered with technological implications. It contained Howe's concept of "megaprojects," primarily in the energy sector, and was co-founded on the Science Council's thrust towards a technology-based strategy.

Resources were to be both extracted and processed in Canada, and not exported in a raw state. High-technology industries would also be encouraged, once the government saw what companies such as Northern Telecom and Spar Aerospace could achieve with government assistance.

Unfortunately, enthusiasm dissipated when energy prices collapsed during the 1981-82 recession. Most of the megaprojects never saw the light of day. By then the government had become newly preoccupied with the Constitution. The Liberals gave up, believing that a comprehensive industrial strategy was beyond reach. Their ambitious plans, which even included public enterprise initiatives to do for manufacturing what the NEP and Petro-Canada had done for energy, were scrapped. The government even gave up trying to pick individual winners.

By 1983, the government of Brian Mulroney, void of any strategic concepts, initiated the Enterprise Development Program (EDP). This fund was designated to assist manufacturing and processing firms at any stage of their life cycles. Not surprisingly, applications for assistance far outweighed the funds allocated to the program. As a result, the EDP became little more than a lender of last resort for firms which were losers in industries designated as winners.

Then, in 1984, Prime Minister Mulroney began setting the stage for the most dramatic shift in Canadian industrial policy since the days of Sir John A. Macdonald. He reversed the mandate of the Foreign Investment Review Agency (FIRA). No longer did it closely scrutinize foreign ventures. Now, it was encouraging and assisting foreigners to invest in Canada. To signal this change, Mulroney changed FIRA's ominous-sounding name to a more positive, proactive moniker: Investment Canada. Within two years, Canada's deficit in foreign direct investment rose by nearly $10 billion to a level of $43 billion—the first significant change in almost a decade!

In 1985, Prime Minister Mulroney disassembled the 1980 NEP. It had effectively held down the FDI deficit by encouraging patriation of Canadian oil and gas assets.

For what was he setting the stage?

THE CANADA-U.S. FREE TRADE AGREEMENT

On January 1, 1989 Canada entered a new age. After resisting the gravitational pull to the south for 125 years—ever since the first talks about Confederation were held in Charlottetown in 1864—Canada formed a continental marketplace with the United States. Free trade was finally here. More than signalling a bold new initiative in industrial and trade policy, it indicated that Canada had come of age. Canadians were secure in their identity; they no longer felt threatened by the giant on their doorstep.

Sir John A. Macdonald, a Conservative, had opposed free trade and was elected on that premise. Sir Wilfred Laurier, a Liberal, had favoured free trade, boasting that it would give the twentieth century to Canada; he was defeated, and the century went to the United States. Brian Mulroney, a Conservative, spoke out against free trade a number of times between 1979 and 1983 before he became Prime Minister. Once, paraphrasing Macdonald, Mulroney said: "Free trade is nothing but veiled treason. I have never been, am not and never will be in favour of free trade and the selling of Canada to the United States."

By 1985, the now Prime Minister was listening to the advice of the Economic Council of Canada: "Economics, geography, common sense and national interest dictate that we try to secure and expand our trade with (the U.S.)." In October, 1987 the Canada-U.S. Free Trade Agreement was accepted in principle with these words from Prime Minister Mulroney: "This is a good deal; good for Canada; and good for all Canadians . . ." He went on to win the 1988 general federal election with a resounding mandate for free trade.

The arguments for and against free trade have changed very little over the last century. Proponents of free trade envision accelerated growth; opponents fear loss of cultural identity and sovereignty. In reality, an increase of duty-free trade of 5% will not likely precipitate either.

The Economic Council of Canada was instrumental in making free trade a reality. But back in the 1970s, it advocated "looking outwards." Canada was to increase trade with Europe and the Pacific Rim, and lessen its dependence upon the falling star of the United States. However, by the 1980s, the ECC was promoting free trade with the U.S., as was the Royal Commission on the Economic Union and Development Prospects for Canada.

Proponents of free trade did not see the choice being between free trade and the status quo, but between free trade and increased U.S. protectionism. This view was supported in 1986 when the U.S. placed a 22% across-the-board tariff on all imports. By 1990, India and China would be net exporters of food; the U.S. would no longer be the "breadbasket of the world." It was also recognized that Japan, despite its phenomenal economic growth, only used 60% of the imported raw materials in 1984 that it did in 1973. The United States was becoming a barricaded island.

Canada *had* to do something. Above all, it was still a trading nation, although its share had dropped from 4.9% to 3.4% in the 100 years prior to free trade. Canada had become a high-cost exporter of products, for which the demand was declining and the world's supply was increasing.

For example, nearly 30% of Canada's exports are based in the auto industry. Considering that auto exports declined 3% in 1987, the nation's overall export gain of 4.3% was actually impressive. Export sales of wheat tumbled 25%, from $3.6 billion in 1985 to $2.7 billion in 1987. On the other hand, forestry exports rose 20%; oil exports climbed 10%; mining exports increased 4%. Of Canada's top 50 exporting firms, 38 sold more products overseas in 1987 than in 1986, and 12 sold fewer. However, only eleven of these were in manufacturing. Canada's trade strength remained in non-renewable resources.

Both sides entered into the agreement fully aware that zones of free trade within the world were becoming a trend. The European Economic Community will fulfill its dream in 1992 with economic unification and total free trade among its members. Figure 12-2 identifies those trading areas within the world which enjoy a free trade environment.

The legacy of 110 years of tariffs averaging 20% is pervasive. In 1988, Canadian tariffs on U.S. imports averaged 6.1%, while United States duties on Canadian exports averaged 4.7%. Company profits have been inflated at the cost of 12-15% less efficiency than their American counterparts. Some industries have become heavily concentrated; many are foreign-owned or controlled. Wages have been inflated. Technology-based productivity is 25-30% lower than in the U.S., while labour productivity is higher. Canada's specialization is low, as is its level of world competitiveness. Over 50% of plants in Canada are smaller than the economically determined *minimum efficient scale*,[55] as opposed to only 20% in the U.S. Tariffs have also provoked retaliation from time to time by other countries.

Theoretically, free trade with the United States will boost Canada's volume of exports, thus increasing production and related employment, if mainly in primary resources. Where Canada does export manufactured goods, it will increase its competitiveness as a result of the economies of scale inherent in longer production runs. More raw materials will be imported and more finished products exported. Consumer prices will drop if cost savings are passed on by industry.[56]

---

[55] The smallest size of plant that can benefit from all possible economies of scale.
[56] Many advocates of free trade believe this will occur with increased consumer selection for most durable goods, as greater numbers of imports are allowed into the country, thus stimulating competition for the buyer's dollar.

Figure 12-2

REGIONAL FREE TRADE AND COMMON MARKET GROUPINGS

1. European Community
   Belgium
   Denmark
   France
   Greece
   Ireland
   Italy
   Luxembourg
   Netherlands
   Portugal
   Spain
   United Kingdom
   West Germany

2. Economic Community of West African States
   Benin
   Burkina Faso
   Gambia
   Ghana
   Guinea
   Guinea-Bissau
   Ivory Coast
   Liberia
   Mali
   Mauritania
   Niger
   Nigeria
   Senegal
   Sierra Leone
   Togo

3. Customs and Economic Union of Central Africa
   Cameroon
   Gabon
   Guinea

4. U.S.-Mexico Pact (being negotiated)
   Mexico
   United States

5. European Free Trade Area
   Austria
   Finland
   Iceland
   Norway
   Sweden
   Switzerland

6. Association for the Integration of Latin America
   Argentina
   Bolivia
   Brazil
   Chile
   Ecuador
   Mexico
   Paraguay
   Peru
   Uruguay
   Venezuela

7. Central American Common Market
   Costa Rica
   El Salvador
   Guatemala
   Honduras
   Nicaragua

8. Lake Chad Basin Commission
   Cameroon
   Chad
   Niger
   Nigeria

9. U.S.-Israel Pact
   Israel
   United States

10. Closer Economic Relationship
    Australia
    New Zealand

11. Caribbean Community
    Antigua
    Barbados
    Belize
    Dominica
    Grenada
    Guyana
    Jamaica
    Montserrat
    St. Kitts-Nevis-Anguilla
    St. Lucia
    St. Vincent
    Trinidad and Tobago

12. Andean Pact
    Bolivia
    Chile
    Columbia
    Ecuador
    Peru
    Venezuela

13. South African Customs Union
    Botswana
    Lesotho
    South Africa
    Swaziland

14. West African Economic Community
    Burkina Faso
    Ivory Coast
    Mali
    Mauritania
    Niger
    Senegal

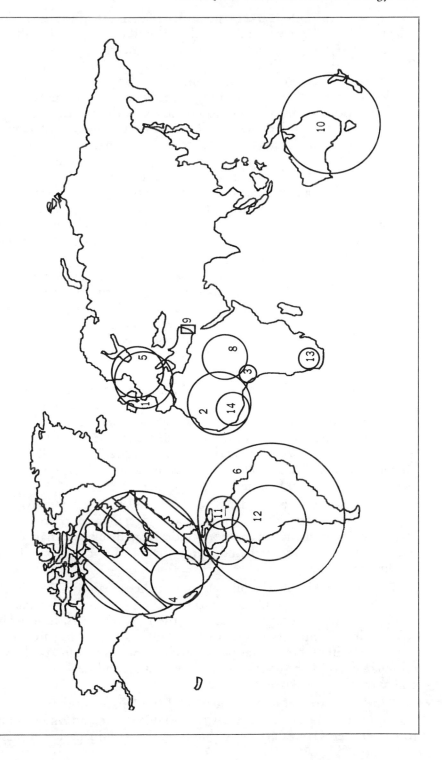

Access to the U.S. market—presently the largest consumer and industrial market in the world at 250 million—will be secured. It will soon be overshadowed by the eventual economic unification of much of Europe. This will add 350 million buyers, further stabilizing Canada's economy and increasing investment opportunities for both domestic and foreign funds. Inevitably, there will be mergers, acquisitions, consolidations, and a general rationalizing of assets to effectively utilize industrial capacity. Finally, free trade with the U.S. will encourage the removal of many of the interprovincial barriers to trade. These were originally erected to preserve jobs in the more disparate, peripheral regions of the country. This will create more centralized industry, as well as economies of scale, lower consumer prices, and increase consumer selection. In the short term, sunset industries will close, creating job losses; in the long term, surviving industries will flourish, creating more employment. For government, lower consumer prices will have the same effect as a tax cut without reducing government revenue.

However, free trade has its costs. The Canada-United States free trade deal by itself will not boost economic growth measurably in Canada. Although Canadian industry will save the $1.1 billion paid in U.S. tariffs in 1987, the Conference Board of Canada expects that the business community will have to invest at least $4.4 billion over the next ten years. Only thus can this country improve technological productivity in order to face greater competition.

Furthermore, by eliminating tariffs, the federal government will forfeit $3 billion in revenue over the ten year phase-in period. It is unlikely that these tariff cuts will be completely offset by federal tax revenue gained from a faster-growing economy. As a result, the federal deficit will rise to $40.9 billion by 1997 instead of the pre-free trade forecast of $36.6 billion. Reducing this additional debt by increasing taxes will negate many of the benefits arising from free trade.

What exactly is free trade? The Canada-U.S. Free Trade Agreement represents the most comprehensive trade agreement ever concluded between two nations. It covers more trade-related subjects than any other economic treaty, and is based upon the GATT criterion of *mutual advantage*.

Free trade is simply the phasing out of the remaining 25% tariffs and quotas on Canadian goods going to the U.S., and the 5% on American-produced goods entering Canada over the next ten years. In some industries, such as computers and whiskey, all tariffs were eliminated on January 1, 1989; in others such as paper products and furniture, tariffs will be eliminated over five years; such items as textiles and steel will have tariffs and quotas removed over ten years.

While investment regulations may differ between the two countries, they must now be applied equally to both Canadian and American investors. Ten years was chosen as the overall phase-in period to ease the adjustments and minimize the disruption free trade will inevitably bring. Investment will shift; jobs will change; technology will increase; trade with the U.S. should increase by about 5%.

The free trade agreement has other safeguards, too. A *snapback provision* allows temporary tariffs to be restored on fresh fruit and vegetables if the phase-in is too disruptive. The garment industry has been allowed some leeway with amounts of imported fabric it can use while still qualifying for duty-free status. Both countries have retained the right to impose punitive measures upon the other if the latter is found engaging in "unfair trade practices." A bilateral dispute settlement mechanism has also been created to hear and settle anti-dumping and countervailing duty cases.

The free trade agreement does *not* prevent the government of Canada from pursuing its own regional economic development policies, its financial support of research and development, its assistance to small business, or its review of foreign investment proposals. Canadian ownership of the banks is protected by provisions of the Bank Act, but competition in financial circles is expected to increase, especially for industrial and commercial loans. "Cultural industries" such as broadcasting, publishing, and the arts are excluded. Social policies such as medical insurance, pensions, and unemployment insurance are also exempt. The Auto Pact remains intact.

Is it really *free* trade? In the true sense of the phrase, no. The agreement provides for *freer* trade between Canada and the United States, but time will tell whether it is *fair* trade.

According to the Economic Council of Canada forecasts, Canada's GNP will increase in *real* terms 3.3% by 1995 under the free trade regime. Without it, the GNP would have increased 2.6%. Unemployment should drop 1.5%, a net increase of 321 000 jobs (150 000, according to the Conference Board of Canada). This is less than the margin of error in the model used to calculate this figure. With or without free trade, inflation will reach 5% by 1995, according to the ECC.

The Conference Board of Canada's projections appear in Figure 12-3. It is debatable whether free trade and its effects will actually increase Canada's industrial efficiency, productivity, or competitiveness. There is every reason to believe that any gains will be negated by what economists call *X-inefficiencies*—the dead weight loss of monopoly market power and profits inherent in an even more concentrated Canadian economy in the 1990s.

Many industries lobbied hard for free trade, anticipating greater sales as their price was reduced for U.S. buyers. In fact, five key industries of Canada's economy, accounting for half of all exports totalling $60 billion in 1986 (75% of which went to the U.S), lobbied very hard. All five industries are in the primary resource sector. The largest of these —the forest products industry, with over $16 billion worth of exports in 1986— is glad to see the end of crippling tariffs and countervailing actions.

Figure 12-3

Canada's Average Annual Forecasted Growth, 1987-1997

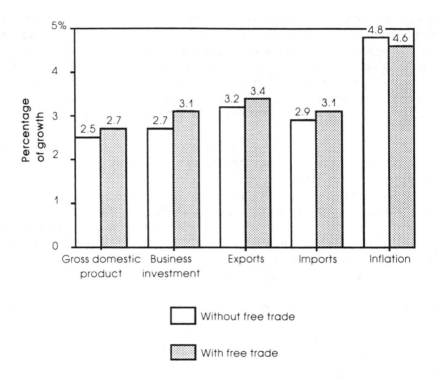

Source: Conference Board of Canada, 1988.

The oil and gas industry now becomes part of a continental energy policy, with Canadian sales expected to increase, but at the possible expense of self-direction. However, gone will be the two-tier system of pricing which placed a premium on the price of exports and subsidized the domestic price of oil. Consumers in Canada and the U.S. will both pay a new "averaged" price, which will be higher for Canadians and lower for Americans.

The Canadian mining industry is the world's largest exporter and third largest producer after the U.S. and the Soviet Union. It supported free trade as world prices for all minerals except gold continued to plummet. The same is true for farm producers, where agricultural prices, except those for livestock, have all declined. (Marketing boards will, however, remain intact in Canada.) Finally, the fishing industry—Canada's first industry—is preparing for increased demand and higher prices under free trade.

Even before 1989, over half of Canada's 75 leading corporations were preparing for a freer trading environment by slashing costs, specializing product lines, and investing in technology. This was, in retrospect, wise. Those companies hurt by free trade will probably find it difficult to borrow money from Canadian banks, since the latter will adjust the risk profiles of the former accordingly. In fact, Ontario grape growers were already denied credit in 1988, as the Ontario wine industry will no longer be protected against U.S. imports by government price discrimination. On the other hand, credit will likely become more available, at less cost, for those highly efficient, productive companies prepared to compete in the free trade arena.

Of course, industries which were highly protected by tariffs and became grossly inefficient opposed free trade and are now terrified by its prospects. For example, garment manufacturers fear losing their markets or, at the least, having to relocate to the U.S. to overcome transportation costs. Other industries with protective tariffs greater than 10% now in trouble are hosiery, shoes, leather goods, cotton textiles, natural rubber goods, consumer electrical items, and household furniture. The only Canadian shoe company welcoming free trade has been Bata Ltd., a globally rationalized multinational. It also happens to be the world's largest shoe manufacturer—but then, that's what free trade is all about — survival of the fittest!

Ontario has expressed the most concern about the vulnerability of its manufacturing sector, a large portion of which is in the inefficient, highly protected industries.[57] The Canadian Manufacturers Association concluded that those industries currently exporting and competing in overseas markets would expand; those that were not would contract, or be eliminated.

Canadian organized labour also vehemently opposed the negotiation and passage of the free trade agreement. Labour felt that Canada's industrial relations system was threatened because management would attempt to "equalize" the Canadian situation with the American.[58] This would equalize costs and improve efficiencies so as to guarantee fair trade. Labour also feared that provinces would bid for new industries and try to retain existing ones by relaxing existing labour relations legislation. Furthermore, the minimum wage could be affected. Canada's minimum wages are much higher than those in the United States; nine southern states do not even have a minimum wage.

Is the threat to labour real? First, almost all federal, provincial, and municipal government employees are unionized in Canada, whereas very

---

[57] Of all the manufacturing jobs in Ontario, 31% are in heavily protected, non-exporting businesses; another 31% in heavily protected, yet competitive industries; and only 12% in unprotected, highly successful operations.

[58] Only 17% of the American labour force is unionized, as union membership has declined over the last 20 years.

few are in the U.S. It is unlikely that these workers and their unions will be de-certified. Second, the largest non-government unions also represent Canada's least-threatened industries: automobiles, steel, oil and gas, petrochemicals, and telecommunications. These industries either welcomed free trade or will not be adversely affected by it. The likelihood of their "bashing" labour in the short term is not great.

Labour probably has a justified concern about wage increases. Economic gains from free trade will arise from lower prices induced by greater competition. For business, these lower prices will also mean narrower margins and thus lower earnings—partially reflected in lower wage gains for workers. In the beginning, wage gains will lag behind increases in consumer prices, thus marginally lowering workers' standards of living. In the long run, lower prices will moderate inflation, and gains in earnings should reflect the lower rate of inflation.

Finally, what effect will free trade have on Canada's regional economic disparities? It has been long recognized that there are more barriers to trade among the Canadian provinces than between Canada and the United States. This is an outgrowth of regional economic protectionism. Free trade with the United States will lower inter-provincial trade barriers; industry will be able to achieve minimum efficient scale to compete in the opened North American market. However, free trade will do little to reduce regional disparity since benefits from the agreement likely will be evenly distributed across the country, thus reinforcing the status quo.

The results of an ECC study (Figure 12-4) show that output and employment in all provincial economies will increase relatively evenly under the free trade agreement. British Columbia, Alberta, Newfoundland, Nova Scotia, New Brunswick, and Prince Edward Island will gain slightly more than the national average, reflecting the relative importance of their resource industries. Quebec and Ontario, as the latter feared, will benefit slightly less, since most Canadian manufacturers are located there. In fact, these two provinces will bear 90% of the adjustment costs under free trade. These statistics confirm the logic of regional economic development policies which capitalize upon regional comparative advantages, rather than the redistribution of income.

IMPLICATIONS FOR MANAGEMENT

Free trade is not an industrial strategy in and of itself, it simply changes the rules of the game with Canada's number one trading partner. Now, however, government has placed the burden of fostering economic growth squarely on the shoulders of the private sector.

A 5% increase in duty-free trade with the United States will neither propel economic growth nor jeopardize our identity or our sovereignty. It will, however, force the very restructuring of our economy. This is essential for Canada to survive in a trade-liberalized world of the twenty-first century, complete with new economic superpowers.

Figure 12-4

Growth in GDP and Employment by Province with Free Trade, 1988-1998

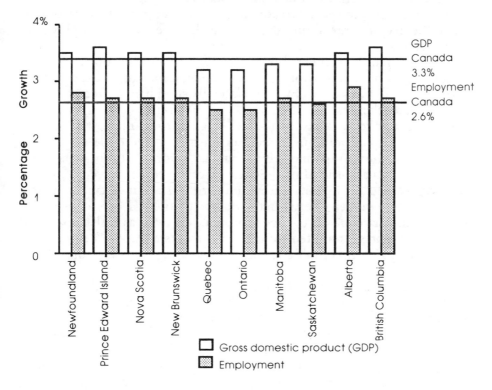

Gross domestic product (GDP)

Employment

Canada had a well-balanced economy which performed well during the late 1960s and early 1970s. Exports grew phenomenally. However, when world markets for Canadian resources and manufactured goods slowed down, Canada's relative world market share in most industries declined. Manufactured exports, commodity exports, and even high technology-based industries suffered during the 1980s. Over the last 25 years or so, growth in Canada's exports has just barely kept ahead of its growth in imports. In fact, the author's 1984 study showed that only 21% of Canada's 500 largest industrial firms exported more than 50% of their total production.

The gamble is whether free trade will allow Canadians to evolve from being "hewers of wood and drawers of water" to something more; whether it will simply make them better and more profitable hewers of wood and drawers of water; or whether it will do neither.

As yet, however, there is no coherent plan for government to continue re-distributing wealth, or to cushion the blow for those who lose their jobs, their investments, and their businesses during the turbulent phase-in period. In fact, a business-labour task force to investigate this actually recommended against such government action. It feared that this would create two classes of unemployed: those who lost their jobs due to free trade, and are thus entitled to special assistance; and those who did not, and were not entitled to special treatment. The deciding factor seemed to be the difficulty of determining causality in the free trade-unemployment scenario.[59]

The free trade agreement also changes the very foundation upon which business-government relations has been built in Canada over the centuries. No longer will Canada be able to unilaterally subsidize, protect, regulate, bail out, or otherwise assist business. As of January 1, 1989, any such government policy will be open to challenge by the United States via the bi-national dispute settlement mechanism in the free trade agreement.

This is further compounded by federal tax reform. Corporate tax rates in both Canada and the United States affect the competitive position of industry—especially manufacturing industries—since investment in these has been the most active between the trading partners. Tax reform in both countries has dramatically changed corporate tax rates, as both Canada and the United States attempted to make the tax system more neutral. *As a result, Canada's competitive edge in manufacturing has been reduced even more!*

Although tax reform in both Canada and the United States was intended to lower the nominal tax rate by reducing or ending exemptions, incentives and credits, the result has been a lower average tax rate, but a higher marginal tax rate. Canada has narrowed the gap in real tax rates primarily by changing its treatment of capital cost allowances. With corporate investment averaging 84% for equipment and 16% for plant construction, and returns on fixed investments yielding a marginal corporate tax rate, this rate has dropped from 6% favouring Canada before reform to less than 1% after reform.

The tax advantage Canadian manufacturers used to enjoy vis-a-vis their American counterparts is all but gone. This despite lower nominal rates in Canada (34.8%) than in the United States (39%). Any incentive to invest in Canadian manufacturing has been significantly reduced by recent corporate tax reforms.

Business-government relations in Canada as we have come to know them may indeed be over. As a result of free trade, business and government are entering a new era of mutual dependency. Never before have communication, co-operation, and understanding between these two institutions been more crucial to national well-being.

---

[59] This, despite the fact that the Royal Commission on the Economic Union and Development Prospects for Canada recommended free trade with the United States in 1985. It was only one part of a twenty-four-part economic plan which included various measures to lessen the blow of the transition to freer trade.

The role of organized labour in all of this cannot be overlooked. Since 1976, real wage gains have been lower than the rate of inflation. A study of 202 collective bargaining agreements by the Canadian Union of Public Employees showed that real wages decreased 6.7% between 1976 and 1988, while production during that time increased 47%. Unions will undoubtedly begin to press for wage gains above the rate of inflation to "catch up," thus fuelling that same rate of inflation. Yet this is exactly what industry doesn't need, as it prepares for free trade by investing in plants and equipment.

Never before has the need for tripartite consensus among business, government, and labour been more critical to this nation's economic welfare. Yet, organized labour wants no part of it. Aware that American unions have been halved to only 17% of the work force over the past three decades, and fearful of losing union members, Shirley Carr, president of the Canadian Labour Congress, proclaimed at the end of 1988 that:

> We have never agreed to concession bargaining and we're not going to start now. We can't have prices sky-rocketing and expect workers to be content with a 25% pay cut just because their jobs are preserved.

Freer trade favours multinational conglomerates and global enterprise. Canadian firms, protected and inefficient, will find it difficult to specialize and become internationally competitive in selected product areas, especially if they compete in a mature society. In due time, newer firms in growth industries will specialize and think in globally competitive terms, but the transition will often be traumatic.

American-owned branch plants face the rational choice between exiting from the Canadian market and exporting from an American base, or creating world product mandates for its Canadian subsidiaries. The balance of activity between these two alternatives cannot be predicted, although withdrawal will be the most devastating for labour.

Is there any hope for an industrial strategy? Can a government preoccupied with employment and redistributing wealth initiate such a mechanism?

The answer is, "not likely," given the apathetic nature of big government. Central agencies now compete with line departments for supremacy in economic policy-making. Different agencies and departments have totally different views of what is needed and what will work. Some do not even believe that an industrial strategy is any longer (if ever it was) needed. Also, given imperfect knowledge, there has been no successful recipe to date for picking winners.

Federal politicians avoid clear-cut strategies with measurable outcomes; they prefer not to be held accountable for their successes or failures. The chances of failure are, in this case, formidable, since industrial strategies must factor in economic forecasting, which is an imperfect science. Politicians also steer clear of picking losers. They have avoided a

comprehensive industrial strategy which would inevitably favour manufacturing in central Canada at the expense of resource development out
west, or vice-versa. That is why Canada, at best, has ten provincial
industrial strategies—each of which cannibalizes the whole—and no national strategy.

Regional economic disparities quite clearly create unequal opportunities among Canadians in terms of education, socio-economic opportunities, career choices, and economic development. Disparities place a
strain on national unity and create feelings of inequity in the less developed
regions. Nevertheless, regional economic disparities in Canada are symp-
tomatic of a greater flaw in the nation's economic structure—a heavy
reliance upon natural resources and protectionism.

Each successive federal and provincial government has been preoccupied with closing the gaps among the regions and provinces—reaching
that mystical, yet elusive national average measure of well-being, rather
than aiming to reduce the gap between each region's potential and actual
economic growth. *Yet, no natural economic law dictates that every region
of a country must have the same average income-per-capita or rate of
employment for each to be well off.* Trying to close the gaps amongst
regions requires the weaker regions to grow at a faster pace than the
national economy; that has proven to be difficult, given the reasons and
history behind regional economic disparity.

One of Canada's two major roots of economic disparity will be removed by free trade with the United States. National protectionism will
essentially become an anachronism. However, inter-provincial protectionism will remain until federal and provincial governments agree on a
common goal for regional economic development. Stimulating economic
activity in "have-not" regions to achieve a national average measure of
well-being simply doesn't work. Further, where free trade eliminates one
root cause of economic disparity, it will intensify the other—this country's
dependence upon natural resources, which essentially guarantees continued disparity.

Regional economic development should continue to follow sectoral
lines, emphasizing regional competitive advantages. It must remain a
policy priority for the federal government, which in turn must provide
strong, central leadership here as it did while negotiating the free trade
agreement.[60] Free trade may not solve the age-old problem of economic
disparity in Canada, but it does shed some light on possible solutions.

The answers to the above questions have not been optimistic, yet the
urgency and need for an industrial strategy remain acute.

Free trade with the United States also creates a whole new set of vested
interests. Regional trading blocs, such as Canada and the United States, are

---

[60] Depending upon the evolution of the Constitutional debates, strong, central leadership
may be in jeopardy.

unlikely to advocate expanding trade further among blocs. Partners in any trading arrangement will want their privileged access maintained. If it is not, they are back to square one. Expanding trade further among blocs—as the U.S. is presently doing with Mexico—jeopardizes the weaker partners. That is why Canada is trying so hard to increase trade with Mexico, too. *A bilateral trade treaty is not an industrial strategy.*

The essential element of an industrial strategy is to have a goal for the economy and a coherent set of policies to achieve that goal. Sir John A. Macdonald had a goal—to build a nation. The National Policy—a joint venture strategy of business and government—built that nation. During the late 1930s and early 1940s, Canada's goal was to win the war. C.D. Howe implemented a coherent set of policies which made Canada the most productive supplier of munitions in the world, with the third-largest merchant marine fleet. In both cases, the goal was to survive—independent of the United States—and to survive the war. *In both cases, business and government worked as partners.*

Canada's goal is the same today—that of survival! In place of a single industrial strategy, Canada must emphasize realistic, attainable economic and social objectives. It must begin to formulate and implement industry-specific or sector-specific policies that would complement, and not contradict, the others. It will be a reactive strategy at best, but then Canada is not in the position to develop a proactive strategy such as that of Japan, which actually shapes the playing field.

The federal government is the only institution in Canada able to create a national consensus in this regard. The business community is the only institution with the capacity to make it work. As in 1867, and during the War, co-operation and consultation remain the key. *Business and government must once again work together as partners.*

SUGGESTED FURTHER READINGS

Consumer and Corporate Affairs Canada. *Competition Law Amendments.* Ottawa: Ministry of Supply and Services Canada, 1986.

D'Cruz, J.R. and J.D. Fleck. *Canada Can Compete!: Strategic Management of the Canadian Industrial Portfolio.* Montreal: Institute for Research on Public Policy, 1985.

Economic Council of Canada. *Looking Outward: A New Trade Strategy for Canada.* Ottawa: Ministry of Supply and Services Canada, 1976.

Economic Council of Canada. *Twenty-Third Annual Review: Changing Times.* Ottawa: Canadian Government Publishing Centre, 1986.

Economic Council of Canada. *Twenty-Fourth Annual Review: Reaching Outward.* Ottawa: Canadian Government Publishing Centre, 1987.

Government of Canada. *The Canada-United States Free Trade Agreement.* Ottawa: Department of External Affairs, 1987.

Green, C. *Canadian Industrial Organization and Policy*, 2nd ed. Toronto: McGraw-Hill Ryerson, 1985.

Lipsey, R.G. and W. Dobson, eds. *Shaping Comparative Advantage.* Toronto: C.D. Howe Institute, 1987.

Kaplan, E. *Japan: The Government-Business Relationship.* Washington, D.C.: U.S. Department of Commerce, 1972.

Keynes, J.M. *The General Theory of Employment, Interest, and Money.* London: Macmillan, 1936.

Magun, S. Rao and B. Lodh. *Impact of Canada-United States Free Trade on the Canadian Economy.* Ottawa: Economic Council of Canada, 1987.

Morici, Peter et al. *Canadian Industrial Policy.* Washington, D.C.: National Planning Association, 1982.

Report of the Royal Commission on the Economic Union and Development Prospects for Canada. Toronto: University of Toronto Press, 1986.

Savoie, D.J. *Regional Economic Development: Canada's Search for Solutions.* Toronto: University of Toronto Press, 1986.

Science Council of Canada. *Report 37: Canadian Industrial Development: Some Policy Directions.* Ottawa: Supply and Services Canada, 1984.

Shearer, R.A., J.F. Chant and D.E. Bond. *The Economies of the Canadian Financial System: Theory, Policy and Institutions.* Scarborough, Ontario: Prentice-Hall, 1984.

Stanbury, W.T. "The New Competition Act and Competition Tribunal Act: Not With a Bang, But a Whimper." *The Canadian Business Law Journal,* 12 (October 1986), 2-42

CHAPTER
13
BUSINESS AS MORAL AGENT — A NOTE

Liberty means responsibility. That is why most men dread it.

George Bernard Shaw, 1856-1950

Power without responsibility— the prerogative of the harlot throughout the ages.

Rudyard Kipling, 1865-1936

It has been over three decades since John Kenneth Galbraith wrote his controversial *The Affluent Society*, in which he documented the "dependence effect" in microeconomics. Essentially, Galbraith posited that as a society becomes increasingly affluent, its members' base wants are increasingly satisfied and replaced by new wants. He predicted greater government investment to provide the services not offered by business in this increasingly materialistic society. He also called upon business to be less preoccupied with economics and more socially responsible.

Social responsibility was easy for business when the self-interest of the corporation and the public were compatible. Today, they are not. Both sectors' ideologies, philosophies, underlying beliefs, and values are mutually exclusive. The corporate sector emphasizes productivity, efficiency, economy, and accumulation of wealth; the public sector focuses on social values such as co-operation, fraternity, altruism, community, self-gratification, and compassion. Leaders of both business and government have assigned varying weights to, and different responsibilities for, these two sets of values, or goals. Consequently, there are tensions and conflicts between these groups.

The concept of efficiency, whether that of the economist or the engineer, directly conflicts with the public sector's primary concern for equity. As the gulf between these two concepts widens, it is only a matter of time before government in Canada shifts the burden of a firm's social costs back onto that firm. Government cannot do much more without forfeiting, through deficit borrowing, its future generations' birthright.

The future of business-government relations must somewhat depend upon business' interpretation of its social responsibility. Specifically, the private sector must accept its share of the responsibility to the community, the natural environment, and the moral fabric of the nation. Today's

217

public demands that business expand its responsibility to the community beyond the payment of taxes. The environment cannot be treated as a "free good" any longer.

Business is no longer value-neutral. Although there are no ready-made solutions to these challenges, it must begin to make more of its decisions from a societal viewpoint. If business is willing to take from government, then in its own interest it had best recognize that its mandate now requires going beyond economic and material satisfaction.

CORPORATE SOCIAL RESPONSIBILITY REVISITED

As mentioned in Chapter 5, the Canadian business community has not embraced Milton Friedman's definition of social responsibility: simply stated, for business to ever increase its profits. Given Canada's neo-corporatist background, the evidence clearly shows that business accepts the role of political mechanisms, as well as market mechanisms, in the allocation of scarce resources. For Canadian enterprise, this is not socialism, as Friedman would suggest, but pragmatism.

However, those who agree that business' only responsibility is to its shareholders, as well as those who argue that business should pay to clean up the world, miss an important point. Profit does not exist except for true monopoly surplus. There are only costs of labour, raw materials, technology, capital, and those associated with future risks and uncertainty. The so-called profit reported in financial statements should really be interpreted as the cost of capital and risk, the latter including the costs associated with tomorrow's jobs.

Not to earn at least the cost of capital is to operate at a loss. For an entire business community, not to earn at least the cost of capital is to impoverish the economy. Despite all of government's recent borrowing, the largest single source of capital with which to finance tomorrow's jobs remains with business, in the form of earnings.

In Canada, net jobs will probably be lost in the textile industry under free trade and a more liberal trading regime worldwide. They will be lost in at least a dozen other sectors and industries, as well. The new jobs of tomorrow will be in environmental protection, waste management, renewable energy, health care for an aging population, alternate food production, and so on. Government alone, however, cannot pay for the transition.

The Advisory Council on Adjustment, chaired by Jean de Grandpré of BCE Inc., recommended that the federal government not compensate workers laid off by free trade. It would be difficult to conclude whether job losses were a result of free trade, GATT, poor management, or something else. It further recommended that training and retraining laid-off workers was the answer, and that business was responsible for this. However, the Council also recommended that government assist business in retraining workers through tax incentives, grants, and revised labour legislation.

Even this is short-sighted, as the costs to the federal government would be at least another $300 million.

The truth is, any firm that cannot cover its own operating costs, cost of capital, and costs of tomorrow's jobs cannot cover its own costs of doing business and the society's costs of doing business. Granted these additional costs are not as easy to determine as the cost of goods sold, but they are as calculable as other costs or depreciation amounts available to cost accountants.

In short, there are the costs of *doing* business and the costs of *staying in* business—the costs of *surviving*. And if the private sector wants to survive in this country, it had best learn this fact of economic life. Business' enemy is not government, but itself and its lack of credibility in the eyes of the public. In a poll conducted by Decima Research in the fall of 1988, 76% thought that government, not business, best protected consumers; 83% thought that government best protected the national interest; and they were split on who could do more to promote economic growth, government or business.

This is not social responsibility in the standard sense, as in product content disclosure, constructive employee relations, or support of local culture. What is being discussed here is *societal responsibility.* Business has a responsibility to operate efficiently and be able to cover costs beyond externalities such as pollution; it must also pay what is required to maintain Canada's standard of living, Canada's position within the world, and its collective future.

Business and government must co-operate to solve society's problems. Honest and open communication between them is necessary for business to know how to help the economic entity known as Canada survive in the years ahead. Performing socially responsible activities in the short run will earn business profits in the long run. Above all, business will be around to enjoy those profits.

Business and government must redefine their interdependent social contract for the 1990s. It is no longer, "What is good for business is good for Canada." Now it is, "What is good for Canada is good for business."

BUSINESS AND THE NATURAL ENVIRONMENT

Deserving special attention in this discussion of business as moral agent is the natural environment. Business owes its very existence to the environment. But no longer can it separate the economy from the environment.

Every day the media reports the latest ecological calamities: marine oil spills, acid rain, ozone depletion, deforestation, soil erosion, the Greenhouse Effect, species extinction, nuclear meltdowns, and growing deserts. For the last couple of years, every newscast also carried positive items on economic growth and increasing prosperity. Hardly ever do broadcasts or articles link the two seemingly disparate phenomena.

Yet, there is a connection. Scientific evidence is both ample and conclusive in documenting the link between economic activities and environmental deterioration. Of course, this is a global problem; but no matter how comparatively small the government of Canada and its business community may be, both can take decisive steps to improve localized ecological imbalances and take international leadership where none exists.

Since the beginning of the Industrial Revolution, environmental concerns have taken a back seat to economic ones. But the climatic warming trend in 1988 produced the most dramatic drop in world grain stocks ever recorded for one year. If this continues, rising food prices and scarcity will threaten our standard of living, as well as the very stability of a world growing by 80 million people per year. To quote former Minister of the Environment Tom McMillan, "Mere tinkering with the status quo is not enough." Every significant economic decision from today onwards must be subject to an ecological imperative.

Earlier, it was clearly stated that business must subordinate its own interest to that of the public to win the ear of government. Putting self-interest aside, business can show government it deserves a say in public policy matters by taking environmentally safe action. Nor need this strain business' bottom line. Ten years ago, urban recycling proved unprofitable for the private sector, and even too costly for local government. Today business is discovering that millions can be made in helping to clean up the environment and reducing industry's impact on it.

To place all of the onus on business in this case would be unfair. Governments pollute and destroy the environment as much as business does. But not only should government clean up its act; it needs to take the lead in weaning both business and the public from their bad habits, whether burning fossil fuels, using fluorocarbons (which it has started to do), wastefully using paper products, or accepting convenience over biodegradability.

For example, Canada's energy policy is an ecological disaster waiting to happen. There is no serious development of alternate, renewable, clean fuel sources in Canada today. Yet the federal government, prior to the 1988 federal election, announced a $1 billion grant and $1.7 billion in loans to the consortium developing the Hibernia oil fields. When these come onstream in the mid-to-late 1990s, they will produce the world's most expensive oil in some of the world's most dangerous waters. This was an uneconomic and environmentally hazardous decision.

No longer can economic growth be viewed as a trade-off for a healthy environment. Economic development and the private sector must help governments harness the means and mechanisms by which to achieve a healthier and safer environment. It is not a question of economic survival; this time, it is a question of survival, period. Canada needs more conservation, research on benign forms of energy and food production, and a massive reduction in toxic emissions and effluents. To achieve these, government must provide leadership, and *business must take the steps to master twenty-first century technology, rather than become custodians of nineteenth-century technology.*

Government must therefore provide an economic climate in which environmentalism is not only altruistic, but profitable. This requires major institutional reform now, before it is too late. If business and government working together could once build a nation-state against all prevailing logic, then it must surely be able to work together towards saving this corner of the planet.

These are tall orders, but a true test for business and government in the 1990s: to turn a real threat into a real opportunity.

BUSINESS ETHICS: DO THE ENDS JUSTIFY THE MEANS?

The Harvard Business School claims that its case method of pedagogy is ethically neutral. However, the "right" solution to a management problem may not necessarily be ethical. Which leads us to examine whether or not the ends *do* justify the means.

If one accepts the above arguments for business' wider role in societal and environmental affairs, then modern business enterprise can no longer afford to be managed in an ethically neutral manner.

Today, business no longer commands an esteemed position in Canadian society. The public no longer perceives it as the sole, legitimate channel of economic growth and prosperity. If the private sector wants to regain its former pre-eminent position, or even be accepted as an equal partner with government, it must be ethically clean.

Like government, business must lead by example. If long-term economic prosperity, full employment, and ecological preservation are the public's concerns, then business must address these issues constructively and ethically. A corporation's ethics will be only as good as those of its chief executive officer. Therefore, CEOs, senior managers, and corporate directors must resist peer group pressure to conform to neutral management technique. If a "bad" law exists, business should pursue getting it changed, not break it. Boards of directors should ask if all laws are being followed, and record management's answers in their minutes. Corporate responsibility should not, however, end with the law.

Ethical behaviour does not stop with good public relations. McDonald's and Dofasco have great public images, yet Dofasco continues to pollute the environment and McDonald's continues to use vast quantities of paper and petroleum-based, non-recyclable packaging materials. Corporate Canada must practise what it purports to be.

For one company to act ethically on all fronts would place it at a cost disadvantage with its domestic and foreign competitors. Yet, if business' full purchasing power were used to convert to environmentally safer processes and materials, economies of scale would be retained. When business works together to improve its ethical conduct, the public will reward it, once again, with the legitimacy needed to influence public policy.

Ethics need also be returned to business' internal operations. If a company issues senior managers stock options as a performance reward, and then its share price plummets shortly thereafter, the company cannot call in those options and re-issue new ones at a lower price.

Let's take another case: this time, a Canadian-born chief executive officer of a foreign-owned Canadian subsidiary given a 15% tax concession for increasing its upstream investment in Canada. Should he object when the foreign owner transfers the tax money saved to itself, without investing another cent in Canada?

Ethics need also be restored to public policy. Is affirmative action ethical by attempting to redress old discriminatory imbalances? Or is this reverse discrimination, ignoring the value of merit? Should the government award contracts on the basis of whether a bidder subscribes to affirmative action or not? Is it ethical for government policy to evolve from assuring equal opportunity to assuring equal results or even equal conditions?

Should Atomic Energy Canada sell Candu reactors to nations it suspects will use the technology to create nuclear weapons? Should a Crown corporation follow the generally accepted practice of bribing foreign officials through a third-party agency to get a sale?

On the other hand, should Canadians sell South African products, or do business in South Africa? If not, what about all the other right-wing or left-wing countries which do not share Canada's regard for human rights? If Canadian companies should avoid dealing with countries which violate basic human rights, then Canadian business interaction will be reduced to only about a dozen Western nations. Is it more ethical to boycott a nation, or to establish business relations in that country, raise the expectations of the oppressed, and indirectly assist evolutionary change from within?

Regardless of business' answer to these problems, it must be able to clearly defend its behaviour on ethical grounds just as easily as it can on economic grounds. Only then might relations with government improve.

IMPLICATIONS FOR MANAGEMENT

Unfortunately this chapter has raised more questions than it has answers. However, its intent was not to provide a formal framework for social responsibility, or to prescribe remedies for every environmental ill, or to define what is ethical in business and what is not. Its sole purpose was to make you *think*.

For the most part, this book has dealt with the concrete, the practical, and the absolute. But business-government relations are not as straightforward as one might have assumed from the first four parts of this book. For that reason, this chapter has indulged in the more abstract.

The arguments for and against business as a moral agent are clear. Those who oppose the concept of business as a moral agent believe that the capitalist system (such as it is) will not survive if firms introduce non-economic values into their corporate decision-making. Those who favour the concept argue that if business, especially big business, does not assume its proper societal, environmental, and ethical responsibilities, society could very well perish.

The answer to this debate is simple. It is in the private sector's *enlightened self-interest* to create a social and physical environment that allows it to stay in business.

Being an executive in either the private or public sector today is not an easy task. However, executives sometimes complicate their lives by dwelling on the immediate and the inconsequential, rather than on what really matters in life. This short chapter is intended to lift the content of this book out of the realm of the immediate and inconsequential, and place it in its true perspective.

SUGGESTED FURTHER READINGS

Aupperle, K.E., A.B. Carroll and J.D. Hatfield. "An Empirical Examination of the Relationship Between Corporate Social Responsibility and Profitability." *Academy of Management Journal*, 28: 2 (1985), 446-463.

Beauchamp, T.L. and N.E. Bowie, eds. *Ethical Theory and Business.* Englewood Cliffs, New Jersey: Prentice-Hall, 1979.

Bell, Daniel. *Cultural Contradictions of Capitalism.* New York: Basic Books, 1976.

Carrol, A.B. *Business and Society: Ethics and Stakeholder Management.* Cincinnati, Ohio: South Western Publishing Co., 1989.

Drucker, P.F. *Management: Tasks, Responsibilities, Practices.* New York: Harper & Row, 1974.

_____. *Managing in Turbulent Times.* New York: Harper & Row, 1980.

Friedman, Milton. "Does Business Have a Social Responsibility?" *Bank Administration* (April, 1971), 13-14.

_____. "The Social Responsibility of Business Is to Increase its Profits." *New York Times Magazine* (September 13, 1970), 32.

Galbraith, J.K. *The Affluent Society.* Boston: Houghton-Mifflin, 1958.

Hay, R.D. and E. Gray. "Social Responsibilities of Business Managers." *Academy of Management Journal*, 17:1 (1974).

Okun, A.M. *Equality and Efficiency: The Big Tradeoff.* Washington: The Brookings Institute, 1975.

Richardson, J.E., ed. *Business Ethics 89/90.* Guilford, Connecticut: Dushkin Publishing Group, 1989.

Schelling, T. "Economic Reasoning and the Ethics of Policy." *Public Interest*, 63 (Spring 1981), 59+.

CHAPTER 14

NOT THE CONCLUSION —BUT A NEW BEGINNING

But what experience and history teach is this, that peoples and governments have never learned anything from history.

Georg Wilhelm Hegel, 1770-1831

The solutions to problems are not necessarily found in new and brilliant ideas. They are sometimes discovered by making the old, proven ideas work.

Author

Sir Wilfrid Laurier claimed that the twentieth century belonged to Canada. Reluctantly, most would say his dream did not come true. What was, and was not, accomplished in this century was, in large part, a result of the actions taken by business and government under the rubric of a "National Policy." Similarly, what the twenty-first century will hold for Canada largely depends on the options that business and government choose during the 1990s. One can hardly suggest that the twenty-first century can "belong to Canada." There is only a hope that Canada will still have a place in the First World ten years from now.

STRATEGICALLY MANAGING THE BUSINESS-GOVERNMENT INTERFACE IN THE 1990s—BACK TO FIRST PRINCIPLES

Most Canadian business-government literature has assumed that prior to the election of President Reagan, the state of business-government relations in Canada was similar to that south of the border. Relations were adversarial, interests of business and government were antagonistic, and each side lacked insight into the role, motivations, problems, and modes of action of the other. Although such was hardly the case in Canada before the early 1970s, Canadian business-government relations did deteriorate thereafter, but hardly to the extent portrayed. Business-government relations improved in the United States under Reagan, while they did not in Canada.

Why was this so? Some blamed business. They claimed that ineffective business leadership at a national level produced fragmentation and a lack of consensus within the business community. Each sector offered its own self-serving option on economic and industrial policies and programs. Alastair Gillespie, then Minister of Industry, Trade and Commerce, had his eyes opened when he met with representatives of the Canadian Manufacturers Association and the Canadian Chamber of Commerce. He discovered that, although the industrial policy they proposed was supported by thirteen of their constituent member organizations, it actually was a compilation of thirteen separate submissions — each pleading for special recognition of its own special needs.

Other critics cited the dearth of effective consultation and co-ordination processes between the private and public sectors. This was seen as compromising the health of business-government relations. Because democratic governments tend to be risk-averse, Ottawa has been slow to take the initiative in business-government consultation when business has lacked enthusiasm for the idea. Still others noted that because of their geographic location, some federal politicians and public servants became isolated from the world of business in Toronto, Montreal, Vancouver, or Calgary.

Overall, there is little evidence to substantiate many of the negative claims made about Canadian business-government relations. In fact, contrary to popular opinion, the most recent empirical research showed that business and government do not perceive their interrelations to be all that bad, but admit there is plenty of room for improvement.

An informed student of Canadian business-government relations would have expected this. If one *understands* the socio-economic underpinnings of business-government relations in this country and its key *players*, and *interprets* data with an eye to context and circumstance, then one becomes aware of how to *manage* this interrelationship constructively and effectively. As *partners*, who understand and respect each other, business and government can turn the economic *challenges* of the 1990s into victories.

Business can take the first step by voluntarily and aggressively offering its advice to government. This must be accurate, objective, and well-documented. Business must also be willing to wait for government's reaction, and to return again and again, if necessary, to get it.

Furthermore, business must show interest in having an impact on a policy decision and being helpful to the decision-makers, rather than just having its point of view publicized. It must know what it wants, and go after it as professionally as it professes to manage its internal operations. Business must visibly perform well its traditional role of wealth creation, and show that it is serving the public interest, however defined by the public policy-makers of the day.

Conversely, government must provide greater access for business and be willing to listen to and digest business' input. Government line departments, which once acted as Ottawa's listening posts for business, no longer influence the policy-making process as they once did. Today, the centralization of decision-making in Ottawa has reduced departments to one of many players in the policy arena today.

This centralization of decision-making authority within the federal government has had a severe, negative impact on business-government relations. There has been a gradual movement away from the mutually dependent department-client relationships which were built up during the 1940s through the 1960s. Today, a less approachable and less comprehensible government-by-central-agency has left most industries and businesses without readily accessible contacts in government who can influence government policy. Cabinet ministers and deputy ministers are now being moved around much more frequently than ever before. This compounds the problem of business' losing touch with government.

If the principal function of economic policy is to create wealth, and the principal function of political policy is to redistribute it, differences are bound to arise between business and government. However, a herculean task awaits them. They must formulate a political-economic framework which balances the creation and redistribution of wealth in a way that both sides and the public can accept. *Although business in Canada does not want government on its back, it does need government by its side.*

The prime requisite for success, however, is political will.

THE FUTURE OF CANADIAN BUSINESS–GOVERNMENT RELATIONS: TWO SOLITUDES OR A NATIONAL PARTNERSHIP?

Above all, Canada has always been—still is—and will continue to be—a trading nation. With the implementation of free trade, further GATT reforms, and Europe '92, Canadian productivity and competitiveness will become very important to this nation of producers, consumers, governors, traders, and tax- collectors. To complicate matters, gains in productivity will be offset in the short term by expected rising inflation. The Bank of Canada is already losing its battle with inflation. Management has two choices: to be less generous on the wage front (a stopgap measure at best), or to dramatically improve technological productivity to compensate for higher wage increases. Either way, becoming more competitive will be difficult to do when interest rates are high.

Ottawa tends to complicate things even further. There is no coherent federal government strategy at present to manage the economy, contain the federal deficit, or help business through the structural transition of the 1990s. In his 1989 budget, Finance Minister Michael Wilson announced new and higher sales and personal income taxes to help offset the growing deficit. Tax increases of this magnitude fuel both the consumer price and industrial price indices, thus adding to inflation. They also reduce disposable income, which dampens consumer spending. As a result, the cost of doing business (particularly manufacturing) increases just when cost-competitiveness is the primary focus for Canadian business. Meanwhile, the federal deficit continues to grow.

Academe also has a role to play. Human resources remain the key to productivity. Both management and labour must work smarter to compete in a freer trade environment, and in an age of rapid technological change. The ability of people to develop, adapt, utilize, manage, and work alongside new technologies will be critical. Schools of management need to develop problem-solvers, leaders, strategic thinkers, and change-agents as much as marketers, policy analysts, and financial whiz-kids.

Innovative organizations survive turbulent times, but even they need change-agents and leadership. Change is not to be feared, but exploited. The Japanese believe that the difference between how Orientals and Occidentals manage change reflects the different ways the two meta-cultures view death. In the East, death is a part of living not to be resisted. In the West, people resist death with every ounce of their strength. As a society, Canadians resist rapid industrial evolution, as they do death—fighting it every step of the way. Japan's ability to manage rapid industrial evolution is similarly grounded in its beliefs about death—something to look forward to, not resist.

Canada has a lot to learn, and so little time in which to apply it. Yet, simplistic, structural, reductionist solutions will not work.

Business must recognize change, plan for it, and be willing and able to cover its costs. Government must financially support and encourage an educational system that will produce the scientific management and labour skills needed to compete in the technological arena. This may well be the greatest challenge facing educators, business, and government in the next decade. It will not be an easy one, as governments at all levels are cutting back educational funding. Yet here is where business should not just tell government how to spend its money, but encourage it to spend *more*—and wisely.

Over a hundred years ago, business and government—working as partners—built a nation out of a wilderness, and kept it from becoming part of the American union. It was a question of survival. Today, business and government must again become partners to rebuild this nation, protect its sovereignty, and secure for its children a leadership position on the world stage. *It is still a question of survival—both for business, and for Canada.*

VI CASES

1. CONSUMERS GAS AND THE ONTARIO ENERGY BOARD

2. NOTE ON THE TRUCKING INDUSTRY

3. CALL-NET TELECOMMUNICATIONS LIMITED

4. RSR ROAD SURFACE RECYCLING INC.

5. BILL C-51: THE TOBACCO PRODUCTS CONTROL ACT

6. THE ONTARIO HEARING AID ASSOCIATION

7. NOTE ON THE ONTARIO WINE INDUSTRY

8. BELL CANADA AND THE CRTC

1 CONSUMERS GAS AND THE ONTARIO ENERGY BOARD

ROSS GORDON KEARNS AND D. WAYNE TAYLOR

During the early part of the 1980s, Consumers Gas, Canada's largest natural gas retailer, was finding it increasingly difficult to supply the required amount of natural gas for the peak demand season. In 1982, it began to consider a number of options to solve this problem. After a lengthy investigation, Consumers Gas decided that building a liquid natural gas storage facility near Cobourg, Ontario, was the answer. In the spring of 1986, it submitted a proposal to the Ontario Energy Board, whose approval was needed to construct this storage facility and to implement a strategy of supply management.

On December 12, 1986, the Ontario Energy Board turned down Consumers'proposal.

CONSUMERS GAS

The Consumers Gas Company Ltd. is a natural gas utility which distributes its product to customers in southern, central, and eastern Ontario, as well as the Niagara region. It is one of three major gas utilities in Ontario. Each has been given an exclusive territory within which it may distribute natural gas for residential and industrial purposes. In turn, the utility agrees to abide by the regulations set out by the Ontario Energy Board Act.

The management of Consumers Gas feels it has had good relations with all provincial government departments over the years. Functionally speaking, its government relations personnel are not centralized within the company because, in many cases, the special knowledge of certain departments is necessary when discussing matters with the government. Therefore, each major company department deals directly with the government when the need arises. Many do so on a regular basis. For example, the human relations department works closely with the Ministry of Labour on such issues as employment equity; the Ministry of Consumer and Commercial Relations is dealt with directly on safety-related matters; and Consumers' engineers work directly with the Ministry of the Environment on environmental concerns.

Various provincial officials also consider working relations between themselves and Consumers Gas to have been very good.

THE ONTARIO ENERGY BOARD

Many business sectors in Canada are regulated—some more so than others. In all provinces where natural gas utilities exist, extensive regulations are in place.

Paramount among the reasons for these regulations is protection of the consumer. This protection includes items such as safety factors (natural gas is a highly flammable and combustible substance); cost factors (large utilities provide economies of scale which keep operating costs—and thus costs to customers—low); and service factors (exclusive territories ensure consistent service and facilities across the system). In addition, the cost of having competing utilities in one district is almost prohibitive. Allowing firms to have exclusive jurisdiction in a region therefore protects the producer as well as the consumer.

In Ontario, the Ministry of Energy is the umbrella department which oversees the operations of natural gas utilities. Under this umbrella are a number of agencies which provide the Ministry with information and recommendations about the sector. One of these agencies is the Ontario Energy Board.

The Ontario Energy Board (the OEB, or the Board) was established under the enabling legislation of the *Ontario Energy Board Act* to regulate the operations of provincial utilities. As with most government regulatory or special-purpose bodies, the powers given to the OEB are broad and vague. Among these powers are the right to approve or fix rates, the authority to allow storage of natural gas, and the right to limit the number of shares one person or group may own of a gas transmitter, distributor, or storage company.

The OEB operates in the following manner: An application may be made by industry or the public to the Lieutenant-Governor in Council (the Cabinet) to have the Board hear a certain case. The Board may also take the initiative, acting under direction from the Minister of Energy or the Minister of Natural Resources. It may also send a resolution to the Cabinet requesting an inquiry into any matter within its jurisdiction. All proceedings before the OEB are public, and all decisions must be published and made available to the public. The OEB can both make and enforce decisions similar to those vested in the Supreme Court of Ontario. Indeed, the Ontario Energy Board is a very powerful government body.

In addition to these powers, the OEB possesses a large degree of discretionary power as a result of its very general terms of reference. Discretion and the power that goes with it exist when rules and generally accepted principles provide little or no guidance; where values, attitudes, and beliefs of deciding officers may affect how they execute their duties; where political or other favouritism may influence outcomes; and where the peculiarities of human nature are often reflected in the decisions made. While the existence of discretionary power is not necessarily wrong, it is often overlooked as an influence on the outcome of a situation. In a situation where a decision-maker has a great deal of discretion, a decision to do nothing, or to do nothing for now, is ten or twenty times as frequent as action decisions.[61]

There is only one route for appeal by those unsatisfied with an OEB decision, and that is directly to Cabinet. Of course, a political cabinet is usually very discretionary. Section 33 of the *Ontario Energy Board Act* states:

---

[61] Kenneth C. Davis. *Discretionary Justice in Europe and America.* Westport, CT: Greenwood Press, 1982.

Upon the petition of any party or person interested, filed with the Clerk of the Executive Council within 28 days after the date of any order or decision by the Board, the Lieutenant Governor in Council may,

(a) confirm, vary or rescind the whole or any part of such order or decision; or

(b) require the Board to hold a new public hearing of the whole or any part of the application to the Board upon which such order or decision of the Board was made . . .

THE PROPOSAL

In 1986, Consumers Gas made a proposal to the OEB to construct a liquid natural gas (LNG) storage facility in the county of Northumberland near Cobourg, Ontario. In the early 1980s, Consumers Gas had found that it was facing a crisis situation regarding its peak season supply of natural gas. As in most Canadian energy sectors, demand is highest in the winter and lowest in the summer. The company felt it had to find a way to supplement its peak season supply to assure its customers of uninterrupted service.

Consumers Gas receives the majority of its natural gas supply from western Canada through the Trans-Canada Pipeline and through the Great Lakes Transmission System. These pipelines are used to capacity throughout the winter months when the demand is highest. Consequently, Consumers Gas cannot obtain enough of its product during this period. In the off-season, the company has, until now, stored natural gas in its underground storage facility, Tecumseh Gas Storage, jointly owned with Imperial Oil Limited. Unfortunately, this facility is also at full capacity and can no longer supply the peak demand period adequately.

As early as 1982, Consumers Gas started investigating options to help close this supply-demand gap. Discussions with the Union Gas Company (the natural gas utility operating in southwestern Ontario), regarding sharing its existing storage facilities, were fruitless. Other studies such as possibly supplementing the natural gas supply with propane, which helps natural gas to burn hotter and more efficiently, also proved not to be reliable long-term solutions. In the end, Consumers Gas decided that extra storage facilities of its own had to be constructed. The only option it felt viable was to construct a liquid natural gas (LNG) storage facility.

A primary reason for choosing an LNG facility was that a larger amount of natural gas can be stored in a smaller area when it is liquid, rather than a gas. The idea behind the plant was that natural gas could be converted to LNG during the summer months and "re-gasified" to supplement supply during the winter. Furthermore, Consumers Gas wanted a facility which it could wholly own and operate.

Once the LNG option had been chosen, Consumers Gas began to prepare a number of reports, plans, and proposals which were specifically designed to maximize efficiency and safety. The project had to meet various government requirements, such as the proven need for the facility, an environmental impact assessment, and contingency plans in case of an emergency or disaster.

Consumers desperately needed the OEB to rule favourably on the need and viability of the project for two reasons. First, speedy approval would mean that construction and implementation could proceed as soon as possible, so that projected excess demand could be met by the end of the 1980s. Second, by having the facility approved by the government, it would signal the surrounding community that the project would be safe for the area.

Consumers Gas anticipated some initial resistance to the project in the local community where the plant was to be located. However, it felt that, with the proper "public participation," people would become more aware of the project, its low-risk profile, and its potential good for the local economy. In an initial survey, Consumers found that very little was known about LNG in the community. It hoped that this participation exercise would help alleviate existing fears in the community, as well as educate residents about plant operations and Consumers Gas in general. By the time the OEB hearings had concluded, community opposition to the plant was limited to a few vocal citizens representing a very small proportion of the population.

THE ONTARIO ENERGY BOARD HEARINGS

The OEB also was concerned about public participation. The Board realized that holding public hearings at its Toronto offices would effectively exclude many local residents from participating. It was decided, therefore, to hold the hearings in Cobourg, about 15 km. from the proposed site of the plant.

The OEB hearing on the LNG project was the lengthiest in the Board's history. The hearing began on April 30, 1986, and concluded on August 25, 1986. Written arguments amounted to 41 volumes of transcript containing 6 889 pages.

The length of the hearings raised a contentious point in the relations between the Board and Consumers Gas. Consumers felt that the Board went to extraordinary lengths to conduct this study. The Board retorted that the project was itself extraordinary and could not be compared with past practices, therefore requiring a full airing of the details. However, Consumers' extensive preparation for the hearing indicated to some that they knew this would be unlike routine applications to the Board. A minimum of six volumes of documentation was prepared just to present the proposal.

One of the findings of the Board that Consumers Gas contested was the actual need for the facility. Consumers was asked to show that the supply of natural gas from both pipeline transmission and underground storage was not adequate during the peak season to meet the demand. After much calculation, the Board ruled that Consumers could not demonstrate adequate need for the project. In fact, it ruled that Consumers actually had an excess inventory of gas from 1977 to 1985.

The Board also felt that Consumers Gas did not utilize properly what the industry called *interruptible supply techniques. Interruptible customers* are industrial customers who contract with Consumers to purchase natural gas in large volumes at reduced rates. In return, Consumers can curtail or cut off supply temporarily to meet retail demand on peak days. The Board inferred that Consumers was not interested in this type of supply-management technique because it did not and would not earn a rate of return as high as it would with the construction of the LNG facility. Furthermore, the Board suggested that Consumers should consider increasing its number of interruptible customers, thereby selling more of its product at a reduced rate, and cutting these customers off when the company faced a peak demand situation.

Consumers responded by insisting that its overall demand had indeed gone up and its ability to service this demand had shrunk. The company charged that this was not illustrated well by the Board's own data because of the abnormally warm winters in the early 1980s. Consumers also stated that the time involved in telephoning up to 500 interruptible customers to find enough supply to satisfy peak need was greater than the time available to do so. In addition, increasing the number of these customers would only add to the time needed to contact them.

Consumers Gas basically wanted to provide a reliable, continuous service to all its customers, while providing its shareholders with a reasonable return on their investment. The Board essentially called for Consumers to spread what supply it could obtain over an even larger number of customers, while maintaining the same level of service.

One of the criteria that the Board used in making its decision was whether the LNG project was in the public interest. The Board defined the public interest in this case to mean:

(a) providing the service at the lowest possible cost to the Ontario customer;
(b) ensuring that security of supply and system reliability and flexibility were maintained and enhanced; and
(c) ensuring that safety and environmental concerns were adequately met.

The Board went on to say that "in this instance, the public interest requires that the Board review other alternatives (sic) beyond those strictly within the control of Consumers and confined in impact to Consumers' customers." The gas company argued that the OEB was now operating beyond its mandate, that this was a shift in Board policy of which it had not been informed in advance. Consumers did not believe that the interests of all Ontario gas customers had to be considered in this case. Such had never been the practice before. Board members insisted that this proposal was unique, and that comparing this hearing to previous Board hearings was like "comparing apples and oranges."

THE UNION GAS ALTERNATIVE

As mentioned earlier, Consumers Gas had discussed its peak demand problems with the Union Gas Company. It had received little, if any, response from Union Gas when the decision was taken to build the LNG plant. It was not until the latter part of the OEB hearings that Union Gas showed up with a storage alternative. To Consumers' dismay, the OEB suspended the hearings into the LNG project to examine this new alternative more closely. It included expansion of Union Gas' underground storage facilities in southwestern Ontario and additional pipeline construction to facilitate transmission of the natural gas to the Consumers Gas system.

The Board rationalized its examination of the Union Gas alternative in two ways. First, the purpose of the hearing was to evaluate the need for a storage facility and to examine all reasonable options. Second, the Board report states that the Union Gas alternative was proposed to Consumers Gas in September, 1985 (fully three years after Union Gas had first been approached). Consumers Gas maintained that it had not been aware of the Union Gas alternative until it was introduced at the hearing.

The Union Gas alternative was evaluated extensively by the Board, especially for cost and environmental impact. As a result, the Board deemed the Union Gas alternative superior to the LNG project. The main reasons for this were a lower net present value of the cost of construction ($155.6 million for Union's proposal vs. $169.8 million for Consumers), and a lesser environmental impact than the LNG plant. Interestingly enough, the LNG proposal also was deemed to have a minor impact on the environment. However, the LNG facility would have no precedents against which to determine the precise environmental impact, whereas the Union Gas proposal involved similar technology to that used elsewhere in the past.

THE ONTARIO ENERGY BOARD DECISION

The final recommendation by the OEB dated December 12, 1986 stated that the proposal by Consumers Gas Company to construct a liquid natural gas storage facility had been turned down. The Board concluded that Consumers Gas had not demonstrated the need for the project, and that the proposal by Union Gas Ltd. to expand its underground storage facilities was more acceptable all around than the LNG plant.

Consumers Gas was obviously not pleased by the ruling of the OEB. The company felt it had been ruled against unfairly on a number of points. It also had had its project effectively neutralized by Union's last-minute proposal. Consumers Gas was left with the same problem it had started with: inadequate supply. Now, however, it had nothing to show for it but sunk costs of more than $5 million! In the words of one Consumers executive, the entire exercise had been "expensive and fruitless."

The OEB ruling was sent to Cabinet, as was an appeal by Consumers Gas to have the decision reviewed. Since the original OEB ruling, Union Gas has had part of its proposal approved by the Board. As of March, 1988 there had been no response from Cabinet on either submission.

Consumers Gas believes that electoral politics may explain Cabinet's silence about the OEB decision. The MPP for the riding in which the LNG plant was to be constructed was a Progressive Conservative—the party in power at the time the proposal was first announced in 1985. While he did survive the 1985 election, his party did not and he became a member of the Opposition. The riding was subsequently won by a Liberal in 1987, when the party obtained a majority government.

As far as the OEB is concerned, it does not think that there has been any erosion in the relations between the Board and Consumers Gas. As for Consumers Gas, it is unsure how to approach the Board in the future.

2 NOTE ON THE TRUCKING INDUSTRY

RUSSELL BRATLEY AND D. WAYNE TAYLOR

On January 1, 1988 federal legislation deregulating the trucking industry in Canada took effect. This, combined with changes in some provincial statutes, was intended to open up the country's private transport network, stimulate competition among companies, and lower prices for shippers and consumers. The deregulation of trucking was the direct result of the lobbying efforts of a coalition of manufacturers and shippers. Opponents to deregulation argue that it will result in the loss of jobs due to industry rationalization and a decrease in highway safety.

With any proposed change in government policy, the outcome is subject to some uncertainty. Deregulation of the trucking industry is no exception. All the various players involved—large and small carriers, shippers, government—perceive the immediate long-term results differently. Not only do those with different interests in deregulation see the outcome differently, but many have drastically altered their perceptions over short periods of time. One trucking executive was quoted in November, 1987 as saying that "the rate structure (of the trucking industry) probably won't change much under deregulation." Four months later, he stated that "predatory pricing will result in a drastic change in the current rate structure of the industry."

BILL C-19

Trucking is the dominant mode of freight transportation in Canada, playing a vital role in the Canadian economy. *For-hire carriers*, which engage in transportation of freight for compensation, generated total operating revenues of $8 billion in 1985. *Private carriers*, who carry their own commodities using company drivers, incurred $5 billion in operating expenses. For-hire and private carriers combined hauled 235 million tons of freight in 1985 and employed 175 000 people nationwide. Ontario, the trucking centre of Canada, accounts for 40% of the total revenues and operating expenses and 42% of the industry's employees.

Deregulation of the Canadian transportation business was enabled by the passage of Bills C-18 (An Act Respecting National Transport) and C-19 (An Act Respecting Motor Vehicle Transport By Extra-provincial Undertakings) in the House of Commons in June, 1987.

Bill C-18 introduced the new National Transport Policy applying to rail, water, air, pipeline, and truck transport. It declares that a safe, economic, efficient, and adequate network of transportation services at the lowest cost can most likely be achieved when all carriers can compete both within and among the various modes of transportation. Although the National Transport Policy is a federal policy, it is administered and interpreted by the individual provinces. The new law governs only interprovincial and international trucking; intraprovincial transport is still governed by each province.

Bill C-19, which relates specifically to the trucking industry, introduced three major changes to the existing legislation. Prior to the January 1, 1988 implementation date of C-18 and C-19, any trucking firm requesting a licence to cross provincial or international boundaries had to prove that the new service was a public necessity. Under the new law, existing firms wanting to block new entrants must prove that the new service will not serve the public interest. This rule will remain in effect for five years, after which new firms need only to show that they are "fit and able." The fitness criteria relate to safety, insurance requirements, bonding requirements, and so on.

The second major change affects the restrictions previously attached to most licences. These limited which cities a company could service, and specifically restricted the types of goods it could carry. Provincial transport boards may now issue licences to, and levy tariffs and tolls on, firms engaged in the inter-provincial transport of goods on terms similar to local transport.

The most dramatic economic change in the new Act involved transport rates. Prior to January 1, 1988 standard rates were set collectively by the carriers and were made public. This practice has been abolished under the new system, making available confidential contracts for shippers and carriers. True negotiations for rates and services will now take place. A "final offer" arbitration and mediation provision to solve disputes between carriers and shippers has also been implemented.

The recent free trade agreement between Canada and the United States further complicates the changes introduced by the new Act. The agreement provides that neither country can change regulatory structures to discriminate against carriers from the other.

REGULATION OF THE TRUCKING INDUSTRY

The basic legislative framework to regulate trucking was established by the railroads in the mid-1930s. Railroad interests were concerned about the "unfair" competition posed by truck transport. The Duff Report of 1932 claimed that:

> because the railways are essential and because the railway rate structure implied conditions approximating to a quasi-monopoly, the railways require, if they are to continue to operate efficiently, a measure of protection from long distance road competition and an equalization of the conditions under which short distance traffic is carried.

The report recommended the filing of tariffs and the application of a test of "public necessity and convenience."

During the 1930s, the trucking industry experienced erratic rates, deteriorating service, high failure rates, and high turnovers. These circumstances led to increased pressure from the railroads to regulate trucking, and most provinces moved to increase licensing restrictions. The provinces directed their regulatory policies without federal co-ordination until 1954, when the government finally addressed the issue of interprovincial transport. The federal government's response was to delegate its responsibilities to the provinces. Therefore, a carrier transporting freight through two or more provinces was forced to justify an application for an inter-provincial route before each provincial regulatory board. This was met with sharp criticism by the Canadian Trucking Association.

Under the 1954 Transport Act, the most important aspects of provincial regulatory policy were:

(a) Controlling entry into intraprovincial for-hire trucking.
(b) Licensing restrictions as to points and areas of coverage, routes, commodities carried, equipment to be used, persons to be served, and frequency of service.
(c) Acquiring by licensed carriers of provincial approval to amend the licence, sale, or transfer of a licence and discontinuance of a service.
(d) Imposing by provinces of rate control, primarily in the form of rate filing.

The effects of regulation on the trucking industry were soon complicated by the different regulatory approaches adopted by each province. The degree of industry conformity to provincial legislation, and the degree to which regulatory boards interpreted, exercised, and enforced their legislation varied dramatically by province.

Despite control of entry, the acceptance rate on applications is at least 80% for most provinces. This rather high acceptance rate, however, must be viewed in its appropriate context. Many potential applicants are deterred by the high costs of applying, the delays of the regulatory process, and the difficulty in meeting regulatory requirements. Furthermore, new applicants tend to have a higher refusal rate than existing firms seeking to expand, which actually represent the majority of licences granted.

Provincial regulatory boards generally interpret public necessity and convenience criteria to mean that the primary responsibility of the regulator is to ensure stability in the industry, and to prevent the recurrence of conditions that led to regulation in the first place.

However, the negative impact of new firms on the financial health of older ones sometimes takes precedence over adequacy of service. Consequently, a new applicant offering to provide a unique public convenience, but one which would adversely affect existing firms, would likely be refused. Similarly, any proposed saving in rates for a service is not considered a factor in determining public necessity and convenience, unless existing rates are ruled to be unreasonably high. Regulators tend to view a proposal for lower rates as a threat to the viability of existing firms. The most acceptable justification for new entry based on "public necessity and convenience" occurs when existing firms are providing inadequate service to an area, or a region experiencing economic growth requires more trucking than is being supplied.

The relatively lax enforcement of regulations and the insignificant fines (averaging $70) levied once a firm is convicted have attracted illegal entrants into the industry. The main deterrent to unlicensed operators is the likelihood that a conviction would prejudice any application for a new licence, endanger any existing operating licences, and result in licence plates being revoked. Unlicensed carriers have been able to evade these penalties by circumventing the intent of the legislation. Leasing and driver pool businesses established as legal entities lease vehicles along with drivers, thereby avoiding the letter of the law. Alternatively, carriers commonly purchase freight at the point of origin and sell it at the point of destination, thus gaining exemption from the regulations as technically private carriers.

As in most regulated industries, the lack of new entrants raises concerns regarding monopolistic pricing. Economic theory claims that prices in a regulated industry tend to be higher than in an unregulated industry. This concern is most apparent in small towns and rural locations with a limited degree of carrier service. However, it is difficult to decide whether the concern is a function of regulation, or a function of limited volume of freight traffic.

Significant disparities exist between carriers who purchase licences at market value, and those who obtain licences from a provincial authority. The market value for a licence can be as much as fifty times greater than if purchased through the government.

DEREGULATION

With the advent of deregulation, most carriers actually preferred to remain regulated, and particularly preferred closed entry. They also conceded that deregulation was inevitable due to market forces and not just government initiative, and were "willing to live with it." As one carrier said:

> The government has no handle on regulation. Single truckers and U.S. operators have been cheating the system for years. Working hour limits are ignored and individuals haul goods that they are not licensed to carry to destinations that they are not licensed to haul to. Safety standards are allowed to deteriorate. The RCMP, which is responsible for enforcing the trucking regulations, is busy giving out traffic tickets at Pearson International Airport. Government's inability to effectively regulate the industry has resulted in unofficial deregulation anyway.

Shippers and producers of goods have generally found the regulated trucking environment to be very restrictive. For firms that rely on other companies to move product, regulation has proved time-consuming. Numerous delays result from restrictions on certain routes for certain products, and the inability to use a single carrier for all products. The lack of rate confidentiality is a major disadvantage for companies producing in cost- competitive environments. Since rates are public information, a large company cannot use its volume or its position as a stable, reliable customer to confidentially negotiate a competitive contract with a carrier.

Although both shippers and carriers find fault with regulated industry rates, one carrier noted:

> Regulation was supposed to eliminate rate competition and place it on the level of service that could be provided. Nonsense! Competition was based on where and how often the customer was taken out for lunch and what gift he was given for Christmas.

Most opinions about trucking's deregulation have come from trucking firms and trucking associations such as the Canadian Trucking Association (CTA) and the Ontario Trucking Association (OTA). Although the CTA and OTA do not oppose deregulation, they believe that federal deregulation has created *de facto* free trade with the United States industry in trans-border trucking services. They also foresee provincial deregulation furthering this process. Passage of the proposed provincial legislation will give U.S. and other provincial carriers easy access to Ontario truck operating rights. Yet Ontario carriers will still find it difficult to obtain operating rights in most states.

One trucking executive predicts that the industry will undergo a major restructuring. It is presently divided into three classes based on firm size:

1. large firms with greater than 20 trucks that tend to specialize in certain routes or goods,
2. medium-sized firms with 15 to 20 trucks, and
3. 1-or-2-truck operations.

He believes that the industry will experience extreme rate slashing over the first two years of deregulation, which will create severe cash flow crises for many of the medium-sized firms. These firms are already plagued with high overhead due to their need for administration, and their lack of economies of scale.

Another executive actually predicts the disappearance of most medium-sized firms, with a serious decline in the number of one or two-truck operations. Large firms that were able to reduce their overhead will be able to grow by acquiring smaller operations. This large decrease in the number of firms available for service will reduce the competitive nature of the industry in the first few years after the initial shock of deregulation. Consumers may find that transport prices initially drop, but as firms exit and the market becomes dominated by a few large firms, prices possibly will rise once again. This was exactly the scenario of the deregulated Australian trucking industry, which is now dominated by four large firms.

However, the chief executive officer of one of Canada's largest trucking firms believes that rates have already sunk in anticipation of deregulation, and are unlikely to go much lower. His concern is that new players entering the market, especially from the United States, will reduce the market shares currently held by Canadian companies. United States carriers say that these fears are not warranted because they already have ample access to the Canadian market. They say that they are unlikely to rush into the Canadian market.

With Canada's major trucking firms accepting deregulation, opposition by the OTA and CTA appears to be primarily in the interest of their major membership— the small to medium-sized firms. This is evidenced in the OTA's statement that "some companies will go out of business, some will go bankrupt, and some will merge." A large portion of the OTA's efforts are also directed toward the uncertainties that free trade will create when combined with deregulation.

Large shippers such as those found in the auto industry feel that deregulation will result in less government intervention and more competition through better service and lower prices. More carriers, they say, whether Canadian or American, can only mean more competition, better service, and lower prices. In fact, most shippers hold this sentiment.

SAFETY

A major concern heightened by the U.S. experience with trucking and airline deregulation is that of safety. Overnight deregulation in the United States resulted in an influx of new entrants into the industry, with drivers attempting to haul as far and as fast as they could in order to meet expenses. Although safety was to have remained regulated, the percentage of tractor-trailers involved in crashes increased substantially after deregulation. This was due to the difficulty in monitoring carrier safety.

Both federal and provincial governments are relying on the new National Safety Code to avoid a similar situation in Canada. The code, to be promulgated by 1989, will limit the number of consecutive hours a trucker can drive and ensure regular inspection of all commercial trucks. Under deregulation and the new safety code, preventive maintenance on equipment to meet safety standards will be necessary to avoid substantial fines. Opponents of deregulation argue that effective, sure safety enforcement is not possible given the overwhelming human factor. With more and more truckers competing for the market, something has to give, and in this instance, it could well be safety.

Economic and safety regulations are related, since economic regulation reduces the intensity of competition and thereby decreases the pressure on firms to compromise safety as a cost-cutting device. Economic regulation gives rise to larger firms which can devote more attention to driver selection, training, and vehicle safety. It also facilitates enforcement by reducing the number of firms and increasing the incentive for carriers to comply with regulations.

However, government believes that economic regulation does not necessarily lead to increased safety. Carriers will spend on safety only while their return is favourable relative to other investments. However, improved safety can provide such economic benefits as better insurance rates and lower operating costs. Both are important in either regulated or unregulated environments.

Canada's largest trucking firms believe that overall safety standards will rise under deregulation. As evidence of this, firms have been updating their fleets for the past five years, not only to provide more efficient operating economies, but to avoid costly replacement of "unsafe" vehicles during times of reduced cash flow.

THE "LEVEL PLAYING FIELD"

Providing a level playing field is a term frequently used to describe the process of removing "unfair" competitive advantages of various players in an industry. The definitions of a level playing field are as numerous as the number of individuals with an interest in deregulation.

Some carriers expect deregulation to create an unequal playing field within an integrated North American market. They feel that equal opportunities cannot exist without certain protective policies. They want reciprocity in market access to be granted on a fast-track basis to carriers from jurisdictions which provide equal access to Ontario carriers. Ontario carriers, they feel, should be compensated for their operating licences lost when securing loans and lines of credit. Carriers also want the tax gap between Canadian and U.S. carriers narrowed. Passage of these policies, they claim, would create a level playing field for Canadian and U.S. carriers under deregulation.

Others believe deregulation will create a level playing field between firms that have operated by the rules, and those that have been cheating the system. Enforcement of the National Safety Code will reduce the number of unsafe vehicles on the road due to firms skimping on maintenance costs. More frequent inspections will force unsafe vehicle operators to improve safety conditions, ensure that operators carry only one licence, and obey the limits on the number of consecutive hours a trucker can drive. Firms that have not already responded to these upcoming changes will likely be eliminated.

During a rate war, firms will have to absorb high costs, both for major fleet overhauls and to hire drivers to compensate for reduced allowable driver-hours. The majority of large trucking firms have already increased their number of drivers and upgraded their fleets. Many have begun to concentrate on specific routes which allow them to haul material in two directions, thus reducing the number of empty-carrier miles.

Deregulation in the U.S. caused a leveling of the playing field between large firms and small firms. Many of the large U.S. trucking firms were endowed with "fat management" and were strongly influenced by the powerful Teamsters Union. Deregulation forced firms to reduce management levels and concentrate on a much narrower profit margin. New, smaller firms entered the market with lean management teams and lower-cost, non-unionized drivers. This trend served to reduce the Teamsters' ability to dominate industry wage rates, and gave smaller firms the opportunity to compete in the market.

The virtual overnight deregulation of the U.S. trucking industry, however, provided no opportunity for opposition or consultation. Nor did it provide legal grounds to challenge the move. Prior to deregulation, one U.S. carrier paid $300 000 for a licence to haul two products through two states. Six months later, the industry was deregulated and one could obtain a licence to haul an unlimited number of products through 48 states for $250.

Most of the changes for the trucking industry were requested by a coalition of manufacturers and shippers. In its opinion, regulation was not working well. Customers of trucking services felt restricted by their inability to negotiate contracts or to control standards of service. They stressed that they must be able to select a service based on quality and cost. For one thing, new inventory management techniques require precise timing of shipments. This demands a higher quality of service than is currently available.

Large trucking firms joined the shippers because they believed that complying with regulation put them at a competitive disadvantage. Truckers and firms that ignored operating regulations (safety, hour logging, licence restrictions) were unlikely to be caught or deterred from further violations. Firms that "cheated" were able to operate successfully with a much larger profit margin. Legitimate firms are now relying upon deregulation to remove "cheaters" from the industry through increased enforcement.

The current state of regulation is seen as "unofficial deregulation" without enforcement. Trucking firms favour the protection offered by regulation in its ideal form, but have come to view deregulation favourably as a return to the "strict regulation" of safety laws that had become unenforceable.

Indications that Canada planned to deregulate the trucking industry were noted by most firms in the early 1980s. The five-year "notification period" has given all participants ample opportunity to express their concerns, opinions, and suggestions. Most Canadian carriers feel they have been given ample opportunity to make adjustments and prepare for the challenge of deregulation. However, Ontario carriers feel that many of their points have not been given adequate consideration.

3 CALL-NET TELECOMMUNICATIONS LIMITED

PETER BROCKMANN AND D. WAYNE TAYLOR

Call-Net Telecommunications Ltd. of Toronto was formed in 1986 with the intention of becoming an "Enhanced Service Provider" (ESP) of telecommunications services. Basic bulk telecommunications services such as OUT-WATS were to be purchased from Bell Canada, and value was to be added through service-enhancing features and then resold to the business community.

Bell Canada brought Call-Net's services and activities to the attention of the Canadian Radio-Television and Telecommunications Commission (CRTC). Bell suggested that, since Call-Net's services were cheaper than Bell Canada's long-distance rates, its services were not, in fact, "enhanced," but basic. Therefore, they competed with Bell in a market where the CRTC allowed Bell a monopoly.

The CRTC agreed and ordered Call-Net to restructure its services so that they were not competitive with Bell's basic long-distance services.

THE TELECOMMUNICATIONS INDUSTRY

Telecommunications in Canada is big business—$10 billion in 1985. It is also a strategic business. More and more corporations depend upon the right information at the right time for competitive advantages. Moving this information requires a complex infrastructure of transmission media—copper wire, fibre optics, satellite, microwave—and a wide array of interconnected devices, such as computers, modems, fax machines, and telephones. Canadian telecommunications is high technology—and highly priced. According to one study:

> The traditional pricing systems for both within and between (telephone) companies favours residential over business users, rural over urban users, and local over toll users. . . . Competition in the provision of telecommunications services is largely, if not wholly, incompatible with the present pricing system.

This cross-subsidization is the biggest barrier to deregulation and more competition. In 1980, Bell's high-priced toll service offset the low-priced local service by $725 million. This practice suits residential consumers just fine, but business' needs are at the bottom of the industry's concerns.

On the other hand, the premium pricing (200% above cost) of long-distance calls makes it extremely attractive to new entrants. Regulation, though, has closed entry and historically guaranteed the phone companies a monopoly within their jurisdictions. Bell Canada is sensitive about its status as a monopoly, and makes great efforts to treat all customers professionally, efficiently, and courteously.

Meanwhile, the Canadian business environment is changing dramatically. Free trade with the United States presents the greatest challenge since Confederation. The American telecommunications industry has been deregulated over the past four years, and the cost of long-distance calls is significantly lower for U.S. businesses than for Canadian firms. At the same time, competition in the United States has created innovative services, encouraged the adoption of innovative technology, and contributed to firm-specific competitive advantages in some information-dependent sectors. Canadian businesses merely point to their U.S. competitors, as they hold up their phone bills and ask: "How can we compete with them?"

THE CANADIAN RADIO-TELEVISION AND TELECOMMUNICATIONS COMMISSION

In the early twentieth century, it was inefficient to allow competition in local telephone service, with several companies' wires entering each neighbourhood. In those simpler times, the focus was on the local network. Regulation, commencing in 1906, sought to protect telephone users from a monopoly price level. Yet it allowed the service providers the opportunity to attract enough income to build the national network that made Canada one of the most telephone-dense nations in the world.

Until 1976, telecommunications were regulated by the Canadian Transport Commission, pursuant to the Railway Act. In 1976, the federal government transferred jurisdiction for telecommunications to the CRTC by amending the Canadian Radio-Television and Telecommunications Commission Act.

As a semi-judicial independent body, the CRTC holds public hearings on issues of public concern regarding the regulation of telecommunications. Responses from the regulated companies are then presented and the Commission announces its decisions in writing. These decisions typically include background information, summaries of positions of the interested parties, a record of process, and the orders of the Commission.

Anyone can appeal the decisions of the CRTC. For questions of jurisdiction and law, an appeal can be brought to the Federal Court of Appeal and then the Supreme Court of Canada. An appeal for any other reason may be brought to the federal Cabinet.

Overall, seven regulatory agencies, one provincial Cabinet, and a number of municipal governments review construction programs, set tariff structures, review customer relations and service quality measures, approve new services, regulate corporate policies, and define the allowed rate of return for Canada's telecommunications carriers.

The ten provincial governments and the federal government agree that the structure of regulation is not the responsibility of the courts or of independent regulators. However, they have not been able to resolve the question, despite almost a decade of negotiations, including six federal-provincial and five interprovincial conferences, as well as innumerable informal meetings. The inability of governments to reach any consensus on the structure of regulation has resulted in both the Supreme Court of Canada and the CRTC usurping government's policy-setting role. Using its discretionary powers, the CRTC, in particular, has set numerous precedents regarding system interconnection, terminal attachments, and most recently interprovincial rates and services.

CALL-NET

Call-Net Telecommunications Ltd. was incorporated in January, 1986 with $3 million in equity to provide enhanced services to small businesses in Ontario and Quebec. The principal shareholder, company President Michael Kedar, had a technical background in electronics. He had worked with Motorola Canada and operated his own telecommunications consulting firm prior to setting up Call-Net.

The company began operating in November, 1986 by providing three services:

- Customer-Dialed Account Recording (CDAR);
- Selective Call Forwarding (SCF); and,
- Voice Messaging (VM).

By having employees of subscribers key in a security or account number before a toll call was connected, Call-Net, acting as a service provider, could generate a custom billing report for subscribers detailing telephone costs by employee and by account code. This CDAR service allowed subscribers to allocate telephone costs, reduce telephone abuse and misuse, and charge telephone expenses back to the client, possibly with some markup assigned by Call-Net's subscriber.

In the SCF service, Call-Net not only let strictly pre-authorized calls be forwarded, but also allowed someone to program call-forwarding numbers from any phone, thus cutting down on the time wasted playing telephone tag.

Call-Net's version of a Voice Messaging system was essentially a sophisticated answering machine that let the subscriber customize the message for a specific caller.

The target market for Call-Net was legal, accounting, engineering, and other professional firms where converting a period expense into a variable cost is advantageous. According to Kedar, Call-Net's CDAR service typically resulted in a 40% reduction in total telephone billings for subscribers, as well as the discount to Bell Canada's long-distance service initially offered by Call-Net.

THE DECISIONS

Two decisions by the CRTC in 1984 and 1985 were the most important events leading up to the company's formation in 1987. These decisions were:

- Telecom Decision 84-18 Enhanced Services; and,
- Telecom Decision 85-19 IX Competition and Related Issues.

Kedar saw these decisions as part of a trend in deregulation, providing improved choice in service configuration and supplier. Bell Canada, before actual service began, complained to the CRTC that Call-Net should not be connected to the network because its service was a basic one, and therefore not allowed under CRTC rules then in place.

Telecom Decision 84-18 defined basic services as:

limited to the offering of transmission capacity for the movement of information. In offering this capacity, a communications path is provided for the analog or digital transmission of information of various types such as voice, data, and video.

Typical basic services were long-distance, WATS, and 800-Service.

The CRTC refused Bell's request. In Telecom Decision 84-18, the CRTC stated that:

> ... as a matter of regulatory policy, it is neither necessary nor desirable that enhanced services provided by parties other than common carriers be regulated ... its (the CRTC's) statutory mandates do not require it to regulate a potentially wide range of enhanced service providers (ESP).

Enhanced services were defined as "any offering over the telecommunications network which is more than a basic service."

Call-Net was considered to be an enhanced service provider, and therefore outside the Commission's mandate. So on December 1, 1986, Call-Net began operations. Three months later, Bell Canada took Call-Net to the CRTC again. On May 22, 1987, the CRTC ordered Bell and CNCP to disconnect Call-Net's lines as of June 22, 1987, agreeing with Bell that the CDAR and SCF services offered were in fact basic services. Call-Net asked the Commission to reconsider its decision, but was denied.

Call-Net's customer base had grown to 450 subscribers. With service definitions as vague as those found in CRTC's Telecom Decision 84-18, it should not be surprising that Kedar took the regulator at face value.

THE APPEALS

Kedar appealed to the federal Cabinet through Communications Minister Flora MacDonald. On November 22, 1987 the Cabinet reaffirmed the CRTC decision and granted Call-Net a 180-day period to conform to the regulations. This Order-in-Council did not explicitly state that Bell should provide Call-Net with any additional services while Call-Net restructured. So when Call-Net asked for more trunk lines to support its restructuring effort, Bell refused. When Call-Net subsequently complained to the regulator, the CRTC agreed that Bell did not have to provide any additional services, but should give "every assistance to Call-Net in making its services conform."

Kedar appealed to the Cabinet a second time on January 21, 1988 asking the Cabinet: (1) to order Bell Canada to provide additional services during the restructuring period, (2) for an additional extension. In return, Call-Net would:

(a) limit its customer base to Ontario, Quebec, and British Columbia;
(b) order no more private line installations for Canadian points outside those three provinces;
(c) not provide services to companies requiring 100 or more lines; and,
(d) set rates comparable to the lowest for direct-dialled long-distance calls offered by Bell Canada in Ontario and Quebec, and BC Tel in British Columbia.

In effect, Kedar proposed to accept more direct regulation in exchange for the survival of the firm, which by now was losing money. Call-Net's annual revenue at that time was approximately $7 million with 800 subscribers.

Cabinet rejected Kedar's four conditions, upholding the original CRTC decision, but took the unprecedented step of reversing its earlier decision, stating that "Call-Net should have access to additional Bell Canada and CNCP Telecommunications facilities while it adjusts its business operations." At the same time, an additional 90-day extension was granted for Call-Net to restructure its operations.

In turn, Cabinet was taken to the Federal Court of Canada by the Telecommunications Workers Union and the Communications and Electrical Workers of Canada, Bell Canada's and BC Tel's unions representing 31 000 employees. They argued that "Cabinet has the right only to issue one Order-in-Council varying or rescinding a CRTC decision, and has no inherent jurisdiction to reconsider its own decision." The Federal Court, however, found in favour of the Government and decided on July 22, 1988 that the Cabinet was not limited in its "ability to further vary a previous Order-in-Council."

In view of all the attention that this matter was receiving, the CRTC on June 10, 1988, issued a public notice soliciting comment on "the whole question of basic versus enhanced services and on Call-Net's role within the regulatory environment." Although more than eighty parties offered comment, on August 16, 1988 (just three days before service was to be cut off) the CRTC re-confirmed its decision that Call-Net offered basic services.

THE RESTRUCTURING OF CALL-NET

Call-Net began to reorganize its subscribers into a long-distance sharing group, which CRTC rules allowed. *Sharing groups*, as defined in CRTC Telecom Decision 84-18, required that the members be jointly and severally liable for the group's phone bill. If a member defaulted on payment of its phone bill, Bell could seek payment from any of the other members.

Bell Canada allowed Kedar a further one-week delay in any service cut-off, while Call-Net proposed to act as the agent for the CDAR/Sharenet sharing group. Members would pay their phone bills, as prepared by Call-Net, into a trust fund, out of which Call-Net's expenses would then be covered once the carriers were paid.

In any event, service disconnection by Bell was not really as bad as it sounded. Call-Net leased discount long-distance lines from Bell, known as WATS or Wide Area Telephone Service. It repackaged the service with the security and account coding features and resold the service as CDAR at a discount to Bell's regular long-distance customers. Most of Call-Net's customers did not have the minimum long-distance bills to warrant leasing a WATS line from Bell. While long-distance tariffs are based upon length of call and distance, WATS generally offers a fee structure based only on length of call. Through Call-Net, subscribers got custom-billing services at a discount of what they were already paying for long distance.

Cut-off simply meant disconnecting Call-Net's WATS lines and reconnecting the higher-priced long-distance lines. Call-Net's margins would be squeezed, but it would not necessarily be put out of business.

A week later, on August 25, 1988, Bell Canada informed Call-Net that Bell would disconnect the services at 5:00 p.m. that day. Kedar went to the CRTC and got an interim order requiring that the service be restored. Bell complied. By this time, Call-Net had a client base of 1000 subscribers, revenues of approximately $8.8 million and employed 75 people in Toronto and Montreal.

The Commission received information from Bell Canada just before the Labour Day weekend that Call-Net was having difficulty acquiring insurance for the sharing group. The Commission announced on the first day back to work— Tuesday, September 6, 1988—that services to Call-Net were to be disconnected immediately. The uncharacteristic speed at which the CRTC reached its September 6, 1988, decision certainly bothered Mr. Kedar: "I cannot believe they have done that," he said angrily. "We were told to restructure and now the Commission is saying it's not good enough . . . I really think this is almost a vendetta against Call-Net. All we're getting is the big machinery of Bell somehow in cahoots with the CRTC trying to squish us in every way."

Call-Net filed a motion on September 7, 1988, with the Federal Court requesting leave to appeal the CRTC's most recent decision. The same day, Kedar also launched an application to the Federal Court requesting a stay of execution order against the CRTC's disconnection order to Bell Canada.

The stay was dismissed on September 9 because the Court decided it could not order a stay of execution against an already carried-out order. On September 21, the Federal Court granted Call-Net leave to appeal the CRTC's September 6 decision ordering Bell Canada to disconnect Call-Net's WATS lines.

Call-Net appealed to the Federal Cabinet on September 12 requesting a retroactive stay of execution against the CRTC's disconnect order of September 6. The Federal Cabinet granted the appeal and issued a retroactive stay of execution on October 17, 1988.

When the Federal Court upheld the CRTC's decision of September 6, 1988, Call-Net appealed to the Supreme Court of Canada. On January 11, 1989, the CRTC issued a public notice soliciting comments from interested parties in a review of the sharing and resale regime. Kedar asked the Supreme Court for a delay to his appeal until the CRTC hearings were completed, hoping the outcome would be favourable to Call-Net. The CRTC's lawyers objected, the Supreme Court sustained the objection, and the case before the Supreme Court should commence shortly.

4 RSR ROAD SURFACE RECYCLING INC.

WARREN M. DUMANSKI AND D. WAYNE TAYLOR

In 1984, Frank Crupi was a man with a dream. His family had been in the paving business for many years in Toronto operating as D. Crupi and Sons Ltd. Crupi knew the paving business and all the advances in technology that affected it.

THE ROAD MANAGER

At that time there existed machines which could recycle pavement *in situ*; however, they left a rough surface which required a new asphalt to be overlaid. D. Crupi and Sons was one of the few companies in Ontario which used this technology. Crupi recognized the limitations of these machines and was determined to develop his own to solve these problems. He reasoned that if such a machine were developed, it would be a great success because of the potential cost savings in resurfacing a road.

Traditionally, roads are resurfaced (as opposed to reconstructed) by stripping the top two inches of asphalt, trucking them to a recycling plant, recycling them, trucking them back, and putting the recycled asphalt back on the road. This is expensive, but less so than putting in new material each time. Crupi's process (see Exhibit 1) would be radically different, because his new machine would do the stripping, recycling, and resurfacing all at once.

Exhibit 1

The Configuration of the Road Manager

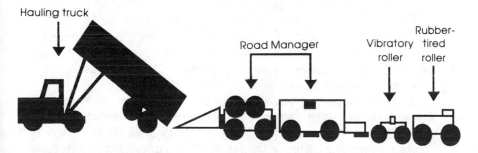

Using this method, Crupi would eliminate the very expensive trucking charges—30 to 40% of the total cost—associated with resurfacing roads. This process would also result in minimal disturbance to the driving public because vehicles could pass beside the machine as it was working. Now all he had to do was build it.

Crupi was very aware that the success of his machine depended upon not only how well it worked, but also on whether it was given work to do. The most logical source of future contracts was the Ministry of Transportation of Ontario (MTO), which was responsible for all provincial highways and cost-shared the work on most municipal roads. Before Crupi started to build his machine, he approached people at MTO. The Ministry's New Products Committee told him it could not commit to the machine until they saw how it worked. The Ministry, Crupi learned, did not get involved with developing technology. Undeterred, he proceeded with his plan.

In 1985, Crupi looked for financial backing from the government. He estimated that his machine would take about three months and $500 000 to build. He was able to obtain a loan of $300 000 from the Ontario Development Corporation (ODC); the rest would be financed personally or through the Toronto-Dominion Bank. He set up RSR Road Surface Recycling Inc. (RSR) as a new operating company and subcontracted the building of the machine to Carruthers Manufacturing in Toronto. As with most new designs, it required many modifications to improve its performance, and these were very expensive. When completed, the machine had taken about three years to perfect and cost a total of $4.5 million to develop.

Frank Crupi was very involved in the development of this machine and did not have much time for D. Crupi and Sons. He quickly fell into debt, which worried his bankers. Still, Crupi was not overly concerned; once the machine was working properly he would make lots of money, or so he felt. To ensure that MTO did not forget about him, Crupi stayed in touch with his contacts and attended many Liberal fund-raisers.

By the summer of 1987 "The Road Manager," as Crupi's in situ recycler was called, was ready to be used on public roads. Frank Crupi was very anxious to get working because of the high debt load he carried; however, the government was indifferent. Apparently, "The Road Manager's" potential cost savings were not enough to convince MTO; Crupi had to prove that his machine could do the job. He was given a special contract to show what his machine could do on a 4.6 km section of Highway 3. Construction reports by MTO indicated that the machine performed very well, but there were a few concerns. Consensus though, was that these problems could be corrected.

Crupi had now become desperate for work, so he took his machine to British Columbia and worked on a few contracts there. He soon became disgruntled, as he felt that he was treated unfairly due to the fact that he was not a local contractor. He also spent time in Quebec where he did several contracts, but was under extreme pressure from local contractors to leave because he was keeping bidding prices low. Frank's family and heart were in Toronto; this was where he

Exhibit 2

The Configuration of the Taisei Rotec Machine

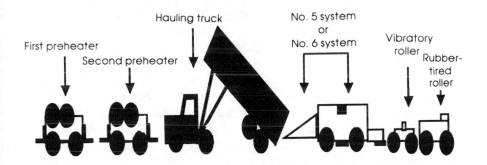

wanted to succeed, but there were no further contracts to come in 1987.

THE COMPETITION—TAISEI ROTEC

Meanwhile, industry giant Warren Bitulithic Ltd. had leased a state-of-the-art *in situ* pavement recycler from the Taisei Rotec Company of Japan.

In the summer of 1987, the Taisei Rotec machine (see Exhibit 2) was granted a test section on Highway 24 in Ontario, and the results were similar to those for "The Road Manager": quite positive, with some small reservations. Government construction reports were very similar for the two machines; one was not significantly better than the other in terms of actual performance. However, Crupi was told by some MTO personnel that Taisei's machine had to be better simply because it was Japanese.

An incident during the summer of 1988 gave Frank Crupi a good indication of his competition. The County of Brant had some resurfacing work to do and was interested in the new technology because of its obvious cost savings. Knowing this, Taisei Rotec, through Warren Bitulithic, paid for a Brant County representative to fly to Seattle to see its machine in operation. Brant County then hired a consulting engineer associated with Warren Bitulithic to write the specifications for the project. When the tender for the job was released, it specified that the machine had to have the items which were unique to the Taisei recycler. In effect, RSR had been "specified out" of the contract. When Crupi approached the provincial government to complain about this, the response was, "Sorry, we can't help you."

One can only imagine Frank Crupi's shock when he learned that the Japanese were beating him in his own province. His dream had been shattered. Crupi could not afford to have "The Road Manager" sit idle in his company's yard. He had too much debt to service. He was forced to take work wherever he could find it.

PREMIER'S COUNCIL REPORT

The Premier's Council was established in 1986 by Ontario Liberal Premier David Peterson. Its mandate was "to steer Ontario into the forefront of economic leadership and technological innovation." The Council, chaired by the Premier, is composed of politicians, business representatives, labour representatives, and academics.

The Premier's Council, in its report, *Competing in the New Global Economy*, concluded that "natural resources and tariff walls are the traditional foundation of Ontario's wealth, but both advantages are disappearing." As these advantages disappear, Ontario becomes very vulnerable to changes in the global marketplace. It was clear to the Council that the provinces and industry had to redirect the emphasis from basic commodities like newsprint and sheet metal to "smarter," more specialized products with higher value-added and a higher technological base.

Of course, the inadequacies of Canada's research and development (R&D) efforts were well-documented. Overall, Canada spends roughly half as much of its Gross Domestic Product on R&D as the other leading industrialized nations (see Exhibit 3). The Council concluded that if Ontario was to maintain or develop a competitive edge in technology it had to encourage more spending in this area.

"If Ontario is to continue to compete internationally, the province must develop more indigenous multinational manufacturing companies operating in high-growth industries." To achieve this, the report went on to say, government must begin to function in partnership with industry and labour.

To specifically encourage R&D and help indigenous companies, the Council suggested that the government should use procurement as a tool:

> The government should move to a system of strategic procurement in government purchasing. This would be a departure from the present practice of spreading the work among dozens or hundreds of small suppliers. The aim should be to use the government purchasing power to help local suppliers upgrade their expertise, improve their products, cut their costs, and gain sufficient scale to compete in world markets . . . In some businesses, new product development is a critical competitive tool. Strategic procurement can help by funding the development of new state-of-the-art techniques, testing prototypes, and making the initial purchase of new products . . . The council also recommends establishing a Strategic Procurement Committee to advise government on the most effective purchasing strategies, and an Enabling R&D Contract Fund to finance prototype research as a prelude to awarding major government contracts and to perform other industry-building functions.

Finally, the Report of the Premier's Council concluded that "the business world's traditional reluctance to deal with government bureaucracy must be broken down, and government's perceived resistance to involving the public sector meaningfully in public policy development must be dissipated."

Exhibit 3

Gross R&D Expenditures as a Percent of GDP
1984

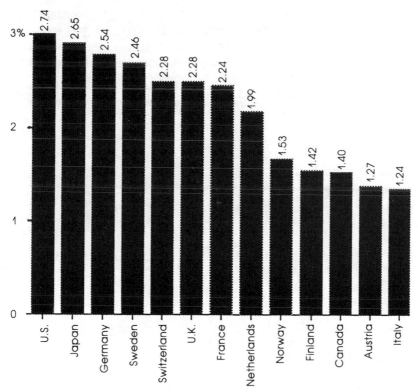

Source: OECD, *Main Economic Indications*, March 1986. OECD, *Recent Results*, 1979-86.

EPILOGUE

At the Ontario Good Roads Association Conference in February 1988, Frank Crupi approached MTO representatives and told them that RSR was unable to maintain its initiative with MTO for in-place recycling; RSR was in receivership. The bank had waited long enough for its payments and had decided to close down Crupi's operations. Unfortunately for the bank, it had accepted Crupi's machine as collateral and was not pleased at the thought of taking control of a 51-tonne machine it had no hope of selling.

Frank Crupi was able to stall the bank by showing them a letter from Ed Fulton, Minister of Transportation, which stated that RSR could count on work from MTO in the summer of 1988. Presumably then, Frank would be able to start paying off the bank. However, despite these promises, no contracts arrived in 1988.

In the fall of that year, Frank received yet another letter from Ed Fulton promising work for 1989. By this time, Frank had seen enough. He had the bank breathing down his neck and he was left with no option but to leave the country. Through an agent, he arranged for several contracts in the Lakeland, Florida area, where he lives today. When Frank Crupi left Toronto in November 1988, his story was told in major newspapers across the country (see Exhibit 4). He was very upset, and rightly so. Initially, he wanted to park his machine on the front lawn of Queen's Park and call a press conference then and there to talk about how the Ontario government deals with new products and new technology. The advertising agency he hired to tell his story talked him out of it.

Today, Frank Crupi is a successful businessman. He has secured contracts through 1989 in Florida. His operation has moved to Lakeland, and he intends to stay there. He has a green card (American working permit) and has about 30 people working for him. Frank's home in Scarborough is for sale.

Exhibit 4

Off the road again . . .

Apathy forces inventor to take machine to U.S.

TORONTO (CP) — A disgruntled Ontario inventor is taking his "revolutionary" road resurfacing machine to the United States because the Ontario government refuses to use it, even though he says the machine could save taxpayers millions.

"There's been only a lukewarm response (here)," said Frank Crupi, president of Toronto-based RSR Road Surface Recycling.

Repaving a road conventionally requires taking off the damaged asphalt, trucking it to an asphalt plant, crushing and recycling it, trucking it back to the site and relaying it.

However, Crupi said Tuesday his machine — dubbed the Road Manager — does the entire process while passing over the damaged area.

He estimated the machine could cut the cost of repaving Ontario roads in 1989 by one-third, or more than $4.5 million.

However, a spokesman for Transportation Minister Ed Fulton called that estimate "superficial."

The ministry is interested in the invention, but John Packowski said that while Crupi's machine does a good job on straight roads, it does substandard repairs on roads with curves or basins.

"His machine has only limited application," Packowski said. "We have been very fair."

But Crupi told a news conference in Toronto that his hulking, 51-tonne machine was being shipped by train to Florida where he has a government contract.

"We're sending it to Florida because it looks like Americans are more interested in saving tax dollars than Canadians."

He said his company spent five years and more than $4-million developing the Road Manager. Crupi said the company is in debt.

Source: *The Globe and Mail*, November 30, 1988, page A10.

5 BILL C-51: THE TOBACCO PRODUCTS CONTROL ACT

LINDA A. CRAENEN AND D. WAYNE TAYLOR

In April, 1987, Health Minister Jake Epp introduced into the House of Commons Bill C-51: The Tobacco Products Control Act. The purpose of this bill was to ban all forms of tobacco advertising in the interests of public health. The tobacco industry was horrified, the advertising industry was horrified, and the government had a majority in the House which guaranteed swift and easy passage of the bill. Or could something be done to change government's mind?

BACKGROUND

Since the early 1960s, research has continued to document the health hazards of both smoking tobacco products and inhaling second-hand smoke. Previously, it was thought that as long as smoking was viewed as a personal issue, people could justifiably argue that the government should not intervene with tobacco use. However, since repeated research has confirmed the negative effects of tobacco smoking, the social perceptions of smoking have changed considerably. Consequently, an anti-smoking lobby blossomed and grew to become increasingly vocal about the social costs of smoking and of tolerating the habit in public places. These groups began to pressure both federal and provincial governments to legislate against tobacco advertising and smoking in the workplace, to declare tobacco a hazardous substance, and to assist tobacco farmers in finding alternative crops or alternative employment. It was this pressure, along with concerns for the rising health costs of preventable illnesses caused by tobacco use, that prompted Jake Epp, Canada's Minister of Health and Welfare, to introduce Bill C-51.

As stated, the purpose of the Act was:
to provide a legislative response to a national public health problem of substantial and pressing concern and in particular,

(a) to protect the health of Canadians in the light of conclusive evidence implicating tobacco use in the incidence of numerous debilitating and fatal diseases;
(b) to protect young persons and others, to the extent that is reasonable in a free and democratic society, from inducements to use tobacco products and consequent dependence on them; and
(c) to enhance public awareness of the hazards of tobacco use by ensuring the effective communication of pertinent information to consumers of tobacco products.''

Measures in the original bill called for:

(a) an end to all newspaper advertising by January 1, 1988;
(b) the prohibition of in-store signs, advertising on non-tobacco goods (for

257

example, T-shirts and lighters), contests, couponing, and product sampling by July 1, 1988. Point-of-purchase material with only the full company name was to be allowed;

(c) the inclusion of new, stronger, rotating health warnings on cigarette packages, also by July 1, 1988;

(d) the indication of levels of toxic contents by manufacturers and importers, as well as reporting of production, import, and sales figures to Health and Welfare Canada effective July 1, 1988;

(e) a ban on magazine, urban transit, and billboard advertising and an end to all brand sponsorship of events by January 1, 1989. "Philanthropic sponsorship" of arts, charity, and sports events would be allowed only under the full company name.

THE TOBACCO INDUSTRY

The tobacco industry comprises tobacco growing, leaf processing, manufacturing, wholesaling, and retailing. The key players in the industry are: (1) tobacco manufacturers represented by the Canadian Tobacco Manufacturers' Council; (2) tobacco growers represented by the Ontario Flue-Cured Tobacco Growers' Marketing Board; and (3) Health and Welfare Canada. The tobacco industry supports nearly 3 000 farm families and over 30 000 transient workers. In addition, 6 800 people work for manufacturers, with thousands more in advertising, distribution, retailing, and related jobs. Either directly or indirectly, manufacturers, farmers, retailers, and government would all be affected by a serious decline in tobacco sales.

THE MANUFACTURERS

Tobacco manufacturing is a heavily concentrated sector of Canadian industry. In 1985, three companies were responsible for 95% of tobacco manufacturing activity. All were subsidiaries of large, diversified, multinational conglomerates including:

Imperial Tobacco (Players, DuMaurier)
Market share 54%
Division of Imasco, 44% owned by BAT Industries PLC of Britain

Rothmans (Rothmans, Craven A)
Market share 28%
Owned 72% by Rothmans International PLC of Britain

RJR-MacDonald (Export A, Vantage)
Market share 18%
Unit of RJR Nabisco Inc. of Atlanta

These companies constitute the membership of the Canadian Tobacco Manufacturers' Council (CTMC), which provides a unified voice for the industry. Members buy their tobacco from leaf processors, who perform the conditioning operations.

Tobacco sales rose yearly for approximately twenty years, until sales peaked in 1982. That year, Canadians purchased 72.8 billion cigarettes. By 1984, this number had declined to 68.1 billion. Manufacturers blamed this decline on both the federal and provincial governments for increasing taxes on tobacco products above the rate of inflation. On average, about 65% of the price of a package of cigarettes goes to pay federal and provincial taxes. According to the CTMC in 1986, Canadians spent $5 billion on tobacco products (1.2% of the GNP), providing $3 billion in federal and provincial taxes (see Exhibit 5). By 1988, even though sales continued to decline, the taxes collected totalled $4 billion.

WHOLESALERS AND RETAILERS

There are three kinds of tobacco wholesaling operations in Canada:

1. those operated by the manufacturers themselves;
2. those by wholesalers, who sell exclusively to one retailing chain of pharmaceutical outlets or grocers; and
3. those by independent wholesalers, who sell to non-related clients.

Wholesaling accounts for approximately 3.5% of the total retail cost of tobacco products. In 1982, there were 30 000 vending machines and 90 000 retail stores selling cigarettes. Two-thirds of all retail sales were made through grocery stores and pharmacies.

THE TOBACCO GROWERS

Ontario farmers grow almost 90% of Canada's tobacco crop. Once tobacco has been picked and heat-dried in curing barns, it is aged for periods of 10 to 12 months. Tobacco auctioning usually begins early in October, with growers guaranteed a minimum price negotiated the previous spring.

The Ontario growers are represented by the Ontario Flue-Cured Tobacco Growers' Marketing Board (OFCTGMB), headquartered in Tillsonburg, Ontario. Major functions of the Board in the 1980s were to help maintain prices and to find new markets in Canada and abroad. Tobacco manufacturers were buying less tobacco from farmers because of declining domestic sales of cigarettes. This they blamed mainly on rising government taxes and increased foreign competition for the export market. (Manufacturers refused to acknowledge that fewer people smoked or smoked less by choice out of concern for their health.[62]) As a result, production of flue-cured tobacco in Ontario has been almost halved in recent years (see Exhibit 6).

Rationalization and diversification have maintained profitability for some tobacco manufacturers, but communities dependent on tobacco growing were suffering financially because they could not sell their crops.

Although the objectives of the OFCTGMB paralleled those of the CTMC, the primary objective of the marketing board was to impress upon the government the concerns of tobacco growers. It therefore felt it essential to warn government that

Exhibit 5
Trends in Tobacco Consumption and Tobacco Prices in Canada, 1980-1986

| | TOTAL TOBACCO CONSUMPTION | | | | TOTAL CIGARETTE CONSUMPTION | | | | REAL TOBACCO PRICE INDEX | |
| | Tonnes | | kg/person over 15 | | Millions of Cigarettes | | Cigarettes/person over 15 | | | |
	Number	Percentage of Change from Previous Year	Number	Percentage of Change from Previous Year	Number	Percentage of Change from Previous Year	Number	Percentage of Change from Previous Year	Index 1981=100	Percentage of Change from Previous Year
1980	64655	–	3.51	–	70085	–	3849	–	99.0	–
1981	66525	+2.9	3.52	+0.3	72159	+3.0	3859	+0.3	100.0	+1.0
1982	66904	+0.6	3.51	-0.3	72818	+0.9	3853	-0.2	104.1	+4.1
1983	64404	-3.7	3.32	-5.4	70010	-3.9	3652	-5.2	115.7	+11.1
1984	62892	-2.3	3.19	-3.9	68521	-2.1	3478	-4.8	123.6	+6.8
1985	61290	-2.5	3.08	-3.4	66642	-2.7	3348	-3.7	139.5	+12.9
1986	58405	-4.7	2.90	-5.8	63544	-4.6	3154	-5.8	157.4	+12.8

Sources:
1. "Production and disposition of tobacco products," Statistics Canada Catalogue No. 32-022, monthly, 1980-1986.
2. "Imports by Commodities," Statistics Canada catalogue No. 65-007, monthly, 1980-1986.
3. "Consumer Prices and Price indexes," Statistics Canada Catalogue No. 62-010, quarterly, 1980-1986.
4. "Postcensal Annual Estimates of Population by Marital Status, Age, Sex and Components of Growth for Canada Provinces and Territories," June 1- Statistics Canada Catalogue No. 91-210, annual 1980-1986.
Reproduced with the permission of the Minister of Supply and Services Canada, 1990.

Exhibit 6

Flue-Cured Tobacco Production (Ontario)

CROP YEAR	CROP IN MILLIONS OF POUNDS
1982	238
1983	215
1984	170
1985	170
1986	130
1987	110
1988	141

if it "legislated" the tobacco industry out of business, it had a responsibility to adequately compensate the producers affected by such action. Under the Tobacco Assistance Program, all available funds had been used with no further funds having been committed. The OFCTGMB further stated:

> We have not been critical of those officials who drafted proposed legislation. We have said that we don't oppose the reasonable legislative controls of the merchandising of tobacco products. We do oppose most vehemently the wording and principles in those sections dealing with promotion and advertising. There can be controls without prohibition.

No other agricultural crop had ever experienced such rapid decline in sales as had tobacco. Over 250 farms had already gone through a crop-reduction program, 98 were in the process of doing so, and 153 were on the waiting list, with more applying each day.

Since tobacco is an international trading commodity, the OFCTGMB advocates that Ontario tobacco growers develop more export markets in order to survive. Worldwide, there is a shortage of tobacco, and with possible export contracts to countries such as Morocco, Algeria, Tunisia and China, it would seem that there is some hope for tobacco growers. Government export and marketing assistance abroad was sought to promote this venture further. However, even if government did assist tobacco farmers, Alvin Lindsay, Chairman of the OFCTGMB, believed that:

> The Ontario tobacco growing industry will continue to slide downward because of anti-smoking propaganda and taxation. . . . If the do-gooders would stay off our backs, then we could keep our heads above water.

THE ROLE OF GOVERNMENT

The role of both the provincial and federal governments in the tobacco industry is quite diverse and complex. Provincial and federal governments legislate and impose excise and sales taxes on tobacco products. Government departments such as Health and Welfare Canada educate and inform the public about the potential hazards of tobacco smoking, monitor the industry, and regulate many aspects of it. Agriculture Canada assists tobacco farmers in diversifying their operations.

In 1987, Agriculture Canada developed the Alternate Enterprise Initiative as part of the Tobacco Transition Adjustment Initiative and implemented it in cooperation with the tobacco-producing provinces, tobacco producers, and manufacturers. This program will inject about $30 million into the tobacco-producing regions of Canada and assist in the orderly transition from tobacco to alternative crops.

The OFCTGMB feels that the problem is not a lack of alternate crops which will grow in the sandy soil of Southern Ontario. It is concerned that the market for these crops (tomatoes, garlic, soybeans) is not as lucrative as that for tobacco. In recent years, tobacco returns had averaged $4 000 per acre, almost ten times the return for alternate crops.

THE ADVERTISING INDUSTRY

In 1986, the CTMC reported that the tobacco industry had spent approximately $79.8 million on advertising and promotions. Consequently, the Canadian advertising industry stands to lose a substantial amount of revenue as a direct result of Bill C-51. The biggest "losers" in the tobacco advertising ban are expected to be the outdoor media. The Outdoor Advertising Association (OAA) feared that 150 people were in danger of losing their jobs, and that 10 to 12 companies could close. As one OAA representative said: "We'll be fighting this thing tooth and nail from a survival and free enterprise point of view."

The objective of the industry was therefore to convince the government that advertising did not entice individuals to smoke. The industry would utilize industry experts and their research. For instance, Dr. Glen Smith of the Children's Research Unit, London, U.K. presented his research findings in an attempt to demonstrate that cigarette advertisements do not have an impact on young people, and therefore the ban on advertising and promotion would have no effect.

The industry also began to send several dozen different form letters outlining its position to members of Parliament (see Exhibit 7).

Peter Gallop, of Gallop & Gallop, a Canadian billboard manufacturer speaking on behalf of forty companies, argued that C-51 was a serious threat to his industry.

Bill C-51 will create several hardships for the outdoor advertising industry in Canada, particularly for newer companies who have not had time to pay off the heavy start-up capital investments with this industry. Many of the smaller and newer companies will not survive under C-51, returning the industry to an effective monopoly.

The outdoor advertising firms proposed a compromise on Bill C-51 that would allow promotion to continue under tougher restrictions and would see a "major media assault" on smoking.

Exhibit 7

Outdoor Advertising Association of Canada · l'Association Canadienne de l'Affichage Extérieur

March 23, 1987

The Right Honourable Martin Brian Mulroney
Prime Minister
Privy Council
Ottawa, Canada

Dear Mr. Prime Minister,

The Outdoor Advertising Association of Canada is made up of
some 37 member companies operating various out-of-home
advertising media products from coast to coast in Canada.

For many years now we have worked closely with the Canadian
tobacco companies in helping them advertise their various
products. This has always been done with good taste,
strictly adhering to the self regulated code of standards
set up by the tobacco industry in 1971. Modifications and
extensions to this code have been made from time to time
throughout the years and these have always been respected.

It is with great concern, therefore, that we view some
rumored legislation from the Federal Government of Canada
which will possibly ban completely the advertising of
tobacco products.

The issue here is not whether tobacco products should be
used. These products are legally manufactured and legally
sold in Canada and therefore their use is a basic freedom
of choice and this is recognized by your Government. It is
therefore, unacceptable that this same government should
introduce measures that would directly impinge on the free
enterprise system on which our whole social and business
structure is built. The Government, therefore, must
respect these basic freedoms and recognize that if a
product is legally manufactured and legally sold that is
must have the right to compete in the market place within
the bounds of good taste.

If any banning legislation is imposed on tobacco
advertising, our industry will be severely damaged.
Substantial revenues will be lost and as a result workers
will be laid off and in some cases some of our smaller
companies will face possible bankruptcy. This must not
happen.

.../2

1300 Yonge Street, Suite 302, Toronto, Canada. M4T 1W6 Telephone (416) 968-3435

- 2 -

For 16 years now members of the tobacco industry in Canada have self regulated themselves with great responsibility. We understand that recently some further voluntary restrictions have been proposed. We strongly urge that the Government of Canada respect these voluntary undertakings and permit the tobacco industry in Canada to continue to take their rightful place in the competitive business environment and that allied industries be allowed to continue to operate in a similar manner.

Yours very truly,

W. A. Leckie
President

WAL:sa

---

1. All people would be eliminated from tobacco ads, and the space allocated for warning would increase to 20%. Content of warning would be controlled by the government.
2. The tobacco companies would pay 15% of their ad spending for anti-smoking or other health-related campaigns, to be administered on behalf of Health and Welfare Canada by government's agency-of-record, Media Canada.
3. Outdoor advertising firms would provide free space to any health campaign, with half the space being tax deductible. Gallop also produced the results of a telephone survey of 440 adults in the Toronto and Hamilton areas. The poll, conducted by Kubas Research Consultants in January, 1988, showed 42% supported the Gallop compromise when it was explained to them, while 36% opted for a complete ban and 18% opposed it.

Further, Gallop suggested the government should "soften" the blow to the advertising industry by:

1. a ten-year phase-in period with one-tenth annual reductions in space;
2. the creation of a Tobacco Tax Transfer Fund that would make up an estimated 50% of the value of lost tobacco ads with advertising for other government programs, health and charitable groups.

Finally, in a speech to the Women's Advertising Club of Toronto, Gallop encouraged advertisers to: "use your influence with the editorial media to cool out the silliness that's been going on with what I will simply call biased and sensationalized reporting on this issue."

THE ANTI-SMOKING LOBBY

As the negative health, social, and economic effects of smoking became increasingly clear, the anti-smoking lobby continued to grow. In the case of Bill C-51, a coalition of health and public-interest groups combined forces to pass it. The key players were the Canadian Cancer Society, The Canadian Heart Foundation, the Non-Smokers' Rights Association, and Athletes to Pass C-51.

The goal of these groups was to build credibility with the press, government, and general public by providing research and accurate information. The Canadian Cancer Society held a joint national press conference with the Canadian Heart Foundation to express its strong doubts that the draft regulations of the bill would be effective. The coalition announced that it would sponsor a national survey to collect information useful to the government in developing stronger recommendations.

These groups were committed. When Simcoe South MP Ronald Stewart spoke out against Bill C-51, the coalition of health groups supporting the bill sent out 33 000 letters (one for every household in Stewart's riding), pointing out that Mr. Stewart owned a tobacco wholesale operation and thus had a direct conflict of interest.

THE MEDIA

The strength of the anti-smoking groups was invigorated by the refusal of several Canadian newspapers, including Toronto's *Globe and Mail*, to accept advertisements for tobacco products. An examination of seventeen editorials in newspapers across Canada discussing Bill C-51 showed that seven newspapers favoured the bill, seven opposed it, and three were neutral. While the number of newspapers for and against the ban were even, their size and influence were not. Canada's five largest English-language dailies supported the bill.

Exhibit 8

Circulation of Newspapers Supporting C-51

PAPER	CIRCULATION
Toronto Star	562 232
Toronto Globe and Mail	326 200
Vancouver Sun	244 153
Montreal Gazette	204 522
Ottawa Citizen	201 554
	1 538 661

Surprising was the fact that a number of newspapers serving the Ontario tobacco belt cautiously came out in favour of the bill as well. Both the *London Free Press* (circulation 131 308) and the *Woodstock Daily Sentinel-Review* (circulation 10 172) were in favour, with the *Simcoe Reformer* (circulation 9 704) remaining neutral. *The Free Press* said that Jake Epp should be "applauded" for taking such a definitive stand. The paper was representative of the "pro" papers in two ways:

1. It urged more government aid for tobacco farmers and expressed reservations about the ban's drawbacks in terms of free speech.
2. It argued that, when health dangers of tobacco are taken into account, a ban is justifiable in a free and democratic society.

"THE BATTLE OF THE TITANS"

The battle over Bill C-51 was one of the most sophisticated lobbying contests the federal government had ever witnessed. The two major players, the anti-smoking groups and the Canadian tobacco industry, utilized a number of highly developed techniques in an effort to achieve their own unique objectives. It was often an emotional and bitter fight.

The tobacco industry's association, the CTMC, hired William Neville, one of the most successful lobbyists in Ottawa and coined as having "gilt-edged" Conservative credentials. Neville had been the Principal Secretary to former Prime Minister Joe Clark, a political organizer for Prime Minister Brian Mulroney, and a speech writer for Health and Welfare Minister Jake Epp. Neville was to save the day for the tobacco industry. As the *Globe and Mail* reported in December, 1987:

> When you've got a bill with broad public support, undeniable health benefits, a Minister committed to it and 200 MPs to vote for it, you'd think it was a sure thing. Under those circumstances, the fact there was doubt the bill would go ahead is quite a tribute to Neville. Neville is a very astute practitioner...he knows you don't go and overtly kill a bull. He will finesse a thing rather than attack it head on.

The objective of the tobacco industry was not to lobby individual MPs, but to try to have the legislation reduced in priority on the government's legislative agenda.

The health groups, on the other hand, joined together to match the tobacco industry "point-for-point, technique-for-technique," if not dollar-for-dollar. The key personality for the pro-Bill C-51 forces was Garfield Mahood, the director of the Non-Smokers' Rights Association (NSRA), and a zealous, occasionally caustic anti-smoker. In typical fashion, Mahood stated the objectives of the pro-Bill C-51 forces' strategy: "We are trying to be sophisticated enough to use our relatively modest resources to blow the industry's multi-million-dollar campaign out of the water."

The CTMC began to organize its attack with a unique and sophisticated mail campaign. It sought to mobilize all those who profit from tobacco, and to broaden support by enlisting those who benefit from tobacco company sponsorship. During the summer of 1987, the industry contacted over 200 000 tobacco industry suppliers, wholesalers, and retailers. First, they received a postal-gram (see Exhibit 9) and then an information kit (see cover letter, Exhibit 10), including a computer-generated letter to the respective MP in the name of the supplier. Finally, three follow-up phone calls encouraged the individual to sign and mail the letter.

Exhibit 9

**Electronic Mail
Courrier électronique**

URGENT

CTMC38 E-MAIL CANADA

FROM: JEAN-LOUIS MERCIER, CHAIRMAN, IMPERIAL TOBACCO LTD.
P.J. HOULT, PRESIDENT, RJR-MACDONALD INC.
P.J. FENNELL, PRESIDENT, ROTHMANS, BENSON & HEDGES INC.

YOU AND MANY OTHER CANADIAN INDIVIDUALS AND COMPANIES ARE ABOUT TO
BECOME THE ECONOMIC VICTIMS OF PROPOSED FEDERAL GOVERNMENT LEGISLATION
. . . FOR ALL THE WRONG REASONS!

AS YOU ARE NO DOUBT AWARE, THE GOVERNMENT HAS INTRODUCED LEGISLATION,
BILL C-51, TO BAN ALL TOBACCO ADVERTISING, PROMOTION AND BRAND SPONSOR-
SHIP BY JANUARY 1, 1989. MANY PEOPLE BELIEVE THE LEGISLATION WILL IN NO WAY
HELP THE GOVERNMENT ACHIEVE ITS STATED AIMS. BUT EVERYONE AGREES THAT
THE BILL WILL WREAK FINANCIAL HAVOC ON PEOPLE SUCH AS YOURSELF. IT IS
IMPORTANT TO REALIZE THAT THIS PROPOSED LEGISLATION COULD SOON BECOME
LAW.

CLEARLY, THE GOVERNMENT THINKS IT IS IN A NO-LOSS SITUATION. THE PEOPLE
WHO WILL SUSTAIN THE ECONOMIC DAMAGE OF THIS LEGISLATION ARE INVOLVED IN
MANY DIFFERENT KINDS OF BUSINESSES AND INDUSTRIES. THAT MAKES IT DIFFICULT
FOR THEM TO FORM AN EFFECTIVE COALITION IN TIME TO STOP, OR DELAY, THE
PASSAGE OF BILL C-51. NATURALLY, THE GOVERNMENT WOULD PREFER THAT THE
FLAWS AND WEAKNESSES AND THE REAL EFFECTS OF THE LAW NOT BE SEEN, SO IT IS
ATTEMPTING TO RUSH THIS LEGISLATION THROUGH PARLIAMENT.

WE THINK THE GOVERNMENT IS WRONG. THERE IS TIME AND THERE IS A WAY FOR
THE PEOPLE WHO WILL BE HURT BY THIS LEGISLATION TO MAKE THEIR FEELINGS
CLEAR TO THE GOVERNMENT. FRANKLY, IT WILL TAKE AN ORGANIZED PROGRAMME.
WE HAVE UNDERTAKEN THE ORGANIZATION. WE HOPE YOU WILL UNDERTAKE TO
OFFER YOUR SUPPORT. WITHIN A DAY OR TWO, YOU WILL RECEIVE A MORE COMPRE-
HENSIVE INFORMATION PACKAGE. INSIDE IT YOU WILL FIND A LETTER TO YOUR
MEMBER OF PARLIAMENT, ALONG WITH A STAMPED, PRE-ADDRESSED ENVELOPE. WE
URGE YOU TO SIGN AND SEND THAT LETTER RIGHT AWAY. PERHAPS TOGETHER, WE
CAN HELP COMMON SENSE PREVAIL. WHILE THERE IS STILL TIME.

Exhibit 10

Canadian Tobacco Manufacturers' Council
Conseil canadien des fabricants des produits du tabac

701-99, rue Bank Street, Ottawa, Ontario K1P 6B9
Telephone (613) 238-2799   FAX: (613) 238-4463

Dear

A day or two ago, you received a postalgram alerting you to the urgency of taking action to stop or delay passage of Bill C-51, the Government's proposed legislation to ban tobacco advertising, promotion and brand sponsorship in Canada.

In the postalgram, we advised that you would receive a comprehensive information kit on this critical issue. You now have the kit in your hands. As you will note, it contains a letter and a stamped, pre-addressed envelope directed to your Member of Parliament. We urge you to sign and send the letter right away. Remember, this damaging legislation could be passed into law soon.

Damaging? Absolutely! Just consider some of the implications of this ill-conceived piece of legislation:

— It will take more than $75 million out of the Canadian advertising industry and throw as many as 2,500 people out of work in the process.

— 40,000 Canadian retailers, many of them small, family-owned businesses, will be hit hard by loss of valuable store fixtures, the cost of restructuring store interiors and the disappearance of $50 million a year tobacco companies spend promoting their brands.

— Canada's sports and cultural organizations will lose up to $10 million a year spent on sponsorship ranging from the Royal Winnipeg Ballet to the Royal Canadian Golf Association.

— Thousands of people in related industries all the way from paper products to freight forwarding will be affected by loss of business and potential job loss.

— Six million Canadians who use tobacco products will be denied their right to information about a perfectly legal product . . . arguably a violation of Canada's Charter of Rights and Freedoms.

Members/Membres   Imperial Tobacco Limited/Limitée   RJR-Macdonald Inc.   Rothmans, Benson & Hedges Inc.

And what would be the benefits of this piece of legislation? Virtually zero! The Government claims that it is taking this action to help reduce the use of tobacco products in Canada. Much of the available evidence suggests it will not happen. Just consider the following facts:

— Numerous studies in countries where tobacco advertising has been banned show that advertising does not stimulate consumption. In countries such as Finland, Singapore, and Iceland, consumption has increased in the aftermath of a tobacco advertising ban.

— Almost two-thirds of the tobacco advertising Canadians see is carried by U.S. and other publications entering the country. A ban on Canadian tobacco advertising won't change that. All it will do is unfairly penalize Canadian newspapers, magazines and outdoor advertising companies. And it will create a market for American cigarettes, where there is none now!

— A recent study conducted among Canadian children by Britain's respected Children's Research Unit proved that advertising has virtually no influence on a young person's decision to smoke. The primary influences are curiosity, peer pressure, and parental and sibling example.

— Under a voluntary advertising code in Canada, cigarette consumption has declined by 17% since 1983 and is expected to decline by an additional 5% this year. In the meantime, in countries where there is no tobacco advertising, use of non-filter cigarettes is much higher than is the case in Canada.

So where are the benefits of Bill C-51? There are none. Yet the economic damage will be massive and widespread. And remember, this piece of legislation could become law in a matter of weeks as the Government tries to rush the legislation through Parliament!

Again, we urge you to sign and send the enclosed letter to your Member of Parliament.

Sincerely,

Norman J. McDonald
President

Along with this unprecedented direct mail campaign, the industry also placed full-page advertisements in most major Canadian newspapers and magazines (see Exhibit 11). These advertisements typified the industry's main strategy, to focus primarily on the "freedom of speech" issue. The CTMC went as far as funding Coalition 51, a group of 56 well-known Canadians who "share a belief in a free Canadian society, and the fear that Bill C-51 would set a dangerous precedent for Canada." No mention was made of the fact that the CTMC funded this group. The assertion that there was no proof that a ban would in fact reduce smoking and save lives, and the issue of corporate sponsorship, were ignored. The fight was about freedom of speech!

The health groups countered every tactic the tobacco industry mounted. In response to Neville's direct mail campaign, Canadian Cancer Society volunteers sent 35 000 black-edged postcards to MPs.

> The Society announced its campaign to the media thus: The Society wants to communicate that although we do not have the vast funds to lobby the government (as donations to the Society mainly support medical research and other programs), we do have volunteers who are willing to try to let the government know that there continues to be strong grass roots support for controlling tobacco promotion.

The Canadian Medical Association asked two physicians in every riding to get directly in touch with their MPs, and also asked all 59 000 physicians in the country to write their MPs in support of Bill C-51.

When the tobacco industry organized a press conference to discuss the freedom of speech issue, the health groups countered with their own press conference. Peter Gallop proposed controlled advertising of tobacco products, with media companies offering public service ads against tobacco usage. The "Physicians for a Smoke-Free Canada" immediately responded with three hard-hitting ads linking cigarettes and death. On January 25, 1988, the coalition of health groups went so far as to take out a full-page newspaper advertisement to point out that William Neville was an influential Conservative, and argued that his assignment was to derail Bill C-51. Douglas Gekkie of the CMA countered the freedom of speech issue with: "After all, how could any self-respecting Canadian who believes in freedom of speech, not to mention freedom of the press, object to advertising a legal (but lethal) product?" Throughout the entire process, this "point-counterpoint" battle ensued.

HOUSE COMMITTEE HEARINGS

By January, 1988, Bill C-51 had passed second reading in the House of Commons. At this time, it was referred to a committee of the House to review it clause by clause before it could pass third reading and become law.

In early January, the Canadian Cancer Society brought a Norwegian Health Officer to testify before the Committee. Dr. Kjell Bjartveit, Chairman of the Norwegian National Council on Smoking and Health, had been involved in a similar debate in the early 1970s, when Norway debated its tobacco ban. Dr. Bjartveit told the Committee that since a similar Norwegian ad ban was implemented in

Exhibit 11a

Every cultural and professional sports group in Canada has the right to accept or reject tobacco brand sponsorship.

The Government wants to take away that right.

The Federal Government has introduced legislation to ban all Canadian tobacco advertising, promotion and brand sponsorship. If this legislation is passed into law, these activities will be illegal by January 1st, 1989.

No matter how you feel about smoking, if you're concerned about civil liberties, you should examine this issue and arrive at your own conclusions.

With brand sponsorship banned cultural and professional groups stand to lose $10 million a year in aid.

WHAT THE PROPOSED LEGISLATION MEANS.

Under Bill C-51, brand sponsorship of professional sports or cultural activities will become illegal. Corporate sponsorship will still be allowed. What does this mean? It means, for example, that Rothmans' sponsorship of equestrian events would be perfectly legal while the duMaurier Council for the Arts would become an outlawed organization. If that seems more than a little silly to you, you're not alone.

WHAT IS THE REASON FOR SPONSORSHIP?

On the one hand sponsorship provides tobacco companies with the opportunity to

WHO WILL THE LEGISLATION HURT?

In recent years, the tobacco industry has provided up to $10 million annually for a variety of sponsorships and grants to cultural and professional sports groups in Canada. These funds have assisted Canadian performers and athletes in many fields to achieve world standards and win international recognition.

Among those who have benefitted from brand sponsorship are:
- *Royal Canadian Golf Association*
- *Tennis Canada*
- *Canadian Race Drivers Association*
- *Calgary Philharmonic*
- *Royal Winnipeg Ballet*
- *Citadel Theatre*
- *Edmonton Symphony*
- *Ontario Jockey Club*
- *Canadian Opera Company*
- *Terragon Theatre*
- *Orchestra London*
- *Ontario Harness Horsemen's Association*
- *Toronto Symphony*
- *Sarnia International Symphony*
- *Cercle Molière*
- *Orchestre Symphonique de Montréal*
- *Théâtre de l'Ile*
- *Grands Ballets Canadiens*
- *Montreal World Film Festival*
- *Neptune Theatre*
- *Maritime Breeders Association*
- *Symphony Nova Scotia*
- *National Darts Federation of Canada*

be responsible corporate citizens, offering financial support in badly needed areas for activities that provide enjoyment to millions of Canadians.

On the other hand, it allows tobacco companies to reinforce brand awareness in the hope that current smokers will be encouraged to try a particular brand.

Will legal corporate sponsorship and illegal brand sponsorship change the whole notion of sponsorship? Yes. Sponsorship is not charity. It is a business and social investment designed to benefit both parties. If the benefits are denied, the motivation is destroyed.

FREEDOM OF CHOICE.

Sponsorship is by definition a relationship of mutual consent. Tobacco companies are under no obligation to sponsor anything and no organization is obligated to accept their sponsorship. Bill C-51 denies that freedom of choice to both parties.

It seems clear in a free society that organizations should have the right to seek or accept sponsorship from a particular company or brand. It seems equally clear that to suggest tobacco brand sponsorship of an opera or a sporting event might encourage people to start smoking, stretches the very limits of credibility.

Brand sponsorship of professional sports events will be outlawed under proposed legislation.

CAN ANYTHING BE DONE ABOUT BILL C-51?

Yes. Public awareness about the extremism of the Bill can be increased. That is the purpose of this advertisement. Concern about the implications of the Bill can be expressed to your Member of Parliament. That way, perhaps Bill C-51 can be stopped or modified before it's too late.

If you would like more information on this issue, or if you'd like to add your voice to those expressing concern, write to P.O. Box 80, Station "H", Montreal, Quebec, H3G 2K8.

Exhibit 11b

There's a major problem with the Federal Government's proposed ban on tobacco advertising.

It won't work.

The Federal Government has proposed legislation to ban all Canadian tobacco advertising, promotion and brand sponsorship by January 1st, 1989.

No matter how you feel about smoking, you owe it to yourself to examine the tobacco advertising issue more closely. You just might find that your point of view could change.

AN ADVERTISING BAN SIMPLY DOESN'T WORK.

It's been tried. Either a total or partial ban. It's been tried in Norway. In Singapore. And in Finland. In virtually every case cigarette consumption has not declined and in some instances it has actually increased. So a ban doesn't work.

In countries where voluntary advertising codes have put constraints on tobacco advertising, consumption has declined. In the United Kingdom consumption declined by 20% between 1979 and 1984. In Canada, cigarette sales have declined by 17% since 1982.

TOTAL VOLUME ——
ADVERTISING BAN IMPOSED 1976

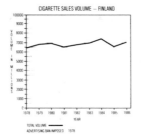

CIGARETTE SALES VOLUME — FINLAND

TOTAL VOLUME ——
ADVERTISING BAN IMPOSED 1978

In the countries noted above, tobacco advertising has been banned for years yet cigarette consumption has increased. In Canada, with a voluntary advertising code, cigarette sales have declined 17% since 1982.

If the Federal Government's aim is to reduce cigarette consumption in Canada, there is clear evidence that current policies are bringing that about.

A BAN WON'T END TOBACCO ADVERTISING IN CANADA.

More than 60% of all the tobacco advertising Canadians see in magazines is contained in publications entering the country from the United States and elsewhere; magazines such as Newsweek, Sports Illustrated, People, Family Circle and Paris Match. A ban on tobacco advertising in Canada won't change that.

Instead, Canadian newspapers, magazines and outdoor advertising companies will lose up to $30 million in advertising revenue. Companies offering internationally advertised brands will have an unfair advantage over companies selling domestic brands. And the Government will have intervened in the marketplace for no good reason.

ADVERTISING DOESN'T MAKE PEOPLE SMOKE. NOT EVEN CHILDREN.

Today's tobacco advertising is designed only to encourage current smokers to try different brands. That's all it does. Ample research is available to prove that advertising doesn't encourage people to start smoking, or to smoke more.

Advertising doesn't even encourage young people to smoke. A recent survey of Canadian children conducted by the respected Children's Research Unit of the United Kingdom makes it clear. The survey shows that curiosity, peer pressure and family example are the primary influences. Advertising's effect is deemed to be negligible.

BANNING ADVERTISING BANISHES JOBS.

Current estimates suggest that a ban on advertising will cost upwards of 2,500 jobs in the Canadian advertising and media industries. But the Government's hit list of people to hurt goes far beyond that.

Among those who will feel the economic pain are people in the following industries:
- Employees of tobacco companies.
- Workers in paper products industries.
- People in packaging companies.
- Employees of freight forwarding companies.
- Tobacco growers.
- Family-owned retail businesses.
- People in the printing industry.
- Manufacturers of promotional materials.

Canada's advertising and media industries will lose some $30 million in tobacco related revenues. But almost two thirds of the tobacco advertising Canadians see in magazines will still enter from outside the country.

IF A BAN WON'T WORK, WHY DO IT?

It's clear that banning tobacco advertising is the wrong way of attacking a perceived problem. It is also a fundamental attack on individual and commercial freedoms guaranteed under the Charter of Rights and Freedoms.

If you'd like more information on this critical issue, or if you want to express your concern about the proposed legislation, write to P.O. Box 80, Station "H", Montreal, Quebec, H3G 2K8.

Exhibit 11c

Why the proposed Government legislation banning tobacco advertising deserves a sensible second look.

Even by people who don't smoke.

The Federal Government has proposed legislation banning all Canadian tobacco advertising, promotion and brand sponsorship.

Whether or not you smoke, if you're a Canadian who cares about civil liberties, you owe it to yourself to examine this issue and come to your own conclusions.

A VIOLATION OF THE CHARTER OF RIGHTS AND FREEDOMS?

Never in the history of Canada has a legal product been totally denied the right to advertise. Bill C-51 denies tobacco manufacturers the right to provide information through advertising and the consumer the right to receive it. So the proposed legislation may well be a direct violation of the Charter of Rights.

Many Canadians believe banning advertising for a legal product is in violation of Canada's Charter of Rights and Freedoms.

REASONABLE CONSTRAINTS YES. OUTRIGHT CENSORSHIP NO.

Nobody questions the need for reasonable constraints on tobacco advertising. Tobacco advertising has been controlled through a voluntary industry code for more than 20 years.

Under the voluntary code, tobacco manufacturers withdrew from television and radio advertising. They limited expenditures, included government health warnings and ensured that outdoor advertising would not appear adjacent to primary and secondary school areas. Within the last year, the industry has further offered to eliminate people from all advertising and enlarge and modify Health and Welfare messages in advertising and on packages. With this record of co-operation and control, is outright censorship really necessary?

WHAT ADVERTISING DOES AND DOESN'T DO.

Today's tobacco advertising is designed to encourage current smokers to try one brand over another. That's all advertising does. It doesn't get people to start smoking and it doesn't get them to smoke more. In countries where tobacco advertising has been banned, such as Norway, Sweden, Finland and Singapore, consumption has not declined, and in some cases, has actually increased.

Advertising also doesn't encourage young people to start smoking. A recent study of Canadian children undertaken by the respected Children's Research Unit of the United Kingdom shows clearly that advertising has little, if any, influence.

JOBS LOST FOR NOTHING.

There is ample evidence to suggest that Bill C-51 will not achieve its aims. What it will achieve is massive economic dislocation. Up to 2,500 people in Canada's advertising and media industries stand to lose their jobs and many other industries will feel the economic impact.

With tobacco brand sponsorship outlawed, organizations such as the Royal Canadian Golf Association, Tennis Canada, the Canadian Equestrian Federation and many major opera companies, dance companies, theatre companies and symphony orchestras could lose up to $10 million a year in sponsorship grants. All in all, a heavy price to pay for ineffective legislation.

TOBACCO ADVERTISING TODAY. WHO'S NEXT?

If the rights inherent in the Charter of Rights and Freedoms can be conveniently trampled upon in the tobacco advertising issue, whose rights will be denied next?

Will alcoholic beverage advertising be made illegal? Will advertising for certain food products be outlawed? Will trade unions be told that they can't plead their case through advertising because the Government doesn't want Canadians exposed to their ideas? Once we start down the road of banning information, where do we stop?

In a study conducted among Canadian children by the highly respected Children's Research Unit of the United Kingdom, the myth that tobacco advertising encourages young people to smoke was shattered. Among the major findings:

- *Peer pressure, parental role models and socio-economic status are the primary influences leading to smoking among young people*
- *Advertising was cited as an influence by less than 2% of the young people surveyed*
- *Cigarette consumption among young people is substantially higher in Norway than in Canada. Tobacco advertising has been banned in Norway since 1975.*

If you're concerned about this basic point of principle, or if you'd like more information on the proposed tobacco advertising ban, we urge you to write to P.O. Box 80, Station "H", Montreal, Quebec, H3G 2K8.

1975, annual tobacco consumption declined from an average close to 2 100 grams per person over the age of 15 to less than 1 900 grams in 1985-86. He also stated that many of the arguments against Bill C-51 were the same as previously used in Norway. Subsequently, he added, no advertising company in Norway had gone out of business. Dr. Bjartveit also condemned the tobacco industry around the world for its deceptive use of statistics to bolster its case. He cited as an example the CTMC ad that ran in newspapers across Canada in July, 1987 (see Exhibit 11), stating that cigarette sales in Norway had increased since 1975.

The day the CTMC appeared before the Committee, the Canadian Cancer Society presented Dr. Bjartveit at a press conference to explain the Norwegian view of the effects of his country's ban. Within a few hours, the tobacco companies had Jean Boddewyn, a Professor of Marketing with City University of New York, presenting a written brief debating the points that Dr. Bjartveit had made that morning. One of Professor Boddewyn's arguments was that the Norwegian ad ban could not be credited with having an effect on smoking because it was not the only factor in the country's anti-smoking policy. The CTMC continued to stress this point along with other negative effects:

> Bans cost jobs, emasculate competition, invite increasing penetration by international brands, threaten financial support of sport and arts events and infringe on basic economic freedom.

The CTMC stated that the industry was "not insensitive to the concerns of Parliament and the Canadian people." It argued in favour of self-regulation—a proposal it had made to Jake Epp in a private meeting in November, 1986. The details of this meeting had not been made public until this time:

1. Not to advertise in youth-oriented publications, in cinemas, or on video-cassettes.
2. To devote 20% of billboard space and 17.5% of space on all print and most point-of-purchase materials to rotating health warnings in large typefaces.
3. To develop public information campaigns directed at retailers reminding them of existing laws against selling tobacco products to minors.
4. To decrease maximum permissible tar levels to 16 mg.

The CMA attempted to keep the scientific facts on the issue before the Government and the Members of the House of Commons by correspondence, by lobbying the Government and Opposition parties, and by making two major presentations to the House of Commons Committee. Near the end of January, the Canadian Medical Association made a dramatic appearance before the Committee. It bombarded the Committee with statistics and graphic slides illustrating the damage done by smoking. As Dr. Athol Roberts, the President of the CMA, testified:

> We are sorry that the slides were so disturbing that one member of Parliament had to leave the room. The CMA may be accused of stooping to sensationalism, but this is a very, very serious subject. We thought it was time that members of Parliament saw

the results of smoking as physicians see them every day . . . You members of Parliament have an opportunity to do more for the prevention of disease and promotion of health than we physicians will have in a professional lifetime. Please do not miss that opportunity to pass C-51 . . . Should Parliament fail to pass the Tobacco Products Act (sic) it would be hypocrisy of the first order and would have been a mockery of the Government's health promotion policies and programs.

In February, 1988, Jake Epp presented the following proposed amendments to the Committee studying Bill C-51:

1. Allow existing promotion of sporting and cultural events using the name of a cigarette brand, but freeze the amount of money that tobacco manufacturers could spend on sponsorship.

2. Reduce the amount tobacco companies could spend on public advertising in 1989 to two-thirds of the amount spent in 1987 and to one-third in 1990 before eliminating all advertising in 1991.

3. Require tobacco companies to include leaflets describing the effects of tobacco on health and the toxic elements in the cigarette.

4. Include the regulations restraining minors from buying cigarettes, previously contained in the Tobacco Restraint Act.

Bill C-51, as amended, passed third reading and became law.

---

[62] 1970—40.6% of Canadians 15 years of age and over were regular smokers; 1977—35.9% of Canadians 15 years of age and over were regular smokers; 1983—31.1% of Canadians 15 years of age and over were regular smokers.

6 THE ONTARIO HEARING AID ASSOCIATION

MARC A. ROBILLARD AND D. WAYNE TAYLOR

The Ontario Hearing Aid Association (OHAA) was incorporated in April, 1967 "for the protection of the hard-of-hearing public." It was formed by a group of hearing-aid dealers who felt that, in the public interest, they should band together as an association and develop standards of training and ethical business conduct. This was instigated, in large part, by the bad press that arose from the unethical behaviour of one dealer (who subsequently left the country), as well as by the unscrupulous dealings of certain fly-by-night operators. These operators would "blitz" certain rural areas of Ontario, sell inferior hearing-aid products, and quickly leave the jurisdiction. Consequently, follow-up assessments were not made and service for the products sold was unavailable. Since such practices reflected poorly upon all members of the profession, the OHAA was formed as a first step to regulate the field and discontinue such damaging practices.

Membership in the OHAA is voluntary; therefore, the OHAA is limited in its effectiveness. It has repeatedly attempted to have provincial legislation passed to regulate the training and licensing of hearing-aid specialists in Ontario.

In early 1967, the Minister of Financial and Commercial Affairs (now Consumer and Commercial Relations) advised the association that the province would soon be developing a licensing program with standards for the performance and conduct of hearing-aid specialists. It would be administered by the provincial Department of Health. No legislation was actually developed, but shortly before the 1971 general election the Minister of Health confirmed that the licensing program would begin shortly afterward. This, again, never materialized.

The association, undaunted, believed that its most important contribution was now to develop an educational program. This would demonstrate to the government of Ontario both its sincerity and its desire to take a proactive approach in the establishment of licensing in Ontario. The program was developed as a part-time course of studies in April, 1975. It later became a full-time program and was taught at Sheridan College of Applied Arts and Technology in Oakville. The content of the course was developed after consultation with medical and academic professionals from both within and outside of the Ministry of Colleges and Universities.

The OHAA has developed a number of committees and programs for various purposes, including:

1. a Consumer Grievance Committee, which investigates justified complaints against members (and at times, non-members) and recommends disciplinary action, if necessary. The Ontario Ministry of Consumer and Commercial Relations has commended the OHAA and has noted that "complaints against hearing-aid dealers are practically non-existent and the credit for this situation must certainly be bestowed to all members of the OHAA;"

2. an Advertising Ethics Committee to screen all advertising used by its members;

3. educational standards which require prospective dealers to complete a one-year (480 class hours) hearing-aid specialists' program. To obtain certification by the Association, graduates must have completed at least 2 000 hours of fitting experience under the supervision of a certified specialist, followed by a practical examination at the end of the training program;

4. an annual upgrading program, where members must attend a specified number of class hours in order to keep abreast of technological and procedural improvements and changes in the testing and fitting of hearing aids; and

5. a standard sales agreement which guarantees unsatisfied hearing-aid buyers a full refund of the purchase price.

THE CANADIAN HEARING SOCIETY

During the early 1970s, another organization, the Canadian Hearing Society (CHS), entered the scene. This non-profit organization began in the late 1950s. Its mandate covers everything from the counselling and education of the hard-of-hearing to their legal representation in court. The CHS receives funding ($800 000) from the Trillium Foundation, the Ministry of Tourism and Recreation (Wintario lottery grants), and from the Ontario Ministries of Health and Community and Social Services.

In accordance with its mandate, the CHS wanted to introduce a three-tier system to test, prescribe, and dispense hearing aids. The process called for a patient to first see a physician, who would determine if the hearing loss could be medically treated. Then, an audiologist would test the hearing and prescribe an aid. Finally, a dispenser would fit and sell the aid. The purpose of the three-tier system was to keep all dealings at arm's length to avoid potential conflict of interest in having the same person prescribing and selling hearing aids.

An audiologist differs from a hearing-aid specialist in that only the former has a Master's degree which concentrates on the diagnostic testing of hearing disorders. The word "dispenser" in the three-tier structure is key, since the process does not include the role of the hearing-aid specialist. By making the testing and prescribing of hearing aids the exclusive right of the audiologist, legislation would effectively reduce the role of the hearing-aid specialist to that of dispenser. A great debate ensued over who was better qualified to test hearing and prescribe hearing aids.

The president of the CHS also contacted the president of the OHAA about another of its concerns: the "rip-offs" of the elderly due to "grossly inflated" private dealer hearing-aid prices. Rather than pursue the matter, the OHAA president responded in no uncertain terms that the matter was not open to discussion.

THE FEUD BEGINS

In public, the CHS proceeded to openly attack the unethical business dealings of some hearing-aid dealers. Though these dealers were not all members of the OHAA, the CHS did not make this distinction. It allowed the public to draw its own conclusions.

> The CHS printed "consumer protection" pamphlets which advocated: "Don't under any circumstances buy a hearing aid without first seeing an audiologist."
> "If you purchase your hearing aid from a dealership, be very careful." "A dealer is not legally required to have any training at all." "Sometimes dealers will try to sell hearing aids to people who have not yet seen an audiologist."

In 1976, the CHS went into direct competition with hearing-aid dealers by selling hearing aids at such reduced prices, private dealers could not compete. Several small dealerships went out of business. The CHS intended to show that hearing-aid prices were inflated by demonstrating its ability to provide them more cheaply. Pleas from both the OHAA and the Canadian Federation of Independent Business (CFIB), on behalf of the OHAA, to discontinue this unfair competition were ignored. The CFIB objected in defence of the independent, small business that found itself competing with an organization subsidized by government.

Throughout this period, rather than becoming involved in a public feud with the CHS, the OHAA concentrated on writing letters and briefs to the Ministry of Health on the subject of licensing in Ontario. The association acquired the services of a former Ontario Cabinet minister to correspond with the Ministry of Health on its behalf. However, throughout the following five years, despite its voluminous correspondence to the Ministry, the OHAA was unable to get recognition as a legitimate player in the profession.

In November, 1981 the Ministry of Health announced that it did not consider the hearing-aid specialist a health practitioner, and that this had been its policy since the issuance of the *Report of the Committee on the Healing Arts.* The Minister of Health went on to recommend that the OHAA's interests would be best served by approaching the Ministry of Consumer and Commercial Affairs. This was quite a revelation to the association, especially in view of the past 11 years' activities.

GOVERNMENT POLICY

Meantime, unbeknownst to the OHAA, the CHS and the audiologists were working their way through the policy-making system of the Ministry of Health. They served as advisers on several committees, where they discredited both the hearing-aid specialists and their community college training.[63]

The audiologists were so successful that government policy was changed to dictate that all government-subsidized hearing-aid purchases required the client to see an audiologist. This meant that all government-assisted hearing-aid purchases through the Children's Assistive Devices Program (ADP) were directed to the CHS, and away from private dealerships who could not compete with the non-profit prices of the CHS.

The CHS's solid standing with the Ministry was made apparent in a statement by then Minister of Health, Hon. Dennis R. Timbrell, on November 9, 1981:

Regarding the Canadian Hearing Society, I would say that it is mentioned in Ministry publications in recognition of the fact that it has been the primary resource in the provision of information and assistance to the deaf and hard of hearing for a number of years.

The reference to "Ministry publications" in the above quote was with respect to a Ministry of Health pamphlet, *Information for Seniors*, which stated that if a hearing aid is recommended, a qualified audiologist should be seen, and that advice was available from the Canadian Hearing Society.

THE SCHWARTZ REPORT

In 1982, the Conservative Government commissioned the Review Committee on the Health Disciplines Act, better known as the Schwartz Commission. The OHAA prepared briefs so that it could once again be considered for licensing under the provisions of this Act. The Ontario Speech and Language Association (OSLA), of which audiologists were members, submitted a brief requesting that only audiologists be permitted to test and evaluate hearing.

Meanwhile, in 1985, the audiologists, believing they had the upper hand, began to select and dispense hearing aids. Many of those employed by the CHS left to open up their own practices. All of a sudden, the CHS's three-tier system was falling apart. Its operations were being scuttled by the very audiologists whom they had supported. The CHS was now in the same predicament as the OHAA. Many audiologists were no longer referring patients to the CHS, but rather to their own dispensers. The CHS was now losing business, too.

In May, 1986, the Schwartz Report was made public with the recommendation to grant full licensing to audiologists. In effect, this was a death sentence to the hearing-aid specialists and their businesses. The President of the OHAA resigned and a completely new board of directors was appointed. Upon further investigation by the OHAA's new president, the Board found that the Commission was only remotely aware of their existence. The new board of directors launched a campaign which involved direct meetings (not mailed correspondence through a third party) with all government players: local MPPs, members of the Schwartz Commission, representatives of the ADP, and the now Liberal Minister of Health, the Hon. Elinor Caplan.

At the OHAA's annual meeting, the Board urged the members to write their MPPs to inform them that this new legislation would in effect put them out of business. Also at this meeting, the Executive Director of the CHS approached the OHAA and asked that the two groups unite against the proposed legislation. The Association of Hearing Aid-Dispensers (AHAD), a group formed by the CHS's hearing aid-dispensers, joined forces with OHAA in October, 1987 to form a new group: the Association of Hearing Instrument Practitioners (AHIP). The CHS reformulated its position, declaring that there might be another way to properly dispense hearing aids, and that perhaps there was a place for hearing-aid specialists in the scheme of things.

THE SECOND SCHWARTZ COMMISSION

With the change in the OHAA's approach and the joining of forces by the OHAA and the CHS, the impending disaster for its hearing-aid specialists was temporarily averted when the Schwartz Commission was reconvened. It was then that the OHAA (representing the newly formed AHIP) made its most convincing argument. Through a three-day effort, during which the OHAA executive contacted virtually all the hearing aid-dispensers in Ontario, they mapped out the extensive distribution network of private dealers across Ontario. This was then compared with the distribution of audiologists in the province. The result clearly showed the Schwartz Commission that the public would not be properly served with the present distribution of audiologists, as they were all located in and around three major centres in the province. The distribution of hearing-aid dealers, on the other hand, effectively covered the entire province. The case for the public to have a choice was made stronger by bringing in individuals who relied on private dealers due to their remote or rural residences.

In December, 1987, the Schwartz Commission released a preliminary decision which recommended against the licensing of audiologists.

In the first week of April, 1988, the ADP announced that those who had been dispensing since October, 1987, could write an exam for accreditation to participate in the Assistive Devices Program. This meant that an individual who passed the exam could test for hearing loss *and* select hearing aids *and* participate in the program. Those not already dispensing as of October, 1987, would not be allowed to do so until a final decision was reached by the Commission. However, regardless of the outcome of the Schwartz Commission, this right would not be revoked.

The Commission's final report is still pending.

---

[63] The number of clinical audiologists in Ontario was growing rapidly, most of whom were American emigrants unable to find work south of the border. The U.S. Federal Drug Administration had concluded that audiological evaluation was not necessary to provide reasonable assurances of the safety or effectiveness of hearing aids. Others came from either Quebec, Alberta, or British Columbia, where hearing-aid specialists were duly recognized, accredited, and licensed. As a result, Ontario had become the "last frontier" for audiologists in North America. Yet, in this province, only the University of Western Ontario has an audiology program. An average of three graduates complete the program every year. Courses leading to accreditation for hearing-aid selection are not mandatory, but rather an option in most university programs.

7 NOTE ON THE ONTARIO WINE INDUSTRY – 1988

JOHN SKILNYK AND D. WAYNE TAYLOR

When the Canada-United States Free Trade Agreement was signed on January 2, 1988, it marked the beginning of a new era of business-government relations in this country. Trade-selective industries such as Ontario's wine industry are presently working with governments to implement necessary adjustment policies. The Ontario wine industry, protected by government regulation since the time of Prohibition, is being forced to become internationally competitive for the first time in its history. Specifically, the industry's current discriminatory pricing, listing, and distribution policies will be phased out over a seven-year period.

Grapes represent the second-largest fruit crop in Ontario, and the wine industry provides between 10 000 and 15 000 full and part-time jobs.

BACKGROUND

The Ontario wine industry has roots which reach back to the year 1811. The first commercial enterprise on record, Clair House, was established at this time near Toronto. Since then, the industry has developed in an environment shaped and dominated by the Ontario government. The provincial government, through the Liquor Control Board of Ontario and Liquor Licensing Board of Ontario, has exclusive control over pricing, quality, and distribution. Its policies have been implemented over the years to protect Ontario grape growers, and have benefited domestic wine producers.

The Ontario grape growers — many with family farms and traditions dating back 200 years — have been represented since 1978 by the Ontario Grape Growers' Marketing Board (OGGMB), an organization representing approximately 900 registered grape growers. The main purpose of this organization is to negotiate annual prices with the wineries and the jam and juice producers on behalf of its members. The OGGMB views the Free Trade Agreement as having a major negative impact on its members and has vehemently opposed it.

Ontario's 18 wine producers are represented by the Ontario Wine Council, a member of the Canadian Wine Institute. The purpose of the Wine Council is to represent the wine producers' viewpoints and concerns when consulting with both provincial and federal governments, and to promote Ontario wines. The Council has also opposed the Free Trade Agreement and is actively consulting with the provincial government on its implementation.

PROVINCIAL LEGISLATION

Historically, Ontario grape growers have been assured of relatively stable livelihoods due to two measures. First, the Wine Content Act and Regulation 947 stipulate that wineries must limit imported grapes to 15% of total Ontario grape purchases, with the percentage of imported grapes in a domestic wine 30% or less. This ensures a demand for Ontario grapes. Second, the Ontario Grape Growers' Marketing Board represents grape growers in negotiating grape prices with representatives of wineries and grape processors. Annual surpluses are bought by the OGGMB, creating artificially high grape prices.

Secondly, in 1927 the government of Ontario created the Liquor Control Board of Ontario (LCBO) to provide a government monopoly over alcoholic beverages. It controls their sources, quality, transportation, price, and point of final sale. The LCBO discriminates against all imports — even those from other provinces. In this way, it protects Ontario grape growers and wine producers.

Protection has come in one basic form: discrimination against imported wines through pricing, listing, and distribution policies. Pricing discrimination involves subjecting imported wines to a provincial markup of 66%, as compared to 1% for Ontario wines. Currently, an average local table wine costs $6.10, whereas an equivalent import costs $7.45 (see Exhibit 12). In contrast, equivalent markups would lower the price of an imported bottle to only $5.30. The LCBO also imposes a minimum price floor on all imported wines to protect lower-priced Ontario products from cheaper European and California wines.

Exhibit 12

Comparative Wine Pricing

	Domestic Table Wine	Imported Table Wine
Size	1000 ml	1000 ml
Markup	1%	66%
Supplier Quote	$2.64	$1.78
Federal Excise (.4472/Litre)	.4472	.4472
Federal Import Duty (.044/L)	0.00	.044
Federal Sales Tax – 18%	0.55	0.41
Freight (Imports Only)	0.00	0.27
Total Landed Cost	3.64	2.95
Markup	.07	1.96
Flat Tax ($1.50/Litre)	1.50	1.50
Levy (.18/750 ml)	.24	.24
Provincial Sales Tax – 12%	.65	.80
Retail Rounded Up to nearest $0.05	$6.10	$7.45

Current listings heavily favour domestic and European wines, and tend to discriminate against American wines. In 1986, the LCBO listed 685 Canadian wines and only 51 American wines. Domestic brands are also offered listings on new products more quickly than are imports, and with a greater variety of bottle sizes.

Exhibit 13

Ontario Wine Sales 1983-1988

(in litres)

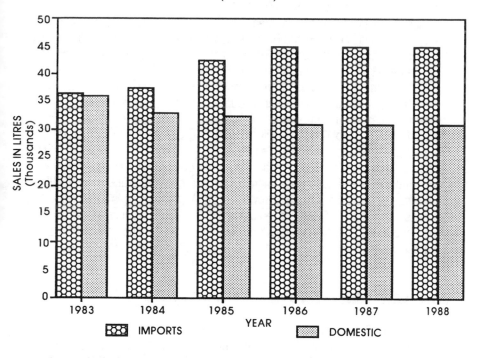

Distribution policies favour domestic wine producers by allowing them to set up their own retail outlet networks with the province. These yield 5-10% more profit per bottle to the wineries. By conveniently locating outlets in shopping malls, domestic wine producers can effectively increase market penetration over imported competition.

Despite these three protective measures, domestic wines have lost significant ground in the Ontario market since 1983 (see Exhibit 13).

FREE TRADE AGREEMENT

On January 2, 1988 the federal governments of Canada and the United States signed a bilateral free trade agreement. Under Article 802, listing procedures for wine and distilled spirits are to be non-discriminatory. Government refusals to list will be subject to appeal procedures that will provide prompt and objective rulings.

Article 803 requires distributors such as the LCBO to charge a price differential of no greater than the actual cost of service. This differential will consist largely of the extra cost of shipping and storing U.S. wines. If there exists a price differential greater than the cost of service, such as Ontario's 65% markup, it must be phased out over a seven-year period. The markup elimination schedule requires 25% of the differential to be removed as of January 1, 1989 and another 25% as of January 1, 1990. The markup must then be reduced by a minimum 10% per year for the next five years. With the elimination of both tariffs and markups, the average bottle of imported table wine would cost $5.20, as compared to $6.05 for an average domestic table wine.

Distribution policies are addressed under Article 804. Private wine store outlets in the provinces of Ontario and British Columbia can still discriminate in favour of domestic wines, but the expansion of private wine store outlets ceased as of October 4, 1987, to abide with the Agreement.

Although the OGGMB presented its position on free trade to the federal government through the Sectoral Advisory Group on International Trade (SAGIT) system of committees, the final text of the Agreement did not give their interests much weight. The Ontario Wine Council, through the Canadian Wine Institute, also presented its position on free trade to the SAGIT committee, but its position, too, was not heavily weighed in negotiating the Agreement. The general consensus was that the beer industry was more important to Canada, and wine was more important to the United States. However, the Agreement does allow marketing boards, such as the OGGMB, to remain in place. Fresh fruits such as grapes have the benefit of a twenty-year adjustment period, during which time tariffs can be reapplied temporarily to respond to depressed market conditions.

ONTARIO GRAPE GROWERS' MARKETING BOARD

The Ontario Grape Growers' Marketing Board represents 900 grape growers throughout Ontario, most of whom are concentrated along the Niagara peninsula and the north shore of Lake Erie. The Board's main purpose is to negotiate grape prices with two representatives of the wine industry and one representative of the food-processing industry.

In 1986, the OGGMB sold close to 77 000 tons of grapes worth approximately $21 million. The wineries purchased 40% of the crop, juice processors 22%, other food companies 14%, and the year's surplus accounted for the remaining 24%. The native *labrusca* grape, used in fortified wines, juices, jams, and coolers, decreased from 65% of the vine count in 1976 to 48% in 1986. *Labrusca* varieties are currently grown above the Niagara escarpment and inland from Niagara township, representing close to half of all grape land — deemed unsuitable for agricultural or urban uses.

Vinifera and hybrid grapes, used in red and white table wines, increased from 24% of the vine count in 1976 to 43% in 1986. *Vinifera* grape production, which represents between 6-10% of all vines and includes Riesling and Chardonnay varieties, is price-competitive with its California counterpart after transportation costs are factored in (see Exhibit 14). *Vinefera* grape production represents the most significant opportunity for Ontario grape growers who want to continue producing in the future.

Exhibit 14

Estimated 1986 Price Declines Required to Meet U.S. Delivered Prices
(Prices are in Canadian $ Per Ton)

Variety	U.S. Price	Delivered Price	Ontario Price	% Decrease Required
Concord	$ 230	$ 270	$271	0%
Thompson/Elvira	90	220	320	31
Grenache/DeChaunac	150	280	340	18
Columbard/Delaware	180	310	565	45
Chenin/Seyval	210	340	600	44
Riesling, White	750	880	783	0
Gamay	470	600	834	28
Chardonnay	1300	1430	850	0

The grape varieties which are not price-competitive are the American and French hybrids grown along Lake Ontario, between Stoney Creek and St. Catharines, and along the Niagara River. They currently comprise about one-third of existing vines. Under free trade, the price declines expected for these varieties would put most hybrid growers in a fairly marginal position. Some farmers with above-average yields might be able to continue operations, but most are expected to leave if their land can be converted to more economical urban uses.

Under the Free Trade Agreement, the OGGMB and the grape growers argue that there is no level playing field between themselves and the U.S. grape growers. U.S. growers have much lower operating costs; fuel and fertilizer cost 40% less than in Ontario. Chemical, heating, and land costs are also much lower in the U.S. California's climate provides longer growing seasons, up to four times Ontario's yield, and better quality grapes. American producers also face lower taxes and a lower or nonexistent minimum wage. Less government interference in terms of environmental protection offers U.S. growers a wider selection of chemicals. The U.S. government also subsidizes water projects and/or support programs geared to encourage wine exports.

The OGGMB views a future under free trade with a sense of impending doom. It expects one-third of the growers to cease operations by the end of 1989. Compensation for these farmers is currently being negotiated with the provincial and federal governments. The OGGMB portrays two scenarios, neither of them positive.

The first would see a few larger growers remaining economically viable, eventually buying out existing growers who do not continue producing. The second scenario involves the survival of a small grape industry that will supply a cottage wine industry, pick-your-own, and/or farm market selling. The OGGMB will still exist; however, its power to negotiate grape prices will be greatly reduced as American grape imports increase.

THE ONTARIO WINE COUNCIL

The Ontario Wine Council, representing 18 Ontario wineries, speaks for the industry when addressing governments and/or promoting Ontario wines. The current industry profile includes four publicly owned wineries: Ridout, Paul Masson, T.G. Brights, and Andres. Barnes Wines Ltd. is a subsidiary of Grand Metropolitan PLC, and Jordan Ste. Michelle Cellars is a subsidiary of Brights. The remaining 12 wineries operate on a much smaller scale and have been in existence for less than ten years. Ontario wineries employed 700 people in 1984, and have not increased employment significantly since then. They produce approximately 45 million litres of wine (10 million gallons) annually.

The Council feels the industry is in no position to compete on equal grounds with its Amercan counterparts. It also believes that the seven-year adjustment period is inadequate to remove existing trade barriers with minimal disruption. Ontario wineries, the Council claims, are burdened with higher grape costs and poorer grape quality than their competitors. Grape costs are three times those of California wineries, thanks to the OGGMB, which supports artificially high prices as a result of government surplus buybacks. Although they recognize the transition domestic growers are undergoing, Ontario wineries feel that future competitiveness will require access to lower-priced, higher-quality California grapes.

Provincial protectionist measures, while promoting domestic wineries and serving local preferences, have also forced wineries to produce while under ten different regulatory environments. Interprovincial trade barriers have prevented Canadian wineries from obtaining economies of scale, since they must produce wine in the province in which they sell. The three largest wine producers in Canada operate 19 wineries; the three largest wine companies in the United States also operate 19 facilities. In the U.S. production from these 19 plants totals more than 200 million gallons; Canada production is less than 20 million gallons.

The Wine Council feels that Ontario wineries are in a better position to deal with free trade than are Ontario grape growers. Therefore, they seek the removal of interprovincial trade barriers, greater access to U.S. grapes and grape concentrate, and more stringent wine quality controls. They are also exploring possible government financial assistance to help firms rationalize their operations.

The Council's most pessimistic scenario under free trade foresees the larger wine producers becoming bottlers of U.S. wines. A few estate wineries may survive by finding market niches for premium table wines.

The Ontario Wine Council has provided a unified voice for domestic wineries throughout all consultations. However, it has had problems obtaining a consensus among its members on the free trade issue. Hillebrand Estates Winery — a cottage firm — approves of the free trade deal, hoping it will force the industry to become more streamlined and efficient. However, Hillebrand probably has more to gain (or less to lose) from free trade than most wineries. It produces a medium-quality, medium-price selection of table wines, and has built or acquired 38 retail stores throughout the province. A similar operation, Reif Wineries Inc., also approves of the Free Trade Agreement.

U.S. BARRIERS TO IMPORTS

The Council and the OGGMB have both expressed concern over U.S. barriers to Canadian exports, specifically the marketing power of U.S. wine industry giant, E. and J. Gallo of Modesto, California. In 1986, Gallo wineries accounted for over 26% of the U.S. market. Even more intimidating, two weeks of production by Gallo would satisfy the entire demand for wine in Canada. Scale economies in bottling, labelling, and administration, and cheaper raw material costs result in a California/ Ontario price gap of between $7 and $10 per case. Since American wine is distributed through independent dealers who work for several competing producers, Gallo has distributors in approximately a dozen markets. For those dealers Gallo does not own, it can use its size to greatly influence distribution decisions and prevent dealers from carrying competitors' products. Thus, the larger Ontario wineries see no major opportunity in U.S. mass markets.

As well, 18 state authorities have imposed discriminatory practices on out-of-state wines, similar to those of the LCBO. These include California, Florida, New York, New Jersey, Michigan, and Maine.

THE GOVERNMENT OF ONTARIO

Two studies regarding the domestic wine industry were commissioned by the Ontario provincial government and were performed by Woods, Gordon Management Consultants in 1987. The first study commissioned was the "Study of the Ontario Beverage Industry." This study concluded that the domestic wine industry faces significant product cost disadvantages as discussed above, along with marketing and brand image problems. The overall image of Ontario wines is improving; however, the product is still considered inferior to European wines. California wines have not had enough exposure in Ontario to create a consumer image. At worst, lower quality California wines will be considered equivalent to comparable Ontario products.

The study summarizes Ontario's overall competitive position as being vulnerable to the California imports, especially in the lower-end, mass-market wine segment. While transportation costs for U.S. products offer some degree of protection, American wines can still enter Ontario at 17% below current, lowest-priced Ontario wines. Domestic producers do possess an important distribution advantage with their private retail networks, and this may help the low-end segment of the market. However, marketing expertise and resources clearly favour large American wine producers.

According to the Woods, Gordon study, comprehensive free trade will lower Ontario wine producers' domestic market share to 27%-40%, from its current level of approximately 48%. California wines could potentially gain between 25% and 50% of the current domestic share, primarily in the lower-price segments. The higher-price segment, dominated by European wines, may also be penetrated by

California wines. Since current U.S. barriers to Ontario wines are quite small, their removal will not present a significant market opportunity to domestic wineries. Brand image will be the key to penetrating the United States.

The overall reduction in employment in the industry is forecast to be approximately 20% by 1995, which could translate into nearly 200 jobs. According to Statistics Canada, every direct job lost in the beverage sector means 2.4 more jobs lost elsewhere in the province. Therefore, free trade has the potential of eliminating between 240 and 480 jobs.

The grape-growing industry is expected to feel the largest impact. Therefore, the provincial government commissioned a second study, entitled "The Vulnerability of the Ontario Grape Growing Industry to Canada-U.S. Free Trade Agreement." This study concluded that grower-controlled marketing boards have pushed some Ontario grape prices well above levels that would remain competitive under free trade. Specifically, the prices of American and French hybrids, such as DeChaunac, Delaware, and Seyval Blanc would have to decline by 18%-47% to become competitive. *Labrusca* grapes would remain in production, since they are price-competitive, and Ontario demand for their use in juice and jams would be unaffected by free trade. Ontario *vinifera* varieties, particularly Chardonnay and Riesling, are currently competitive with their U.S. counterparts and should remain in production. However, current marketing board prices do not provide much incentive for planting these varieties.

A final decision on what policy changes the provincial government will pursue is pending further discussions with the OGGMB and the Ontario Wine Council. All areas of the Liquor Control Act and Wine Control Act are being examined, and an alternative 12-year adjustment period may be amended to the Agreement. This amendment will be the subject of the first hearing of the International Trade Commission in March, 1989.

8 BELL CANADA AND THE CRTC

DARREN FARRUGIA AND D. WAYNE TAYLOR

On October 15, 1988 the Canadian Radio-Television and Telecommunications Commission (CRTC) ruled that Bell Canada had earned "excess profits" of $63 million in 1985, $143 million in 1986 and was on the way to earning an excess of $234 million profit in 1987. As a result, the CRTC ordered Bell Canada to immediately rebate its seven million customers $206 million and reduce its long-distance charges by 20% effective January 1, 1988. The total cost of the two orders represented $400 million in lost revenues to Bell. It was the largest rate decrease ever ordered and the very first retroactive order for a profit rebate.

Immediate market reaction to the decision was harsh. The stock of Bell Canada Enterprise Inc. (BCE) — the parent company of Bell Canada — hit a twenty-month low of $34.25. The Dominion Bond Rating Service lowered Bell's mortgage rating from the AAA rank to the AA rank. Standard & Poor's bond rating service in the United States also reduced its rating of Bell's bonds and debentures. As a result, Bell would have to pay a higher rate of interest for any future debt financing; so, in effect, the CRTC ruling probably would cost the company about $500 million or more!

BELL CANADA

Bell Canada is the largest telephone company in Canada. Its territory covers much of Ontario, Quebec, and the Northwest Territories. There are a number of small, provincially regulated telephone companies within these areas that operate independently from Bell. Bell Canada is a wholly owned subsidiary of the recently formed holding company, BCE Inc.

Bell Canada, in its 1986 fiscal year, received operating revenues in excess of $6.2 billion, earned operating income in excess of $1.7 billion, and pocketed a net income of $711 million. This profit figure made it the most profitable business operation in Canada, although its results are not reported separately from its parent, BCE Inc.

The company operates from an asset base of approximately $12.7 billion with 7.4 million lines, which represents 58.8% of all access service in Canada. With a work force of 51 370 Bell's total employment represents 48.8% of all workers in the Canadian telecommunications industry.

Bell's parent company, BCE Inc., is the only Canadian company to record annual profits in excess of $1 billion. With total employment of 110 000, it is Canada's largest corporate employer.

THE CANADIAN RADIO-TELEVISION AND TELECOMMUNICATIONS COMMISSION

As its name implies, the Canadian Radio-Television and Telecommunications Commission (CRTC) is the federal regulator of several communications industries.

The CRTC department responsible for telecommunications is the Telecommunications Directorate. The directorate has a full-time staff of 63, and is divided into three branches: Economic, Social, and Technical Analysis; Financial Analysis; and Operations.

The CRTC accepted responsibility for telecommunications on April 1, 1976. This responsibility was previously held by the Canadian Transport Commission. As a result, much of the CRTC regulation of common carriers is derived largely from Section 321(1) and (2) of the Railway Act:

> All tolls should be just and reasonable and shall always, under substantially similar circumstances and conditions with respect to all traffic of the same description carried over the same route, be charged equally to all persons at the same rate.

According to the 1987 Annual Report of the CRTC, its mission as the federal government's communications regulator is:

> to preserve and enhance communications systems in Canada in the interests of the Canadian public. In carrying out this commitment, the CRTC will foster an environment characterized by a wide diversity and availability of Canadian services and facilities offered by adequately resourced entities.
>
> Furthermore, in pursuit of this commitment, the CRTC will act in an efficient, proactive and adaptive manner supported by the fullest possible public participation.

The intermediate goals of the CRTC in the field of telecommunications are based on the objectives and policy elements contained in its enabling legislation. They are to:

1. ensure the provision of efficient, justly and reasonably priced telecommunications services;
2. ensure universal accessibility to basic telephone services;
3. ensure that telecommunications carriers do not unfairly take advantage of their monopoly or dominant market positions in dealing with subscribers, other carriers, or competitors;
4. ensure that telecommunications carriers are financially viable and able to provide basic services of adequate quality to meet subscriber needs, and;
5. determine where regulation could be eliminated, reduced, or made more flexible and, in particular, where regulation could be replaced/supplemented by reliance on market forces.

Federal jurisdiction covering just two of Canada's telephone companies, Bell Canada and British Columbia Telephones (BC Tel) accounts for 77% of all subscribers, 75% of industry revenues, and 70% of the assets in the national telecommunications industry (see Exhibit 15).

It is the opinion of the Commission that Canada has one of the world's most advanced communications systems. The level of technological innovation in this country is extremely high, with Canada at the leading edge in worldwide telecommunications developments. As a result of these continuing developments, the Commission is charged with carefully examining the opportunities that arise from

Exhibit 15

Regulatory Jurisdictions in Telecommunications

Regulator	Telephone Company
Federal Government — through CRTC	Bell Canada B.C. Tel. CNCP Telecommunications Teleglobe Canada Telesat Canada NorthwesTel Cantel
Provinces — through the Public Utility Boards or Commissions	Saskatchewan Telecommunications Newfoundland Tel Island Telephone (P.E.I.) New Brunswick Tel Maritime Tel and Tel Manitoba Tel Alberta Government Telephones Northern Telephone Thunder Bay Telephone Quebec Telephone Telebec Other independent telephone companies in Ontario, Quebec, and British Columbia
Municipalities	Edmonton Telephones Prince Rupert City Telephones

new technologies, and balancing market dynamics and public concerns with the need to provide comprehensive and affordable service to Canadians. This concern must be addressed in terms of all Canadians within the federal jurisdiction, regardless of their location.

UNIVERSAL ACCESSIBILITY, CORPORATE FINANCIAL HEALTH, AND CONSUMER WELLBEING

Three of the most important objectives of the CRTC are to ensure universal accessibility to telephone services, to maintain an environment in which operating companies remain financially healthy, and to guard the consumers' wellbeing. The CRTC and Bell Canada seem to score well on all three criteria.

Canada enjoys one of the highest rates of access to telephone service in the world. Ninety-eight percent of all Canadian households have telephones. This is a substantial accomplishment considering the diverse geographical conditions and long distances that the country encompasses. Since the cost of providing the service is not currently reflected in the price charged to any individual consumer, the price of the service does not appear to be a prohibiting factor in universal accessibility. If one were to assess Bell Canada's accessibility, one might consider that since its territory includes the two most heavily populated provinces, with only minor geographic hindrances in other areas of the country, Bell should be providing as high a level of accessibility as the national average.

In order for telephone companies to continue to upgrade equipment and perform research into new technologies, they must be allowed to operate from a sound financial position. If one accepts the premise that the performance of a corporation's stock on the open market is a good indicator of corporate health, then Bell Canada is definitely in an attractive financial position. Bell Canada's shares have been described as the perfect stock for "widows and orphans." This description arises from the relatively safe, almost recession-proof nature of the investment. In the history of organized stock-trading in Canada, Bell has never failed to pay its dividends, and with the CRTC deciding on the rate of return on shareholders' equity, its earnings never fall below present levels.

BCE Inc. shares, of which Bell Canada is a major influencing factor, are the most widely held shares of any Canadian corporation, having some 350 000 Canadian shareholders. No single institutional shareholder controls more than 5% of the stocks outstanding. Its blue-chip nature is further supported by its wide use in most pension funds that look for long-term growth and stability in their investments. It is also the only Canadian stock listed on fourteen world stock exchanges, and the first to be listed on the increasingly powerful Tokyo Stock Exchange.

Finally, a survey was conducted by members of a major Canadian graduate business school in March, 1988 to gauge consumer opinion about the operations and quality of service of the telephone company.

On average, those questioned believed that the quality of service provided by Bell Canada was "good" in both general and specific terms. The average number of days of unexpected service interruptions was less than one. The cost of the service was perceived as slightly higher than reasonable. Given the findings of similiar surveys about various consumer products, public opinion towards Bell appeared to be quite favourable. Bell was generally seen as providing a good quality product at a reasonable cost.

RATE SETTING

The cost of Bell's "local telephone service" (the term given to usage of the telephone system covered by a fixed monthly charge) is based on the area that can be accessed without incurring long-distance charges. The charge must be consistent within Bell's area of operations and cannot discriminate on the basis of cost. The CRTC has continually monitored these charges very closely, with the help of a number of public-interest groups. These groups, including the Consumers' Association of Canada and the National Anti-Poverty Organization, make regular presentations to the CRTC through public hearings. The Commission uses these to facilitate public input into the decision-making process. The objective of the Commission is to ensure that universal access is not restricted on the basis of cost.

Historically, long-distance charges have been used as a source of funds to support the cost of local service. Bell Canada claims that each $1 of revenue earned from local service costs the company $1.96. Long-distance service, on the other hand, costs $0.31 to generate $1 in revenue. In effect, the CRTC regulates a cross-subsidization of telephone services to the benefit of users of primarily local service.

Bell Canada sets its rates by making annual submissions of "tariff notices" to the Commission, forecasting total operating costs and revenues based on current or proposed rates for local and long-distance service. The company also suggests a reasonable range for its return on average common equity, the financial ratio that the CRTC uses to determine the allowable profit level for Bell. This ratio is calculated by dividing after-tax-profit by the total common shareholders' equity.

The Commission examines the data supplied by the company and can respond in a number of ways. It can approve the submission as received; it can question the company on some or all of the submission; it can advise changes and call for a re-submission; or, if the matter is of significant importance, it can call for public hearings. In the event of a hearing, the CRTC informs known public interest groups as well as the general public and requests their comments to the Commission. Any group or individual submitting comments may be asked to give sworn testimony and answer questions before the Commission.

The Commission has the authority of a superior court, with legal and quasi-legislative powers. The decisions of the Commission are binding unless one of several avenues of appeal available to regulated companies or to the general public are followed. The first and most direct process of appeal is to request that the Commission review its findings and decisions. New data or re-interpretation of received data can be submitted for consideration.

The second avenue of appeal is to the Federal Court of Canada, Appeals Division. The court can only rule on matters of law and will not make or alter decisions of judgment. This alternative is chosen only if the Commission is thought to have intervened in an area that it may not legally be entitled to, or the Commission is suspected of having made an error in law in reaching its decision. The decision of the Federal Court also can be appealed. Appeals of Federal Court decisions must go to the Supreme Court of Canada. In order for the Court to hear the appeal, it must first be convinced that there are implications of national importance in the decision before it will agree to hear the case.

The third alternative is to appeal to the federal Cabinet. The Cabinet does not have the authority to strike down or change CRTC decisions, but it can apply strong pressures to force the Commission to reconsider its actions. Supreme Court of Canada decisions can also be appealed to Cabinet; but rarely are such appeals considered today.

INDUSTRY-GOVERNMENT INTERACTION

The procedures required to be followed are set out in the Regulations and are very structured. There is, therefore, a great degree of interaction between Bell Canada and the CRTC. Both entities describe their relationship as amicable. The CRTC acknowledges that Bell routinely follows the outlined procedures and quickly fulfils the Commission's requests for information. All CRTC decisions that are not appealed are implemented as per instructions. The Commission understands the objectives of Bell Canada in these interactions and is therefore not disturbed by some of the demands of the company, even if they are not in line with the direction that the CRTC is attempting to follow.

Bell Canada, on the other hand, is sympathetic to the Commission's role of balancing consumer welfare and corporate viability. Bell believes that the CRTC's approach to regulating the industry is reasonable. The Commission ensures that the company operates in an efficient manner and charges reasonable rates for the services it provides. In so doing, it also allows Bell to earn sufficient profits for reinvestment purposes as well as achieving above-average returns for investors.

Bell admits that the Commission forces the company to act as if it were in a competitive environment. Methods of tracking efficiency and quality of service have been developed by Bell which have been approved by the Commission. These methods are constantly being updated, and the methods used and results of the tests are filed annually with the Commission.

There are several examples of how regulation by the CRTC has forced Bell Canada to become more efficient. Bell has undergone a voluntary hiring freeze over the past six years which reduced employment by some 9 000 employees. Bell's rate increases are historically below levels experienced in other regulated industries in Canada, and have been held well below the rate of inflation.

In 1983, however, Bell Canada underwent a major corporate restructuring in a move to reduce the scope of the regulatory influence of the CRTC. The move to restructure was based on the CRTC's decision, and the subsequent Federal Court's upholding of the CRTC decision, that any revenues generated by Bell in any way related to telephone operations would be applied as if they arose from everyday operations. These could be applied against normal operating costs in the return-on-equity calculations. The case in point was Bell Canada's sale of telephone equipment, installation charges and operations-training fees to Saudi Arabia, profits of which the Commission decided to apply against Canadian operating costs. Under the new corporate restructuring of BCE Inc., any future ventures of this nature are not expected to fall under CRTC jurisdiction.

THE CRTC RULING

The Commission had not reviewed Bell's financial situation in detail since 1981, when it reviewed projections through the 1985 fiscal year. In early 1985, Bell submitted an application for, and was granted, an interim rate increase of 2%. The Commission held a series of public meetings to address the rate increases, to determine if the interim rate increase should be rescinded or made permanent. This interim rate increase was suspended in September, 1985. A number of delays in the tariff approval process resulted in the Commission not filing its findings on the tariff submissions until a year later.

Bell Canada's faith in the CTRC's process was shattered on October 15, 1986. The Commission ruled that the interim rate increase was not justified, and that since the tariff applications has not been approved for the years of 1985-1987, pending the results of the review, the CRTC had the authority to adjust Bell Canada's profits retroactively to the date of the last approved tariff. The orders were the result of the Commission's findings that Bell had earned a 14.2% and 14% rate of return in 1985 and 1986 respectively — well above the allowable rates of 13.75% and 13.25%.

BELL'S APPEAL TO THE FEDERAL COURT OF CANADA

Bell Canada believed that the CRTC had no administrative authority to act in a retroactive manner, and that imposing such an order would have detrimental effects on all regulated industries. For this reason, Bell decided to bypass the CRTC and appeal directly to the Federal Court of Canada.

Bell also believed that the ordered rate reductions on long-distance charges were overly harsh, and asked the CRTC to review its ruling in this matter. Bell stated that the decreases called for by the Commission would result in Bell receiving the lowest rate of return of any major North American telephone utility.

The Federal Court granted Bell Canada the right to appeal the CRTC ruling on rebates. It also gave Bell 90 days after any decision to make rebates, but said that the amount of the rebates would have to include interest.

The CRTC, on the other hand, received the enthusiastic support of both the Consumers' Association of Canada and the National Anti-Poverty Organization in its defence of the rebate order.

While the Federal Court of Canada was hearing Bell's case against the CRTC, the appeal to the CRTC on long-distance rate reductions was completed. The Commission ruled that the reductions were justified, and that Bell would have to comply with the earlier decision. Although Bell was disappointed with the outcome, the company stated that it would comply with the order.

On Friday, July 10, 1987, the Federal Court produced an 80-page decision. The judgment stated that the CRTC had no authority to act retroactively, and that Bell Canada was not bound by the Commission's earlier rebate order. The decision of the Court could be appealed by any group to the Supreme Court of Canada, but submission of a request for appeal had to be filed by October 31, 1987.

THE CRTC'S APPEAL TO THE SUPREME COURT OF CANADA

It took the CRTC less than a week to apply to the Supreme Court of Canada for the right to appeal. The Commission felt that the decision of the Federal Court seriously impeded its mandate to regulate telecommunications carriers' rates.

At the present time, the CRTC has been awarded the right to appeal before the Supreme Court. The Court will probably begin hearing the appeal in late 1988 or early 1989, with no decision expected before the summer of 1989. In the meantime, Bell is not required to make any rebates to its customers, but it must track the whereabouts of all customers on record as of the initial CRTC decision so that it can fulfil its requirements if the Court rules against the company.

INDEX